The Multi-coloured
GARDEN

By the same author

FERNS
ORNAMENTAL GRASSES
THE PRIVATE LIFE OF PLANTS
GROW YOUR OWN VEGETABLES
BOTTLE GARDENS
THE NATURAL GARDEN
TREES FOR SMALLER GARDENS
THE 2-HOUR GARDEN
FRESH FROM YOUR GARDEN
SHRUBS AND DECORATIVE EVERGREENS
HOW TO GROW FRUIT AND VEGETABLES
YOUR GREENHOUSE
THE COMPLETE HANDBOOK OF GARDENING
GARDENING IN COLOUR
THE PERFECT LAWN
MAKING AND PLANNING A SMALL GARDEN
GARDENING FOR BEGINNERS

The Multi-coloured GARDEN

A New Approach to Gardening with Coloured Foliage

ROGER GROUNDS

PELHAM BOOKS

For Stephen Taffler
who has introduced so many
good variegated plants

First published in Great Britain by
PELHAM BOOKS LTD
44 Bedford Square
London WC1B 3DU
1982

British Library Cataloguing in Publication Data
Grounds, Roger
   The multi-coloured garden.
   1. Garden—Design   2. Flower gardening
   I. Title
   712'.6   SB454

ISBN 0 7207 1388 9

Photoset in Great Britain by
Rowland Phototypesetting Ltd, Bury St Edmunds, Suffolk
Printed by Hollen Street Press Ltd, Slough
and Bound by Hunter and Foulis Ltd, Edinburgh.

Contents

Colour Plates

29 *Aptenia cordifolia* 'Variegata', *Phormium tenax* 'Purpureum' and *Fatsia japonica*.

30 *Acorus calamus* 'Variegatus'.

31 *Ricinus communis* 'Gibsonii'.

32 Massed plant materials give a hint of the excitement of the multi-coloured garden.

33–4 Two views of a multi-coloured scheme designed by the author and created with the kind co-operation of Hillier Nurseries (Winchester) Ltd.

CHAPTER ONE

The Multi-coloured Concept

You probably picked this book up expecting it to be about flowers. It is, in fact, about plants with coloured foliage, and how they can be used in a very particular style of gardening. The aim is not to deny the value of flowers in the garden: merely to assert that they may not be the most important element in the making of a modern garden.

The purpose of a garden is to rest the mind and please the senses. That purpose is more likely to be fulfilled in a garden in whose design foliage plants play a dominant role, especially if that design is disciplined to achieve a deliberate end. If that end is the multi-coloured garden, then the prime means are plants with coloured foliage. Foliage plants are plants grown primarily for their foliage, and plants with coloured foliage have leaves any colour other than green (which is not to deny that green is a colour – merely to assume that you already have plants of a diversity of greens in your garden).

It is a basic tenet of this book that most of us garden in a style that neither rests the mind nor pleases the senses, and that at this moment a new and more cohesive style of gardening is being born. The style in which most of us garden is what might be called, for want of a more precise term, suburban traditional. It is a style that is not without merit. It enables us to garden in a diversity of ways: the extrovert can show off his front garden in a blaze of colours changing with the seasons; the introvert can collect together in his back garden treasures that none of his neighbours knows nor appreciates; and the non-gardener can put the whole thing down to lawn, weeds and a few tough if unlovely shrubs and not feel ashamed. It is a style that draws on most of what is best in our gardening heritage and owes much to William Robinson and Gertrude Jekyll. It is essentially eclectic, and its essence seems to be that if a sufficient number of different plants are thrown together promiscuously in the same bed, the results may be pleasing. Then again, they may not. It rather depends on how much of the mix took its inspiration from the cottage garden and how much from the aesthetics of Miss Jekyll.

One of the most notable deficiencies of the twentieth century is that, while it has produced a number of amazing things – world wars, atom bombs, space travel, radio, television, aeroplanes and even the microchip (to name but a few) – it has conspicuously failed to produce a new style of gardening. That is not surprising:

gardeners tend to be a conservative lot – at least about gardening. The finest gardens made in this century contain no new concepts: Hidcote, Sissinghurst, the Savill have nothing new to offer. They are merely the finest examples of their style. Yet we live in an age and in a world when more than ever before it is desirable that a garden should indeed rest the mind and please the senses. Ours is a world of increasing stress, strain and pressures, of increasing turbulence and violence at all levels and of all kinds, and a world in which, if the sociologists are right, we shall all have increasing (if at times involuntary) leisure. Now more than ever before we need a style of gardening which can really rest the mind and bring pleasure to our senses. That style of gardening is the multi-coloured garden.

To explain the multi-coloured concept it is necessary to go back to Brown or Repton. If you have ever seen a Brown or Repton landscape in its 'unimproved' state (that is, without the addition of copious quantities of rhododendrons) what will strike you most is the simplicity of the design. It is that simplicity which calms and delights. Pure Brown and pure Repton are simply landscapes with all the scrub and clutter removed to reveal the natural beauty of the lie of the land; a little extra work was done to enhance the contours (the curve of a hillside or the extent of a stretch of water) and this effect was deepened by having certain areas grazed and others left rough, the whole design being pulled together by the skilful positioning of clumps of trees.

When we look at a mature Brown or Repton today we tend to assume, quite naturally, that the great land-owners who commissioned such men did so for aesthetic reasons. That is only part of the story. There were also forceful economic factors at work. Both Brown and Repton swept away the high-cost labour-intensive knot gardens and parterres that had till then been the fashion, and replaced them with gardens needing relatively minimal upkeep. The multi-coloured garden does much the same in modern idiom and on a smaller scale.

The great master of this new style of gardening is Roberto Burle Marx, who readily acknowledges Brown as the source of his inspiration. Where Brown or Repton used differing textures of grass to create bold but simple effects, Burle Marx uses colour, great sweeps and curves and curls of it (often skilfully interlocking) to create enchanting spatial relationships. Working in South America, with a wealth of tropical foliage plants, he uses, for example, plants such as the vivid violet *Setcreasea purpurea* in a great, bold curve, with a lawn of *Stenotaphrum secundatum* 'Variegatum' in front of it and *Coleus* 'Roi des Noires' behind it, and then ties those disparate colour bands together with clumps of pampas grass in much the same way that Brown would have used clumps of trees.

Such simplicity is stunningly effective, and it works not only in vast landscapes but also in small gardens which are all too easily over-planted. It works with the sort of colour-leafed plants that can be grown in cool temperate climates just as well as with tropical plants, though the colours are necessarily more subdued and probably more restful and more pleasing for that.

The essence of such a garden is a disciplined simplicity of design combined with a new approach to plant materials. The plant materials are necessarily plants with coloured leaves and plants, moreover, that are capable of keeping most of their own weeds down most of the time. Yet it is not a style which denies the keen plantsman his pleasures. Indeed, it is also the essence of such design that the simplicity of the bulk of it is enhanced by pockets of intensely promiscuous plantings, the random nature of these only emphasising the unmuddled simplicity of the rest of the garden.

The general arguments in favour of foliage plants can be quickly explained. The contribution that flowers make to a garden is, by and large, a fleeting one. No single flowering plant contributes much to the garden as a whole for much of the year. Foliage, by contrast, is there for very much longer, usually from its rising-up in spring till its dying-down in autumn; evergreens, of course, are with us the whole year through. Over the year as a whole, foliage contributes far more to a garden than flowers. Indeed, it is the dominant visual element in almost every garden. That being the case, it does far more to determine the particular qualities of a garden than flowers ever can.

Besides, where flowers contribute to the garden only once in the year, and in only one way, the foliage of most plants makes a contribution more than once in the season, and in more ways than one. Most foliage emerges one colour in spring, changes to another colour by summer and then, even in those plants not noted for their autumn colour, gradually subsides through shades too numerous to name as winter approaches. There is no flower that changes with the seasons.

A leaf, moreover, even the dullest, simplest leaf, has two surfaces, an upper one that is usually glossy, and a lower one that is usually matt, and the contrast between the two is a delight in itself. In some plants the difference between the two leaf surfaces is so clear, so distinct, that the plants are grown for that quality alone.

The problem, of course, is that where you have a garden made solely of foliage, if that foliage is merely green the effects created between the differing degrees of green may be too subtle for our sensibilities. We still need the vitality of colour. If that colour can be supplied by foliage plants, the effects that can be achieved are among the most rewarding that any gardener could seek.

Let us take, by way of example, a composition of intrinsically interesting foliage plants, but one in which all the plants have green leaves, and then let's see what happens if we use instead forms of the same or similar plants but with coloured leaves. Picture in your mind's eye a mature grouping of phormiums and fatsias, ferns and hardy palms with a backdrop of bamboos, standing in a ring of rough grass towards the edge of a well-kept lawn. It is essentially an interesting picture. What makes it interesting is primarily the variation in foliage form: the sword-shaped leaves of the phormium are in sharp contrast with the glossy, digitate leaves of the fatsia; the deeply cut leaves of the fan palm make a further contrast with the feathery lightness of the ferns; and the delicate drooping leaves of the bamboo afford yet a further contrast. Even the rough grass in which the planting stands contributes to the effect, the spiky

leaves of the grass complementing the phormiums and yet making their contribution in a different way, not singly but by sheer force of numbers.

Now let's recreate that picture in colour. The hardy palm can only be green, but it is
an interesting, very dark green, and the leaf is of a sufficiently distinctive shape for
that green to be enough. With the fatsia you have two choices: it can be either green or
slightly variegated white; not an outstanding variegation, but pleasing in its quiet
way. So let's opt for the variegated form – it has a general greyish appearance from a
distance. Again, the choice is limited among the ferns. There are only two that have
much to offer in the way of colour. The most exciting of these is the Japanese painted
fern, *Athyrium nipponicum* 'Metallicum' (*A. goeringianum* 'Pictum'), a beautiful,
low-growing, slowly spreading fern whose fronds are basically silvery-grey with a
rich, red midrib. The other is *Dryopteris erythrosora*, whose fronds are a rich coppery
colour for most of the year, and emerge in spring a deep, glowing pink. Since we
already have a grey element in the variegated fatsia, let's opt for the copper-coloured
dryopteris. Then there's the bamboo, which could present a problem. While there is
quite a number of variegated bamboos in cultivation, only two are widely known
and grown, the variegation on the majority of the others being rather academic. The
choice is between the white-variegated *Arundinaria variegata* and the yellow-
variegated *Arundinaria viridistriata (auricoma)*. Since we already have a white
variegation in the fatsia, we'll go for the yellow. In fact it is the brightest colour of all
so far. That leaves the phormium which could be grey, green or purple or variegated
white, cream, yellow, pink or bronze. I would choose the purple form, *Phormium
tenax* 'Purpureum', a plant with sword-shaped leaves of a marvellous deep-
mahogany reddish bronze. There is one further element to which we could add
colour – the rough grass. There is a diversity of grass-like plants with coloured leaves
which one could use from the rich golden-yellow of *Carex stricta* 'Aurea' to the bright
blue of *Festuca caesia* or, more dramatically, the black of *Ophiopogon planiscarpus*
'Nigrescens'. The black-leaved ophiopogon would be useful here, since it is good in
both sun and shade.

Colouring that picture at once produced a more interesting planting, one that
has the chance of both resting the mind and pleasing the senses. But it
is nothing new. It is merely what is called a colour group. The problem with such
groupings is that, because only individual plants are used most of the time, the effect
can be garish, almost shocking; acceptable in a public place where you pass it once in a
while, but too violent to live with, at peace, in your own garden. Its discordance is
merely a product of its promiscuity. Such a group lacks the essential simplicity of
good design.

The first principle of design is restraint, not indulgence. A quiet but deliberate
statement is usually far more effective than a strident striving for effect. It is, from a
purely design point of view, something of a misfortune that the cool, temperate
regions of the world will grow with such ease such an abundance of good garden
plants. It is all too tempting simply to keep piling one good plant into the garden after

another, year after year, until the garden is filled with an indecent, undisciplined ebullience of flowers and foliage. What one misses by such indulgence is the serenity of a scene that has been deliberately created.

No doubt most of us create our gardens in ways that come about largely by chance. We usually set out with some basic design in mind, some general interrelationship of lawns and borders, but the way we fill those borders leaves too much to chance. It is usually determined by such simple things as what the local garden centre actually has to offer, and on seeds and cuttings offered by friends because those plants looked good in their garden. We tend to forget that in their garden they were being grown in a different setting.

There are ways of handling the problem of promiscuity. Let us take a suburban front garden as an example and see how that might be handled.

A front garden presents problems. In the first place you have to decide whether to lay it out so that it looks better when seen from the house or from the street – or so that it looks equally attractive from both angles. Whichever decision you take is going to make a statement about you, and this is probably why many people simply put the front garden down to lawn.

'Suburban traditional' seems to offer most people an acceptable compromise. The tradition is to put a border along the front of the house, a border along the hedge or wall by the road (or whatever front boundary there may be) and usually another border along the boundary with one neighbour. Keen gardeners tend also to have a border beside the drive. The convention further requires that one has a square lawn in the middle, and a hedge (usually green and usually privet) along that boundary. Your neighbour on the other side will usually have done the same so that you have hedges (usually green and usually privet) on both sides of your front garden. People who want to break with convention and assert their individuality usually plant, instead of the common green privet, its yellow form, *Ligustrum ovalifolium* 'Aureum', a plant of chlorotically jaundiced appearance. Even that has now become a convention for the unconventional. It always helps to know the conventions: it makes them easier to break.

A fairly straightforward multi-coloured alternative would consist merely of spaces which need to be filled with plants with coloured foliage, each space with one plant only (Fig. 1, overleaf).

To demonstrate one further point, let's use the same plants that we used in the original promiscuous colour group, and see how different they look when massed. The circle in the lower left-hand corner (1) is packed with *Phormium tenax* 'Purpureum'. It will in time make a large clump of sword-shaped leaves as much as 2m (6½ft) long of a rich, reddish mahogany colour. The second area (2) is filled with *Arundinaria viridistriata* 'Feesey's Form' (a dwarf form, growing to about 60cm [2ft]), which is a brilliant bright yellow all year round. In the top left-hand corner (3), which tends to be a little dark anyway, we plant a carpet of *Ophiopogon planiscarpus* 'Nigrescens' : its sheer blackness not only supplies a dramatic contrast to the bright

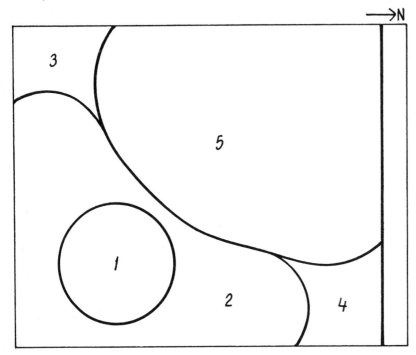

→N

FIGURE I
Key
1 *Phormium tenax*
  'Purpureum'
2 *Arundinaria viridistriata*
  'Feesey's Form'
3 *Ophiopogon planiscarpus*
  'Nigrescens'
4 *Festuca caesia*
5 *Holcus mollis* 'Variegata'
or
1 *Canna indica*
  'Le Roi Humbert'
2 *Iresine herbstii*
  'Aureo-reticulata'
3 *Coleus* 'Roi des Noires'
4 *Helichrysum mycrophyllu*
5 *Chlorophytum elatum*
  'Variegatum'

yellow of the bamboo, but also makes a virtue of the darkness of that corner. In the bottom right-hand corner (4) we can plant either brilliant blue *Festuca caesia* or *Bergenia crassifolia* whose virtues are its round leaves which flush purplish in winter and its rich pink flowers, borne very early in the year. Finally there is the area that is left (5) when those shapes have been filled. The obvious solution would be to put it down to lawn; an alternative would be to plant a brilliantly white-variegated grass that can be mown once established, *Holcus mollis* 'Variegata'. This is a bright little grass, growing to about 30cm (1ft) and spreading slowly but steadily. It runs just enough to make turf but not enough to be a nuisance, and when trimmed over with shears not only remains a brighter colour the whole year through, but also spreads to form a denser turf. After a couple of seasons it can quite readily be mown.

The above example illustrates the qualities of the multi-coloured garden. Its strengths are its simplicity, its total lack of promiscuity: every element is planned; nothing is left to chance. Furthermore, it looks good from every angle.

You may of course feel that that is not really gardening, but merely making patterns with plants, like modern non-figurative painters. But what Brown and Repton were doing was simply imitating paintings. They were trying to bring into being the sort of scenes that men like Claude Lorraine were painting. Painting has moved on since then, however, and so has gardening. If you feel that to garden in that idiom would leave you no scope to exercise your cultural skills you could not easily be so wrong: it will stretch them to the limit. Furthermore, a garden designed in this idiom both needs and provides pockets of intensely promiscuous plantings: they are the jewels of such a garden; the rest is merely a rather finer setting than most gardeners give to their most treasured plants. The very simplicity of the general scheme shows off the detail of your own little corners to perfection.

It may be that in spite of the effectiveness of curves and curls of colour, your taste or your house or your existing garden calls for something more formal. In this case you could divide the whole front garden up into a series of squares, like a chessboard, and then carry the theme through by planting alternate squares black and white (Fig. 2). You could use *Ophiopogon planiscarpus* 'Nigrescens' for the black squares, and *Holcus mollis* 'Variegata' for the white squares. If you need a boundary between the garden and the road, use a tabletop hedge of alternating dark and light colours: *Buxus sempervirens* 'Suffruticosa' would provide the darker colour, and *Buxus sempervirens* 'Elegantissima' (a beautiful white-variegated form) could provide the lighter squares. Keep the tabletop trimmed to whatever height you want it, though it should not be above 2ft high to marry well with the chessboard lawn. In a very small garden it could be effective to use a similar but simpler approach, merely straight parallel lines of alternate black or green and white, using tabletops again to define the boundary (Fig. 3, overleaf) but this time keeping the whites in line with the whites, instead of alternating them.

All this may sound at first a far cry from our great gardening tradition. It is not. It is

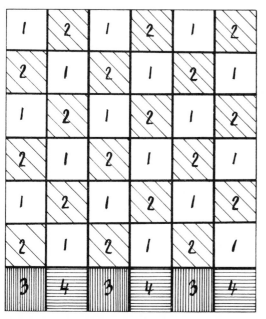

FIGURE 2
Key
1 *Holcus mollis* 'Variegata'
2 *Ophiopogon planiscarpus* 'Nigrescens'
3 *Buxus sempervirens* 'Suffruticosa'
4 *Buxus sempervirens* 'Elegantissima'

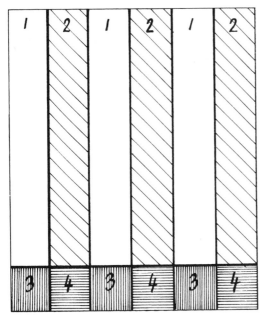

FIGURE 3
Key
1 *Holcus mollis* 'Variegata'
2 *Ophiopogon planiscarpus* 'Nigrescens'
3 *Buxus sempervirens* 'Suffruticosa'
4 *Buxus sempervirens* 'Elegantissima'

merely a development of it, drawing its inspiration from the two main strands of our gardening heritage, the English landscape movement and carpet bedding. What one is doing, in essence, is carpet bedding with permanent plants, and setting the plants out in freehand curves and contours borrowed from the landscape movement.

Carpet bedding is now a much-denigrated manner of gardening, and like most much-denigrated forms of gardening is considered fit only for public places (though that is not the reason one tends to see it only in public places). In its heyday carpet bedding must have provided many marvellous sights: its sheer scale was impressive, but the complexities of the patterns in which most of the plants are laid out would be beyond the competence of most gardeners today. Pattern books were published, showing ever more and more complicated patterns and demanding ever more and more plants. One of the main reasons why carpet bedding fell into decline was indeed a consequence of the numbers of plants needed to do it on the grand scale: some schemes called for 20,000 or 30,000 plants. The expense was immense; not only did one need acres of glass in which to raise sufficient plants, one also needed a veritable army of gardeners to tend them. Few people today could calmly countenance such extravagance.

Just to emphasise the similarity between the multi-coloured concept and carpet bedding, let's re-do that front garden (Fig. 1), this time with accepted carpet-bedding plants. We replace the clump of purple phormium with the purple of *Canna* 'Le Roi Humbert', with its big, bold leaves and bright red flowers; the golden bamboo with

Iresine herbstii 'Aureo-reticulata', a brilliant plant too seldom seen, with vivid yellow leaves overlaid with a network of bright red veins. Then we replace the black of *Ophiopogon planiscarpus* 'Nigrescens' with the rather flat black of *Coleus* 'Roi des Noires'. Next we replace the blue of *Festuca caesia* with a silver, *Helichrysum microphyllum*, a delightful little grey-leaved trailing plant, very similar to the better-known *Helichrysum petiolatum* but with tiny leaves and a more decidedly trailing habit. Finally, we replace the white-variegated *Holcus mollis* 'Variegata' either with a variegated bedding grass, such as *Stenotaphrum secundatum* 'Variegatum', or with the grass-like spider plant, *Chlorophytum elatum* 'Variegatum'.

Even to carry through a scheme like this, however, you need quite a lot of glass to bring the plants on, and you need to go to some expense to bring them safely through winter. Meanwhile that area of glass cannot be used to grow other things, which in its turn helps to highlight why the multi-coloured concept offers such an excitingly viable alternative. Working with permanent plants you start with a small number and just keep multiplying them until you have sufficient for a particular area.

So far we have really only looked at the multi-coloured concept in terms of the patterns drawn on the ground. But there is more even to carpet bedding than merely that. One needs a vertical accent here and there, and changes in level as well. Let us take a further example: a square front garden, with a logarithmic spiral whose tightest point is up near the top right-hand corner of the plan (Fig. 4). The lowest-growing element is *Festuca caesia* (1), with its steely blue needles. The next

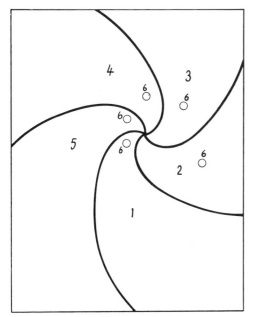

FIGURE 4
Key
1 *Festuca caesia*
2 *Carex buchanani*
3 *Euonymus* 'Emerald 'n Gold'
4 *Cotinus coggygria* 'Royal Purple'
5 *Juniperus squamata* 'Chinese Silver'
6 *Juniperus scopulorum* 'Skyrocket'

element is *Carex buchanani* (2), with its brilliant, foxy-red leaves. Then in complete contrast there are the rounded leaves of the bright yellow *Euonymus* 'Emerald'n Gold' (3), the purple-leafed *Cotinus coggygria* 'Royal Purple' (4), and finally the tallest of the basic pattern colours, the bright silver of *Juniperus squamata* 'Chinese Silver' (5). That is a pattern, but it is a pattern in height as well as in spread. The final ingredient, the one that links all the other elements together, is the use of a vertical accent, a series of sentinel-like *Juniperus scopulorum* 'Skyrocket' (6) striding across each element of the pattern and in so doing tying them together into one cohesive visual entity.

That is essentially all there is to multi-coloured gardening. But since plants are the main visual element in any garden, and since multi-coloured gardens are made up mainly of plants with coloured leaves, we need to look at those plants best suited to the purpose before turning to further plans.

CHAPTER TWO

Multi-coloured Plants

You might think that multi-coloured plants are just what you need for a multi-coloured garden. In fact the great majority are an absolute disaster when massed. Let's take just a few multi-coloured plants and see which are good for massing and which are not and, if possible, why.

Bugle, *Ajuga reptans*, is a common, lowly little plant with few pretensions to garden worthiness, at least in its wild form. But it has sported a number of exciting colour-leafed forms, of which two are outstanding. The first is *A.r.* 'Burgundy Glow' whose leaves do indeed glow a rich burgundy colour. In fact, the leaf is very multi-coloured, the overall colouring being made up of four or five different colours of which blue, pink, mauve and purple are the dominant ones, along with a pale greyish-white haze just masking the green. The second of the multi-coloured bugles is variously known as 'Harlequin', 'Rainbow' and 'Multicolour'. In this form the leaves seem to be completely lacking in green, the background colour being a greyish-white which is marked and splashed red, pink, mauve, blue and orange. It is a very colourful leaf, far brighter than that of 'Burgundy Glow'. When massed, it is 'Burgundy Glow' that is the more effective, the mauvish colouring coming over clearly when the plant is growing densely across a large area. The overall effect of 'Multicolour' is off-white, the brightness being lost at a distance and in quantity. Both are easy to grow, happy almost anywhere, and show their colour best in good light.

Moving up a little in size is *Calluna vulgaris*, one of the calcifuge heathers. There is an outstanding form called 'Multicolour', whose leaves are variously yellow, red, orange, bronze and old gold, all these colours appearing on the plant at the same time, with a slight shift of emphasis from summer to winter. It is a veritable riot of colour and, because the colours are all related, falling within the same relative band of the spectrum, it is singularly effective when used in vast quantities, an almost internally illuminated bright orange colour predominating. It is an altogether excellent plant for massing, growing to only 15 or 20cm (6 or 8in.) and is completely weed-proof once established. It does best on a light, sandy soil, but even heavy clay can be sufficiently improved for it to thrive. Like most coloured plants, it needs full sun to colour well.

The genus *Cornus* is full of good things. *Cornus florida* is one of the so-called flowering dogwoods, and it is the one with the twist to the bracts; *C. kousa* has untwisted bracts, while *C. nuttallii* has much larger, showier bracts. *C. florida* has two good multi-coloured forms. The first is 'Rainbow' in which the leaves are green, strongly marked with a white variegation which fades to a rich, pink flush towards the centre of the leaf. The second is 'Tricolor', in which yellow is the dominant colour (where white is the dominant colour in 'Rainbow'). In both the flowering bracts are white, but are rather lost against the brilliant leaves. Both have brilliant autumn colour, both are desirable plants, but neither amounts to much when massed. The beauty is all in the individual leaf, which makes them fine as focal-point plants. They need good cultivation, and show their colouring best when grown in a slightly shaded and definitely sheltered position. Both come readily from late June cuttings, a method of increase much to be preferred to grafting: grafted plants invariably sucker considerably.

Another multi-coloured cornus is *C. mas* 'Elegantissima'. *C. mas* is the male cornus or Cornelian cherry, grown normally for its bright show of tiny yellow frost-resistant flowers in February. It slowly forms a rather twiggy, shrub-like small tree. In the form 'Elegantissima', which is far slower-growing than the typical plant, the leaves are variegated yellow and rose pink, with just a touch of green at the centre. Because the leaves are small and the yellow a strong colour, this is a plant that is effective when massed since, seen from a distance the overall impression is of a yellow-variegated plant. It is only when it is seen at close quarters that the detailed beauty of the leaves can be properly appreciated. Sadly, it is quite a rare plant, presumably because, being slow-growing, there is little propagating material on it. It is a plant to treat well, with carefully prepared soil and an annual mulch of leaf mould; it prefers a position in slight shade – the leaves scorch in full sun.

Hypericum is, to far too many people, just that frightfully dull thing they grow in public places instead of weeds, with more or less evergreen leaves and bright yellow flowers for much of the summer. That hypericum is *H. calycinum*, and I rather like it. There is a hybrid between that and another showy hypericum, *H. patulum*, known as *H.* x *moseranum*, of which there is a variegated form called 'Tricolor'. In this the leaves, which are relatively narrow, are variegated brightly with green, white and pink. Seen at a distance, the overall effect is of a white-variegated plant, and because the white is so dominant, it is excellent for massing. Unfortunately it lacks the running qualities of *H. calycinum*, so that one needs a lot of plants in order to mass it, but it can be increased readily from August cuttings or division, and is happy in almost any soil. In cold areas it tends to behave more like a perennial than a shrub and, even where it is decidedly shrubby, benefits from having the previous season's growth clipped off: this seems to make the colouring brighter.

Pelargoniums are what most people call geraniums (though geraniums are a far finer thing) – a group of plants typified by those forms with bright scarlet blobs of flowers much used for bedding. There is, however, a considerable diversity of pelargoniums, with a great variety of leaf and flower forms and colours beyond the range usually grown. *Pelargonium* x *hortorum* 'Mrs Henry Cox' has the same rounded leaf as the typical bedding geranium, and the same scent to the leaf, but it is richly variegated yellow, cream, white, pink, red and purple with, just occasionally, a little green, the colours being presented in concentric bands. It is a somewhat unstable plant, given to throwing odd shoots of completely cream leaves, but a good leaf of it is a beautiful thing, about as multi-coloured as a leaf can be. A small, well-grown, well-balanced plant is a joy to see. Massed, it is a mess. No one colour dominates sufficiently for the plant to be effective. *P. x h.* 'The Czar', on the other hand, is very effective when massed. It too has the typical rounded leaf of the bedding geranium, with a base colour of a rich, strong yellow: about two-thirds of the way from the centre of the leaf to the margin there is a band of maroon, with the interfaces where yellow and maroon meet being brightly brick red. Both need the same treatment as other pelargoniums.

Pseudowintera colorata, formerly *Drimys colorata*, is one of those plants whose leaves are naturally coloured, no green-leaved form being known. The leaves, which are thick and fleshy, are an extraordinary pale yellow flushed pink and edged with crimson: the underside is glaucous. It is a small shrub, slowly growing to perhaps 1.3–1.6m (4–5ft) high and rather more than twice as much across, but very slow. Seen from a distance, the overall effect is of a pale yellow plant – yet there is something about the yellow that tempts you to look closer. If you can give it the conditions it needs – a semi-shaded position with shelter from cold winds – it is excellent for massing. It is essentially a woodland plant, and woodland conditions are what you must replicate in your garden if you are to succeed with it. It is well worth the trouble of preparing the soil for it thoroughly by mixing in copious quantities of leaf-mould or peat, and then mulching it annually with one or other. The roots are thick and fleshy like those of magnolias (to which it is closely related) and, since these rot very readily if damaged during planting, it is always best to plant it rather later than other shrubs, and certainly not until it is in growth, since then any damage done to the roots will be quickly repaired.

Pyracantha coccinea 'Harlequin' is always billed as a multi-coloured plant, and strictly it probably is, since the leaves (which are just like those of any other pyracantha) are margined white and flushed pink with a green centre. The overall effect, however, is of a white-variegated shrub, and a very effective one at that. Part of its appeal is that it is far brighter than the usual green-leafed pyracanthas and can be grown, just as they are, in dry, poor soil at the foot of a drafty north wall. It flowers and berries as well as other pyracanthas, but the variegation is a decided bonus. It should be good for massing, but in fact fails for the same reason as other pyracanthas when grown away from a wall: it flops all over the place, even as a small plant. The only way it can be used in quantity is to ensure that it does its flopping early in its life, and then to give it an occasional trim to keep it in bounds. It is happy in any reasonable soil, and comes readily from late June cuttings, or cuttings taken from then until winter.

Rubus is the genus that embraces such fruit-bearing plants as the raspberry, loganberry and blackberry. It also includes a large number of excellent ground-cover plants. One of the most curious of these is a diminutive species known as *Rubus microphyllus*, of which the form 'Variegatus' has exceptionally brightly multi-coloured leaves. These are narrowly triangular, bright green splashed with red and white. It is a slowly-suckering shrub that gradually builds itself up into little mounds of rather congested growth. The overall effect of a large area of it is pink – an unusual colour for massing. The colour shows best when the plant is grown in full sun, and especially when the plant is cut to ground level each year. It will grow happily in any fertile soil, and needs little fussing. It can be increased by layering, division or cuttings taken in late summer.

The multi-coloured charms of *Saxifraga stolonifera* are very low-key compared with the jazzy brightness of *Rubus microphyllus* 'Variegatus'. The leaves are round and subtly marbled grey, white and pink, with a deeper pink at the margins. It is a plant that is frequently grown on a windowsill, where the bright red stolons, with their little plantlets at the tips, can be allowed to hang down. In the garden the stolons spread horizontally, the plantlets rooting and throwing out more stolons. Its stoloniferous habit makes it a quite rapid coloniser, though never invasive and never likely to become a nuisance. It is not wholly frost hardy, though it is very seldom that a whole colony is killed outright. *S. stolonifera* grows best in a moist, shaded spot, under shrubs (preferably evergreen), or at the foot of a north wall, and needs a light soil with plenty of leaf-mould or peat mixed in and lying on the surface to grow well. An established colony is always a delight. It is readily increased by detaching the plantlets and potting them up before planting them out.

Tovara virginiana (which may or may not now be *Polygonum filiforme*) 'Painter's Palette' is another low-key multi-coloured plant. It is an herbaceous perennial with a clump-forming habit that throws its leaves up rather later in the year than most perennials. The leaves are broadly oval, variegated ivory-yellow, grey and red with, about half-way along the leaf, a clearly defined, broad, inverted V of deep brown marked red and pink. The colouring is palest in spring, gradually growing richer as the year advances. There is a plant sold as *T.v.* 'Variegata' which is similar but less strongly coloured. The leafy stems of both grow to about 60cm (2ft) in height, and the clumps are slow to spread but, if you divide regularly, you can soon build up sufficient stocks to mass them. They grow best in a position in which they get sun for about half the day, preferably the second half, and need a good fertile soil containing plenty of organic matter. The overall effect of a massed planting is a curious brownish-grey. I have never seen the plants flower, but the flowers are described as tiny, dark brown and totally insignificant.

What emerges from this brief survey of multi-coloured plants is that it is those multi-coloured plants in which one of the colours predominates that are of some use for massing, and those in which the colours are fairly evenly distributed that are of little use. If you use multi-coloured plants in quantity in a multi-coloured garden, they are best used near the house, or near a sitting area, where you can enjoy both their effect when seen from a distance as well as the beauty of the details of the individual leaves.

CHAPTER THREE

Vari-coloured Plants

If you are going to spend good money on good plants, and if you are going to take the time and trouble to plan your garden properly, prepare the ground thoroughly, plant the plants with care and cultivate them with skill, it is worth spending that money on plants that will give you more than one season of pleasure in the year – plants, for example, whose foliage is one colour in spring, another in summer and yet another in autumn. Such plants have a particular value in the multi-coloured garden, their varying colours providing different colour schemes at different seasons in the one place.

An extreme example of variability in leaf colouring occurs in those plants grown for their autumn colouring. Such plants, of necessity, are deciduous, so that in addition to their summer and autumn colours, one has the further season of interest when they are stripped to their skeletal winter form.

The Japanese maples are among the most brilliant of all plants in the intensity of their autumn colouring. What never ceases to amaze is that, although one knows perfectly well that they have dazzling autumn colour, one has almost forgotten, from one year to the next, just how intense it is: the plants glow, as though illuminated from within with an intense fieriness that is almost shocking. The term Japanese maple is usually taken to include two quite distinct species and their forms. The first is *Acer japonicum*, a species which slowly forms a small, much-branched tree and whose leaves are rounded in outline. The second is *Acer palmatum*, again a small, many-branched tree, but differing in that the leaves are distinctly five- or seven-lobed. They are not easily confused once you know them.

The most useful of these maples in the multi-coloured garden are the cut-leaf forms. The term cut-leaf maple in fact embraces not only *Acer palmatum* 'Dissectum', but a whole group of clones all of which have in common very finely cut leaves. Typically, the leaves are composed of anything from five to nine lobes, each of which is cut almost to the midrib. *Acer palmatum* 'Dissectum' itself has light green leaves and is worth growing in the multi-coloured garden on that account. *A.p.* 'Dissectum Atropurpureum' (which seems to be the same plant as *A.p.* 'Purpureum') has the same cut leaves, but of a good rich horticultural purple. 'Dissectum Nigrum' has very much darker leaves and is even more desirable. 'Dissectum Flavescens' has leaves that are euphemistically described as 'soft yellow': the colour is not strong. 'Dissectum Ornatum' has leaves that are neither green nor purple but appear to be green with an overlay of purple: it tends to be disappointing. 'Dissectum Variegatum' has a basic leaf colour of a good strong purple, and the segments of the leaves are tipped and margined rose-pink and creamy white. It sounds a mess but is actually extremely effective in the garden.

You could make a colour band or block of any of these and gain pleasure from it all summer through as a green or a purple or a near-black, and then enjoy it all over again in autumn as a band of fiery scarlet burning brilliantly as though on fire. Then there is a short season when the sere leaves still hang on the shrubs, before the winter form of the twigs adds yet another season of interest. All grow into mushroom-shaped bushes with their lowest twigs trailing on the ground and, if planted close enough, will run one into another. This creates the effect of a series of mounds within a colour band, an interesting quality to exploit in its own right. If you want the colour band to look as though it were one solid, continuous level, you need to plant in a quincunx formation.

These cut-leaf maples will grow on any fertile soil so long as the drainage is good. They benefit from a liberal treatment of the ground before planting, and plenty of leaf-mould used as a mulch each year. What they will not tolerate are cold winds or draughts, and it is important to bear that in mind when siting them. If they can be protected from cold winds with a taller colour band of contrasting colour they will give of their best.

There are two other very small maples which are so brilliantly coloured in autumn that they are worth including, even though it may be a year or two before you can obtain them. The first is *Acer circinatum* 'Little Gem', which originated as a witch's broom on a tree in Canada. The leaf is typical of the species, but about half the normal size, and the plant is extremely slow-growing, putting on only a couple of centimetres a year, and gradually forming a well-rounded little bush. In autumn the whole plant becomes a ball of brilliant scarlet. The other is *A. ginnala* 'Durand Dwarf', which forms a mound-like bush about 1.6m (5ft) across and 1m (3ft) high after ten years. The leaves, which are narrowly triangular in outline and three-lobed, become the most intense, self-illuminating crimson in autumn, every leaf changing to the same colour at the same time. In that respect, there could scarcely be a better maple for massing for autumn effect.

After the elegant refinement of the maples, bergenias seem coarse, crass plants. Yet it is precisely the boldness of their foliage that makes them of such value in the garden. The roundness of their leaves makes them excellent companions for irises, phormiums and any other plants with sword-shaped leaves.

The most valuable of the bergenias for the multi-coloured garden are those whose leaves turn rich purplish tones in winter. Probably the most widely grown of these is *Bergenia cordifolia* 'Purpurea', with big, rounded, glossy leaves up to 75cm (2½ft) long and 60cm (2ft) across, which turn a vivid purple in winter: the flowers are a good magenta colour, and the plant has the further merit of making excellent ground cover. *B. crassifolia* has somewhat smaller leaves of a less tough texture which turn mahogany in winter rather than purple. It is altogether a slightly smaller plant. If I had room for only one, I would go for the first: given more space I would grow both for the contrast in winter colouring.

By far the finest of the bergenias in winter colour is *B. purpurascens*. It differs from the two previously mentioned first in that the leaves are somewhat spoon-shaped, second in that they are slightly hairy and third in that they are a little smaller. From October till April they turn the most vivid, glorious beetroot red, a colour unsurpassed in the genus. The flowers are mauvish, held on red stalks, one of the most vivid flower colours in the genus. *B. beesianum* (which botanists have now relegated to a position where it is conspecific with *purpurascens*) is in effect a dwarf form of *purpurascens*, and this dwarfness makes it useful in smaller gardens.

There is also a number of excellent hybrid bergenias that colour well in winter. Probably the most popular of these is 'Ballawley' which has very large, very rounded, very glossy leaves which squeak if you rub them against each other and turn a vivid, almost hectic liver-red in winter. The flowers, which are borne on tall stalks, are bright crimson. The only disappointing thing about this plant is that the leaves are not wholly frost hardy, so that unless it is grown in a relatively sheltered position or under large, spreading evergreen trees, some of the leaves may be turned to pulp by frosts. More effective in this respect is the hybrid 'Sunningdale', which is thought to be a cross between *cordifolia* and *purpurascens*. As such it should be stunning – and it is: it has the winter colour of *purpurascens* and the ground-covering capabilities of *cordifolia*, and the flowers are of a good lilac-carmine.

All the bergenias grow well in any fertile soil, in sun or shade, though they only show their best winter colours in sun, and are readily increased by division, preferably in spring. They are tolerant of poor growing conditions, but definitely thrive best when treated to generous cultivation.

The Japanese cedar, *Cryptomeria japonica* (which is not a cedar at all but a relative of the swamp cypress), has a number of cultivated forms noted for their winter colouring. *C.j.* 'Elegans' is probably the best-known of these, forming in time a large, bushy shrub or small tree with perpetually juvenile foliage which turns to a glowing bronzy-red all winter. Nurserymen have a way of making it sound a highly desirable plant: it isn't. Given a good few years' growth, a couple of gales and a light fall of snow, the whole plant splays open like the wreck of the *Hesperis*. *C.j.* 'Elegans Compacta' is not much better.

The two forms of *Cryptomeria japonica* which do make excellent vari-coloured garden plants are *C.j.* 'Compressa' and *C.j.* 'Vilmoriniana'. Both are very slow-growing, tightly congested little bushes, packed with foliage, which in forty years will form flat-topped domes less than 1 m (3 ft) high. The foliage of both is dark green, turning a rich, reddish-purple in winter. Both are neat, tidy plants, excellent for massing in colour blocks or bands, and easily raised from cuttings.

Dacrydium laxifolium is variously known as the pygmy pine and the mountain rimu. It is certainly pygmy, though not a pine at all, and it is naturally the smallest conifer in cultivation. A wiry-stemmed little shrublet that crawls over the ground, it adds only a couple of centimetres to its spread each year, and takes about thirty years to attain a spread of 1m (3ft) and a height of 10 or 12.5cm (4 or 5ins.). The leaves, which are tiny and sharply pointed, are decidedly glaucous in summer, but in winter the whole plant turns the most amazing bright violet-purple – quite unlike the winter colouring of any other hardy plant – and at that season it is even more bewitching than in summer. It has the bonus of decorating itself, even when very tiny, with minute, bright red cones. Because it is so slow-growing you need a large number of plants to achieve much effect, but it comes very readily from November cuttings, so the only problem is obtaining sufficient propagating material. It seems happy in any fertile soil in a sunny position.

An excellent companion for *Dacrydium laxifolium* is *Larix decidua* 'Corley', a miniature larch which is winning in every way. It slowly forms a leaderless little bun of a bush, growing to only a couple of feet in height, but spreading about twice that. Like those of the larger larches, the twigs have a purplish hue in winter when massed, then in spring the whole bush is the most vivid green, passing to a deeper, though never dark green in summer: it is in autumn that this larch is at its most spectacular, turning a glowing, burning yellow. A colour band of it is a breath-taking sight. Its sole problem is that it is a plant that can only be increased by grafting, which tends to make it expensive to mass.

Another genus noted for autumn colour is *Liquidambar* which, though closely allied to *Hamamelis*, is frequently confused with *Acer*. *Liquidambar* differs from maple in having the leaves alternate instead of opposite. The majority of species and forms are large-growing trees, typically tall and narrow until maturity, when they become spreading. There is just one form that is dwarf enough to mass in small gardens – *Liquidambar styraciflua* 'Red Dwarf', which grows into a compact, perfectly rounded little ball that in autumn turns into a blaze of reds, yellows and oranges, a veritable ball of fire. It has only recently been introduced to cultivation, but has great potential in the multi-coloured garden as a colour-band element. It needs an acid, fertile soil and is readily increased from cuttings.

Microbiota decussata is another of nature's relatively small-growing conifers, seldom exceeding 30cm (1ft) in height, and making a spread of about 2m (6½ft) each way across the ground. The foliage is bright green, soft and feathery, held in flattened sprays, and turns a rich bronze throughout winter. It is easily grown in any soil, in full exposure even in the coldest areas, and the only reason it is still rare is that it is fairly new to cultivation, having only been introduced in the late 1960s. It is also rare in the wild, being found in only one valley to the east of Vladivostock in coldest Siberia. It can readily be propagated by cuttings taken almost any time in winter, and also layers itself readily.

The ironwood tree, *Parrotia persica*, is scarcely a tree at all, at least not in this country where it usually forms a multi-stemmed shrub of enormous size with a good spring show of bright red staminoid flowers, bark that exfoliates like that of the London plane, and brilliant autumn colour. It is too large to mass in most gardens, but there is a more or less dwarf form, *P.p.* 'Pendula' which, provided you grow it on its own roots and not grafted on top of a 1.6m (5ft) stalk, sprawls over the ground in serpentine fashion with no inclination whatever to grow upwards. By the time it has humped itself up to 30cm (1ft) in height, it will have spread at least 5ft across the ground. If you grow a mass of it, with one plant running into another, it in time forms a weed-proof carpet of humps and valleys, and in autumn the whole lights up with fiery scarlets, crimsons, oranges and yellows. There is no other garden plant which can create that brilliancy of autumn colour at ground level. It needs acid soil and good cultivation, and can be increased reasonably easily by mid–summer cuttings.

The genus *Pieris* stands in the same degree of pre-eminence among spring foliage shrubs as *Acer* does among autumn-colouring shrubs. *Pieris* is a genus of evergreen ericaceous shrubs whose flowers resemble those of lily-of-the-valley and whose new growths are almost invariably bright red. It is for these brilliant red new leaves that it is grown, rather than for the flowers which, while they would be exciting on any other shrub, pale into insignificance beside the vividness of the new growths. The finest plant in the genus is *Pieris formosa forrestii* which, under optimum conditions, can grow up to 7m (22ft) in height and produces in spring new growths that emerge bright scarlet, then gradually mature through crimson to pink, then to a yellowish-white, then yellowish-green and finally dark green – but by that time in the season a second flush of scarlet new growth has usually started to show itself. The only problem is that the plant is not bone hardy, though tough enough for most of us most of the time. It comes readily from seed, and a number of seedlings have been selected and named as being superior in one way or another: 'Charles Michael' has the largest individual flowers; 'Jermyns' has the largest and showiest flower truss; while 'Wakehurst', which may possibly be a hybrid, is smaller in stature, with smaller leaves but has possibly even more brilliant new growths. 'Forest Flame' is similar to 'Wakehurst' but freer in flower. *P. japonica* is a smaller, wider-growing plant, whose new growths are merely copper-coloured, as is the case with most of the other pieris species and forms. Two forms of *P. japonica* are, however, of outstanding interest. These are *P.j.* 'White Swan', whose new growths come through a brilliant and totally unexpected white, and *P.j. pygmaea*, a tiny little plant, scarcely recognizable as a pieris at all, growing to only about 30cm (1ft) in ten years, with minute leaves and a very neat and compact habit. The new growths of the latter are red rather than copper, but not so brilliant as the various *forestii* forms. It is, however, so useful in a small garden for massing that this slight loss of intensity of colouring is tolerable.

All the pierises need cool, moist, woodland conditions to thrive, and a very definitely acid soil. They can be readily increased by seed, soft tip cuttings or by layering. They are at their loveliest used as colour bands at the edge of woodland.

Moving from colour bands to accent plants, the neatness of the shape of the spruces makes them absolutely ideal for this purpose, especially in smaller gardens. There is something very satisfying about their symmetry. The common Christmas tree,

Picea abies, has a clone, 'Aurea', which turns yellow in winter, but the colouring is not really fine enough to commend it. Far, far better, not only in the intensity of the colouring, but also in the density of the foliage and the compactness of the plant, is *Picea orientalis* 'Aurea', whose shoots emerge creamy-yellow in spring and mature to a rich, bright yellow by mid-summer, after which they fade to green. It is an ideal plant to use as a series of specimens striding across colour bands and linking them together.

Few pines have the symmetry of habit of the spruces and the Scots pine least of all, but it does have a form that turns an intense yellow in winter, *Pinus sylvestris* 'Aurea', an indispensable plant in a vari-coloured garden. It is really just like an ordinary Scots pine though rather slower in growth, but at the first frost of winter the needles start turning yellow and then quickly change to a deep, rich golden yellow across the whole plant. The new growths also emerge a brilliant yellow, and the summer is half-gone before they have faded to green. This pine will grow in almost any soil, but needs sun for the winter colouring to show brightly: the side of the tree away from the sun is decidedly less yellow than the side that is in the sun. It does not make a particularly attractive tree, and is preferable grown as a bush so that you look down on it. All you need do to keep it low, multi-stemmed and bushy is pinch out the leading shoot as soon as you buy the plant and then keep pinching out growths. If you do this, it can be used to stunning effect as a colour band.

There is an even more brilliantly winter-coloured pine in the pipeline, a golden form of *Pinus radiata*. Not only is the colouring very much more intense than *P. sylvestris*, but it also has its typically very leafy habit, which makes it even showier in the garden.

There are two forms of *Thuja orientalis* which change colour in winter and which are restricted enough in size to make colour bands in small gardens. The first is *T.o.* 'Juniperoides' which, as its varietal name suggests, has prickly foliage like a juniper and really does not look like a thuja at all. It slowly forms a conical bush, about 2m (6½ft) high by 1m (3ft) across, and, while the leaves are a soft, blue-green through summer, they change to a curious mauvish colour in winter, unique and very striking. The other form is *T.o.* 'Rosedalis' which has foliage that is both soft to look at and to touch and a rounded habit, slowly growing to about 1m (3ft) in height by 45cm (18ins.) across. Unlike most vari-coloured plants, which have only two colours, this one goes through three quite distinct colours each season. It is bright yellow-green in spring, mid-green in summer, and plum-purple in winter. Both grow happily in any fertile soil, and colour well so long as they are in sun.

Thujopsis dolabrata 'Nana' is a low-growing, wide-spreading little bun of a bush with bright green, fresh foliage presented in flattened sprays, the sprays held somewhat upright on the bush, and the whole plant turning to a rich, glowing coppery-orange through the winter. In ten years a plant will make about 1.5m (4½ft) spread and about 0.75m (2¼ft) in height. This makes it ideal for use in colour bands or blocks. It is very easily increased by cuttings taken in November.

Departing from foliage, though not from the multi-coloured concept, mention must be made of the dogwoods. This genus, some of whose members have beautifully coloured stems, outshines all others in winter. The coloured stems appear to become more and more brilliant as winter goes on: the worse the winter, the better they seem to be. Perhaps the most typical of the colour-stemmed dogwoods is *Cornus alba*, whose stems are a deep, rich crimson through winter. There are forms with variegated leaves, both white and gold variegations, but if you want to grow your dogwoods for their winter bark, you need to coppice them every other year, and it is no good doing that with the variegated ones. *C. alba* 'Siberica', sometimes also known as 'Westonbirt', has the brightest stems of all – clean scarlet. The two together make an interesting contrast, but to get the very best from them you need something more subdued to show them off, and the almost black-purple stems of *C.a.* 'Kesselringii' make the perfect foil. A second species of cornus, *C. stolonifera*, provides yet more colour-stemmed dogwoods. *C. stolonifera* itself has dark red stems – rather a heavy colour, but useful. *C.s.* 'Flaviramea' has bright yellow stems and is exceedingly showy. There is also a form with stems of the brightest imaginable pea-green, *C.s.* var. *nitida*, which sadly is little-known (though it is occasionally sold as 'Flaviramea' – a disappointment if you want bright yellow stems). The green needs to stand in front of the scarlet or yellow to be really effective. There is a further species with green stems, *C. paliophylla*, which is even brighter. All these dogwoods come readily from hardwood cuttings.

If you use your vari-coloured plants with skill you can have two gardens in the one place, and more than double the pleasure your garden will give. The trouble is that you will need to plan the garden twice, once working it through for the plants in their summer colours, and a second time for the plants in their winter colours. The challenge of making such a garden, and making it well, is almost irresistible, especially when you consider the diversity of plants in this chapter alone. But before you rush out to make your vari-coloured summer/winter garden, read on: there is more, far more to come.

CHAPTER FOUR

Creams and Whites

There are relatively few plants whose leaves are variegated with a true, clean white. The great majority of whiteish variegations are in fact creams, so it makes more sense to lump cream- and white-variegated plants together than to try to split them, especially as with so many plants the colouring of the variegation changes as the season progresses, usually starting quite a deep cream and gradually fading to white as the leaves mature.

Acorus calamus 'Variegatus' is an exception to the generality. Though the variegation is a singularly clean white in mid-summer, it shows no hint of cream earlier in the season: the bias is, unexpectedly, towards pink. The new leaves in spring emerge a bright, deep pink, which gradually fades as the leaves get larger, revealing first the green part of the leaf and then paling away to leave the white variegation. The mature leaves on an established plant are sword-shaped, as much as 45cm (18ins.) long and 5cm (2ins.) across, each leaf being longitudinally divided equally into green and white halves. On young plants the leaves are very straight and stiff-looking, but on established clumps they arch gracefully outwards. *A.c.* 'Variegatus' looks for all the world like an iris in leaf, and indeed you might easily mistake it for one, but there is something about its way of growing that seems wrong. It is wrong: the plant is in fact a member of the aroid family; if you grow it under glass you just occasionally get little flowers that look like those of an arum, but in miniature. All in all, it is one of the most striking plants you can grow in a really wet situation, either in boggy ground or at the edge of a pond or stream. *Acorus gramineus* 'Variegatus' is by contrast an almost tatty-looking little plant. It is very much smaller, with leaves only about 15cm (6ins.) long and scarcely 6mm (¼in.) wide; these are green with a thin white margin along one side. It is quite useful when massed, giving a grassy appearance, and is particularly effective when used to fringe rocks or stone artefacts. It too needs wet ground to thrive.

If the idea of using ground elder as a ground cover horrifies you, it is worth bearing in mind that in situations where it has gone wild, it does make a very effective ground cover. There is a brilliantly white-variegated form of it, *Aegopodium podogaria* 'Variegatum', which is far less vigorous and invasive than the green-leaved weed and a highly desirable garden plant. The leaves are just like those of ordinary ground elder but smaller, margined, splashed and striped bright white. The leaves are presented more closely than on the green plant, so that they are more effective, and the plant does not run so vigorously. It will grow happily in any fertile soil in sun or semi-shade, and the only attention you need give it is to check it once or twice a year and cut it back to size. It is important never to let it get its roots into a lawn, since once it does that it will keep growing back out of the lawn into borders, but beyond that it is no trouble. It is a useful and unexpectedly decorative plant for a confined situation – in a small border, for example, hemmed in between a building and a concrete or crazy-paving drive.

Arrhenatherum elatius is unquestionably one of the dullest grasses around. It is also, as its common name, onion couch, suggests, one of the most invasive. There is, however, a sub-form, *A.e.* forma *bulbosum* of which there is a stunningly white-variegated variety. *A.e. bulbosum* does not run. Instead it produces bulbils – a somewhat eccentric proclivity in a grass. All through the growing season the stems fatten until at the end, when the rest of the plant is withering away, all that is left of the stems is a mass of small, rather elongated bulbs, each of which could form a new plant. Happily they usually fall in the middle of the old plant and never get a chance. The white-variegated form, *A.e. bulbosum* 'Variegatum' has this same bulb-forming habit, which makes it on the one hand non–invasive, but on the other extremely easy to increase when you want to. It is one of the most brilliantly white-variegated grasses in existence. The leaves, which are long and narrow, are conspicuously striped and margined bright white, and the overall effect is stunning. It grows to little more than 30cm (1ft) in height and about the same across in six or eight years, but is easy to increase into clumps or colour bands where it can be left to grow ever more and more dense. It really is one of those plants that is only seen at its best in quantity, which makes it ideal for our purpose. It needs to be grown in sun to look really bright, preferably with a dark background.

Bamboos are, of course, only grasses, but they differ in that they are, as it were, the shrubs of the grass world, forming a semi-permanent infra-structure of canes. One of the finest of all bamboos for garden use, and excellent for massing, is *Arundinaria variegata* (*A. fortunei*), a relatively low-growing bamboo with a decidedly clump-forming habit. Given good cultivation it will normally grow to about 1m (3ft) in height, with a spread of about 1m in ten years. Near water it will tend to grow a little bigger and run a little more, but it is never one of those uncontrollable bamboos that take over your whole garden without your consent. Its main decorative merit is its white-variegated leaves, the variegation occurring in stripes and bands running down the leaves. The variegation is extremely constant, even over quite large plantings. And it never reverts. There is, so far as we know, no green-leaved form for it to revert to. So it just remains delightfully white-variegated for ever. If you want to mass it, plant pot-grown stock, with just under 1m (3ft) between the plants in each direction, and mulch the ground well with leaf-mould. The clumps will join up within three or four years. If you are using it in a colour band, all you need do to keep it under control is cut the edges of the planting back to shape with a spade every spring. And if you want to get a dense, weed-proof thicket of canes quickly, it is worth cutting the plant down to 15cm (6ins.) or so above ground every spring. There is also a dwarf form of this bamboo, which seems at present to be known merely as *A.v.*

'Dwarf Form' (now *Pleioblastus chino* f. *angustifolia*). It grows to only about 30cm (1ft) and is proportionately less spreading. There are other white-variegated bamboos around, but none is so good as *Arundinaria variegata* or its dwarf form.

We seem to have struck a rich vein of *Poaceae*, so we might as well stay with it. *Arundo donax* 'Variegata' is the finest variegated grass in the world. I defy you to find anything more stately or stunning. Given good, fertile soil, a sheltered position and adequate moisture at the roots, it will run up to 3m (10ft) or more, with elegant, arching leaves as much as 5cm (2ins.) across and 1m (3ft) in length equally spaced up the stems, each leaf dramatically marked with a broad white marginal variegation and striped and shaded white: as much as three-quarters of any leaf is white. The variegation even extends to the ligules. It is the perfect, totally unexpected, accent plant for the multi-coloured garden, ideal on a patio or in some similar sheltered area, sprouting up out of a low, dense ground cover of bronzy acaena or one of the foxy-red New Zealand sedges. Its brilliance is marred only be a regrettable lack of hardiness. It will survive, to a greater or lesser extent, out of doors in the open, given a light covering of straw or bracken to protect it through the winter, but is really safer in the shelter of a warm wall. It is so dramatic that it is worth this little trouble.

In the same star category of breath-taking brilliance is *Brunnera macrophylla* 'Variegata'. *Brunnera macrophylla* itself is a marvellous ground-cover plant with big, heart-shaped green leaves and large sprays of tiny forget-me-not-blue flowers very like those of the true forget-me-not. It is much loved by flower arrangers both for its flowers and for its foliage. The variegated form is a far finer thing, the leaves boldly margined, splashed and shaded creamy white. The sheer size of the leaves, as much as 15cm (6ins.) across, and the contrast of the darkness of the green with the brightness of the variegation, combine to make this one of the most exciting and desirable of all variegated plants. It is one of those that definitely grow best in a lightly shaded position: the variegated parts of the leaves scorch readily in full sun. On the other hand, it will not tolerate dry shade, so a site must be chosen for it with care. And it certainly rewards good cultivation, producing larger and more luxuriant leaves. Like many stars, however, it has its tricky side. If you damage the roots while weeding, it is likely to throw green leaves where the damage was done. Since you may well do more damage in removing the green-leaved piece of the plant, it is likely to go on throwing green leaves. But if you persevere, you can get rid of the green-leaved parts and keep the whole clump variegated. Once established, *B.m.* 'Variegata' will keep most of its own weeds down and the problem of reversions will not occur.

Turning from the temperamental and tricky to the reliably robust, you will find that the genus *Buddleia* contains many good things beloved of butterflies. The common buddleia, *B. davidii*, has two variegated forms, one of which is superb, the other practically worthless. The good one is *B.d.* 'Harlequin', which has leaves conspicuously variegated a pleasing creamy white. The poor one is *B.d.* 'Variegata', which has occasional white markings on the leaves. 'Harlequin' is good enough to go to the trouble of planting and pruning properly, with large, well-prepared planting holes, liberal mulches once planted, and vigorous removal of old wood every season. It is the strong new growths that carry the brightest variegation, so they are worth the trouble of caring for correctly. You usually see 'Harlequin' grown as singletons – they lack the structural dignity to be called specimens – but they are stunning when massed. If the plants are spaced about 2m (6½ft) apart, pruned hard every year and fed regularly, they make a marvellous coloured display. It is worth growing some knock-about ground cover under them, though nothing too good since you are going to have to walk on it to prune the buddleias – *Hypericum calycinum*, for example, or a variegated dead-nettle. 'Harlequin' will grow on almost any soil almost anywhere, but shows its colour best in sun. It is readily propagated by cuttings taken almost any time.

The Japanese use the term 'Benten' to denote any plant that is variegated, so when you come across a plant called *Camellia japonica* 'Benten' expect a variegated form of *Camellia japonica*. It has the typical *Camellia japonica* leaf in shape and texture, though a little smaller than usual, strongly splashed, mottled and margined white on a very dark ground; the habit is more open than with other forms of *Camellia japonica*. The flower is pink. *C.j.* 'Variegata' has sometimes been confused with 'Benten' but is really quite distinct. The leaf is much broader, and the variegation is far more mottled and speckled than in 'Benten', and has a decidedly creamy colouring about it; and the flower is red. Both seem to be only marginally less hardy than other cultivars of *Camellia japonica*. *Camellia sasanqua* 'Variegata' is a disappointment by comparison. The leaves are long and narrow, with a thin white marginal variegation which scarcely shows against a basically grey leaf. The habit is strong, open and straggly. It needs to be grown in a warm situation – the foot of a west wall, for example. While the two variegated forms of *Camellia japonica* are excellent for massing, needing only a neutral to acid soil, plenty of humus and some shade, the variegated sasanqua is absolutely useless and totally ineffective in the mass. *Camellia japonica* can readily be increased from cuttings taken in August or November and rooted in heat.

Carex comans is a delightful little New Zealand sedge with almost weeping, tress-like foliage, the thread-like leaves rising up out of the centre of the plant then arching outwards and trailing on the ground. It forms, in time, a little tuft, about 20cm (8ins.) high but rather more across, since the leaves grow up to 45cm (18ins.) long. What makes it desirable in the multi-coloured garden is that the leaves are coloured a curious self-white. Even more strongly coloured, and again coloured white, is *Carex albula*, which differs in that the leaves are slightly broader, slightly shorter, and of a stronger white. Both seem to be frost hardy, to grow almost anywhere so long as the soil is not dry, and both come readily from seed. They are lovely used in quantity, but not too vast a quantity: they just don't have the quality to justify it.

Carex ornithopoda 'Variegata' is quite different: the leaves are green with a white margin, and a bright and striking white it is too, but the plant is much too small and weak-growing to mass on any scale. A square metre (9 square feet) of it would be quite enough. It is slow to increase, but a well-established clump will yield quite a large number of plants.

Carex riparia 'Variegata' is a monster by comparison. It is the most vulgarly rampageous ground-consuming carex in cultivation. A small plant in a pot is very winning. The tall, narrow leaves rise straight up for about 18 ins., then arch over gracefully and sway languidly in the breeze. And the variegation is stunning, the narrow leaves being margined brightest white. It is included here merely as a warning. If you like it, keep it in a pot. If you treasure your garden, don't plant it: if you do, you will rue the day for years to come, because it will advance in all directions at the same time and completely take over before you have had time to find out how to get rid of it.

By contrast, *Carex siderostica* 'Variegata' might be considered to have a disappointing variegation. The light green leaf, which only grows to about 10cm (4ins.) long, is very broad (nearly 2.5cm [1in.] wide), deeply pleated along its length and with a strong central fold to it, and the margin is lightly lined with white. It is enchanting in a delicate way, but not dramatic. Its most impressive season is spring when the new leaves emerge, pink in colour. It is a spreading sedge, though never vigorous, always remaining in a relatively tight clump, and ideal for massing in a small way at the front of a border or the edge of a path, where not too large an area is needed and its delicacy can be appreciated.

The Indian bean tree, *Catalpa bignonioides*, is one of the finest specimen trees for growing on a lawn that you could possibly have. The architecture of its branching system in winter is a fascination in itself, the light green leaves are large, heart-shaped and as much as 25cm (10ins.) long and 20cm (8ins.) across, and the flowers, which are very like those of the horse chestnut (but better) are produced in a large, loose panicle in late summer, and have the bonus of a fine scent. The 'beans' from which its name is derived are the seed pods, which do indeed look very like runner beans and create a striking effect in autumn when they remain on the tree after the leaves have fallen: they are only produced after good summers. While the typical green-leaved plant is excellent in every way, the variegated form is far superior. *Catalpa bignonioides* 'Variegata' has the same large leaves but boldly margined with a broad band of creamy white, with a yellowish centre. The leaf is very striking and the effect produced by a whole tree covered in these dramatically variegated leaves is extremely impressive. There is some question as to whether *C.b.* 'Variegata' is the correct name for this plant. There is also a plant known as *Catalpa bignonioides* 'Variegata' which has the most appalling yellowish white blotching to the leaves, a dreadful thing.

To get catalpas to grow well, you need to prepare the ground for them thoroughly and site them where they are open to the sun but not in a position too exposed to cold winds. And you should be warned that what you will get for the £10 or more that you have to pay for your variegated catalpa will be a little stick in a pot: it is usually sold as a grafted plant. (This is odd, since it comes readily from cuttings taken in spring, as soon as the wood is firm enough, and rooted in gentle heat.) If you then plant this little stick and leave it to its own devices it will form the most enormous shrub you have ever seen, because, like all catalpas, it totally fails to make a leader. You only have to look at a catalpa to understand why: on not a single twig, even on a large plant, will you ever find a terminal bud (a bud at the tip of the twig) but only side buds. In consequence, instead of each shoot producing a single extension growth, the catalpa produces two or three shoots obliquely to the axis of the original shoot. To train the plant up as a tree, you need to stake it securely and, each season, select the strongest of the two or three new shoots, trim away the weaker ones, and tie in the strongest shoot to train up as a leader. You may find that some of the soft, vigorous growth induced at this stage causes a little die-back each winter, but do not despair – it will get there soon enough. Ideally you need to train the leader up clean to about 3m (10ft) so that the tree can spread and its branches droop down, as they naturally do.

Catalpa bignonioides is a North American tree – most of the catalpas grown in Britain are North American. In fact the genus has more species in China, of which the finest so far introduced is *Catalpa fargesii*, a much smaller tree but with delightful pink flowers. There is a subspecies, *duclouxii*, also with fine pink flowers and exceedingly long beans – up to 45cm (18ins.) – which differs only in the absence of the stellate hairs of the type. There is a very interesting white-variegated form of this, with the leaves margined and marked white and grey. It is sadly little-known and not yet in commerce, but no doubt if enough people ask often enough someone will settle down to propagating it for the nursery trade.

If you are interested in dwarf conifers you'll know what I mean when I refer to Lawsons: Lawson's cypress, or, to be more correct, Lawson's false cypress *Chamaecyparis lawsoniana*. Although this is a single species, you will find, if you have a plant, that when you sow seed from it no two seedlings will be quite alike. Scarcely surprising then that it has given rise to well over two hundred recorded varieties, with more coming on the market every year, and enthusiasts eagerly arguing over their identification. Certainly many Lawsons do not look like Lawsons. Some grow into narrowly pyramidal trees over 30m (100ft) high, while others form low, spreading bushes, gradually rising to 60cm (2ft) or so if you are lucky.

A word of warning before commending any Lawsons to you. There is a group of Lawsons with a spire-like habit and an erect branching system that used at one time to be extremely popular. One can only presume that such popularity arose because no one had ever seen a mature plant. All the Lawsons with this almost vertical branching habit look elegant when young. As they get bigger, however, you have to keep tying the branches back in to stop them flopping outwards. Eventually they get out of reach and you just have to let them go, at which point, if it has not already happened, they will just fall apart at the seams, revealing great tracts of bare brown branches within, and the only thing to do with them then is to cut them down. Plants to avoid particularly are 'Erecta Viridis', 'Erecta Aurea', 'Potenii', 'Erecta Alba' and the still popular 'Erecta Filiformis'.

There is a large number of Lawsons with creamy or whitish foliage or variegations, some of which are among the best of relatively dwarf conifers for massing. 'Albospica' is semi-dwarf, reaching about 3m (10ft) in ten years, with congested growths which are liberally spattered with white patches, mainly at the growing tips. It is not sufficiently well variegated to look much when massed, but makes quite an interesting dot plant. 'Albovariegata' by contrast is excellently variegated, with big, bold, white patches on the foliage, about half-white, half-green. It is a slow-growing plant, of rounded form, reaching about 70cm (2⅓ft) in ten years, and is a good plant for massing in a colour band, though the white in the foliage is inclined to scorch if you plant it in full sun. 'Fletcher's White' is also a fine variegated form, again with about half the foliage clearly marked white, but the habit of growth is completely different, forming in time a small, upright bush, fairly narrow and a bit untidy in habit, about 1.6m (5ft) high. 'Gold Splash' is completely misnamed: it is not gold at all but variegated a good deep rich creamy colour. It is slow-growing, again reaching about 1.6m in ten years, but has an open habit of growth, the twigs pointing upwards and creating a flat-topped effect. It is an excellent plant for massing, and far less liable to scorching in sunlight than many. 'Pygmaea Argentea' is very popular, and people are inclined to gush about its merits, giving you, if you allow them the chance, a veritable encomium on the plant. It does not deserve such lavish praises, though it is no doubt a good thing if you do not know any better. It is a slow-growing bun-shaped bush, making about 38cm (15ins.) in height in ten years, but is bulbous in habit, the fatter parts filling out to 1m (3ft) or more in the same period, a characteristic which becomes more pronounced with age: it is positively obese in its senility. Its reputed charms are that the outer margins of its foliage sprays are brightly creamy white in spring and summer (less so at other seasons). The trouble is that it needs full sun from dawn till dusk to perform this well. Given a little shade it is a great disappointment. If you could give it full sun, perhaps it would be good for massing: it should be – the habit is right and the colour a useful one. If you want to try it, do: don't let me put you off. Everyone else likes it.

By contrast 'Silver Queen' is a plant about which I could wax lyrical. It is another relatively slow-growing Lawson, reaching about 3m (10ft) in ten years, though ultimately about 10m, and forms a symmetrical, pyramidal tree, with good, soft, Lawson foliage but of a quite unique silvery greenish-white colouring, brightest in the spring when it is making its new growth, but good at all seasons. It is an excellent Lawson for massing, one of the best.

'Snow Flurry', a relative newcomer which originated in New Zealand in the late fifties, is so good that it has rapidly become popular. It is usually sold as a dwarf, but it is really only semi-dwarf, reaching about 3m (10ft) in ten years. The variegation is creamy white on a blue background, which makes it outstandingly effective, and about half the foliage on the plant is variegated. The foliage is juvenile. As with so many white-variegated conifers, the white areas tend to scorch in full sun or strong winds, so that it is really a plant that needs some shelter from wind and a position where it is only shaded for part of the day. It would be an ideal conifer for massing in the right position. If you do not have the right position, it would be better to use it as a dot plant.

Chamaecyparis pisifera differs from the Lawsons (and other false cypresses) in its sharply pointed, scale-like leaves with distinct white marks on the undersides, in its very small cones and in its ultimately much larger size. It is a native of Japan, where it has been cultivated time out of mind. In its own country it will grow to 50m (165ft) and in cultivation is quite capable of reaching 30m (100ft). Happily there are a number of clones which are much smaller growing, and a couple which are eminently desirable. (It is worth noting here the remarkable fact that not only *Chamaecyparis lawsoniana* but almost all the chamaecyparis species have given rise to vast numbers of good garden clones: you might call it a sporting genus.) *Chamaecyparis pisifera* 'Snow' is a delightful little clone which frequently turns up in garden centres where, if you see it when it is freshly in from the growers, looks highly attractive, and indeed it does have much to commend it. It has fuzzy foliage, greyish greenish white on the inside of the plant and pure white on the outside. Though rated as a dwarf, it will reach 2m (6ft) in ten years (you seldom see it at anything approaching that size, however). It sounds perfect for using in big, bold groupings. In fact, it is an extremely difficult plant to grow well, and no plant is worth massing unless you can grow it well. It scorches more readily in sun, wind or frost than any other dwarf conifer I can think of. It really needs a sheltered, somewhat shaded corner on a rock garden to succeed.

If you tour around some garden centres one afternoon, you might come away with the distinct impression that two quite different plants are being sold as *Chamaecyparis pisifera* 'Snow'. You would be right: the other one is properly *Chamaecyparis pisifera* 'Squarrosa Sulphurea', which is a stronger-growing plant with little inclination to scorch in sun, wind or frost. It is also a little less exciting in its colouring. The foliage is of a soft, feathery type, a little larger than that of 'Snow', and the plant will grow slightly larger. The foliage is bright greyish cream in spring, passing to a paler colouring by winter, when it is sometimes tinged with bronze. It is a much better garden plant than 'Snow' and good for massing: indeed, that is the most effective way of growing it.

It is one of the tenets of the multi-coloured garden that stunning effects can be achieved by using quite common plants in uncommon ways. The genus *Cornus*, already considered in Chapter Three, is full of good things, a fact so universally recognized that several have become quite common. Among these are two of the white-variegated forms of *Cornus alba*, the red-stemmed dogwood. The finest of these is *Cornus alba* 'Elegantissima' (also known as 'Sibirica Variegata'), with the leaves boldly marked, margined and mottled bright white. Slightly inferior and probably more often seen and sold is *Cornus alba* 'Variegata', in which the leaves have an overall greyish-whitish colouring and an irregular creamy white margin. It is not so fine, but still worth garden space. Both grow to about 3m (10ft) and slowly form quite extensive thickets (nothing you can't control if you want to), and both have stems that, though more or less green in summer, are a rich maroon-red in winter. Both are seen to best advantage when massed, though you need some dark background to show them off. It is popularly believed that these two plants will only thrive in wet soils, but in fact they are just as happy in really quite dry soils.

Cornus alternifolia 'Variegata' ('Argentea') is very elegant, by comparison. It is known as the wedding-cake tree – an apt name. The plant grows with its branches distinctively arranged in a series of horizontal tiers. The leaves are small, very similar in shape and size to those of *Cornus mas*, and conspicuously variegated with a wide white margin. It is one of the finest of all white-variegated small trees, outstandingly good at all seasons. Though not fast growing, it will ultimately get up to about 3m (10ft). It is quite easy to grow in any fertile soil, but your problem will be obtaining a plant in the first place, though it is not rare: it just does not seem to have caught on with the garden-centre trade yet. Once you have a plant it is easy to increase, since any branch that touches the ground will root readily. You could easily mass it merely by pegging down the lower branches until they root, and keeping on doing this until you have covered the area you want to fill. However, it would not be an ideal plant for massing: the rather unique tiered effect of the branches would be lost. Much better use it as a specimen or series of linking specimens spaced out through other colour bands or blocks.

It is a curious thing that those people who think highly of *Cornus alternifolia* 'Variegata' are inclined to dismiss *Cornus controversa* 'Variegata' as a rather coarse plant, while those who adore *Cornus controversa* 'Variegata' find *Cornus alternifolia* 'Variegata' too dainty and delicate-looking. I like both, but for different reasons. *C.c.* 'Variegata' (formerly *Thelycrania controversa* 'Variegata') has stunningly variegated individual leaves, which emerge in spring strongly marked a rich yellow-cream and fairly rapidly mature to a fine white variegation. The drama of the variegation is probably best appreciated on a small plant, but a large plant – and it will grow to 21m (70ft), given a generation or two – is almost unbelievably good: it is as rich and lush in its production of foliage as *Cornus alternifolia* 'Variegata' is sparing. Given room for both, I would grow both. Not only that, I would grow yet another white-variegated dogwood too, *Cornus mas* 'Variegata'. This makes a large shrub or small tree of typical Cornelian cherry shape and size, but has leaves strongly variegated bright white. After the superlatives already lavished on the other white-variegated dogwoods it is difficult to convey just how good this one is: it is stunning. And what is more, it will grow well and show its variegation at its best in quite dense shade, so long as it is not too dry at the roots.

It is almost a relief to leave the brilliant dogwoods behind and turn to something more subdued. The pampas grasses hail from the pampa prairies of South America and it is surprising that they are so hardy. But hardy they are, and popular: on a recent sortie into the uncharted deeps of inner suburbia I counted a pampas grass in about one in every five front gardens. So it would be pleasant to grow one that is a little different, and a pampas grass with white-variegated leaves is just that. This is *Cortaderia sellowana* 'Albo-marginata' (=‘Albo-lineata’) which has leaves like those of a typical pampas grass but margined white. It grows to about the same size as *Cortaderia sellowana* 'Pumila' but is not perhaps so hardy. It is not an outstanding variegation, but it is a plant that looks lovely massed, and is particularly effective with clumps of purple phormium behind it or among it. And while we are on pampas grass, a word of warning to the unwary. Never plunge your bare hand into the middle of a clump, not even to cull a plume. The edges of the leaves are sharply saw-toothed, with the teeth slightly angled outwards. As you thrust your hand inwards, the teeth can and will cut deeply and viciously. I know one nurseryman who learnt this lesson as a youngster, and at seventy still bears the scars.

If you were to come across a plant of *Cryptomeria japonica* 'Knaptonensis' on the show bench, and it was a perfectly grown specimen, I think you would be so taken with it you would order enough to make a colour band of it. Sadly, it would let you down quite dreadfully. 'Knaptonensis' is a dwarf, congested form of the Japanese cedar whose young growths are brilliant white, the older growths tipped white and the inner leaves green. If you can grow it in a pot by your back door, and pinch out any shoot that is green or that turns brown on you, you will have a gem of a plant. If you can't do that you will probably end up with a rather bare, bald dwarf conifer that looks as though the parts of it that have not been scorched by sun, wind or rain, have been bleached. Lovely though it is, it is totally unsuited to massing.

Should you still be at that happy and uncomplicated stage of your horticultural development and education at which you find flowers important, you are scarcely likely to find the genus *Euonymus* exciting – the flowers are green and tiny. If you want effective foliage plants for massing, however, it is a genus with which you need to be familiar. *Euonymus fortunei radicans* is an extremely hardy and useful plant in all its forms, lending itself readily to being grown as a trailing ground cover (rooting as it goes) or allowed to climb by means of its aerial roots: if you let it climb, it will run up to as much as 6m (20ft). There is a number of variegated forms, all of them good. 'Emerald Gaiety' is very effective massed, though it does not look much as a small plant in a pot. It has a greyish-white marginal variegation, with a little white speckling in the leaf: it looks rather insignificant at close quarters. Seen from a distance, it is extraordinarily good. It is more of a shrub and less of a trailer than the majority of the others. 'Silver Pillar' has small oval leaves strongly margined and splashed white, but its very upright habit makes it less suitable for massing than other forms. 'Silver Queen' is again a shrubby form but brilliantly variegated, the young leaves in spring unfolding rich creamy yellow and later settling down to a strong marginal white variegation and with a little white in the centre of the leaf, and a touch of red or pink as well on some leaves: excellent for massing, in sun or shade. The finest of the truly trailing sorts is 'Variegatus', which has a smaller leaf than most with a clearly defined white marginal variegation and splashes of white on the leaves, and again the leaves are often tinged pink. It is probably the best of all for massing, though it is not a fast-growing plant, so you need plenty of it. Happily, it comes very easily from cuttings and any branches pegged down can be relied on to root.

The difference in habit of these euonymuses needs explaining. Like the English ivy, *Euonymus radicans* has a juvenile phase in which it runs or climbs and an adult, arborescent stage in which it flowers and fruits. The trailing or climbing forms are juvenile; the shrubby forms adult.

Euonymus japonicus is, in some of its variegated forms, seen almost as often as the variegated forms of *Euonymus fortunei*. It is, however, a decidedly shrubby shrub with no inclination to climb – or even to crawl. There are several white-variegated forms around, but one is outstanding. This is *Euonymus japonicus* 'Macrophyllus Albus' (formerly 'Latifolius Variegatus'), which has quite large oval leaves with silvery-grey and white markings and conspicuous creamy-white margins. The variegation is equally good in sun or shade, though in shade it may become a little less dense than it does in sun – but never straggly. It will grow up to about 2m (6½ft), with a spread of about twice that. It looks even more dramatic in bulk than it does as an individual.

There is nothing stunning, breathtaking or even particularly eye-catching about *Fragraria vesca* 'Variegata', a delightful little variegated strawberry, but everyone who has it seems to adore it. It is just like the ordinary cultivated strawberry, but smaller in all its parts and the leaves are variegated white. It sends out long red trailers in all directions, and produces little plants at the end of them, but it is never vigorous or invasive. It certainly grows best where the soil has been well treated over the years, whether with manure or leaf-mould and, though it seldom makes a dense patch of colour, it will run about among other plants quite happily, popping up here and there, which seems to be how most people like best to grow it. It is not a plant that you will find very often in commerce, but anyone who has a piece will readily be able to spare you a rooted offset.

Most people are familiar with ground elder, but may not be so familiar with ground ivy, an almost equally obnoxious weed where it is native. It has small rounded leaves with a slight scallopping at the edges, and it spreads by means of overground runners: when it is happy in your garden it spreads quite fast. Unlike ground elder it is quite easy to get rid of, since it has relatively little in the way of roots. As with ground elder, there is a fine variegated form, *Glechoma hederacea* 'Variegata', the leaves edged and marked with clean white, a very pretty and most effective little ground-cover plant, especially in a small garden where you can control it. It seems to need no very special cultural skill to grow, though on the whole it seems to prefer a soil enriched with leaf-mould, and a little shade.

If you have a small garden you will not welcome plants that are inclined to invade areas for which you never intended them, but if your garden is large, you will find *Glycera maxima* (formerly *aquatica*) 'Variegata' almost indispensable. It is not to be confused with another grass, the one usually known as gardener's garters (for which purpose it is, incidentally, absolutely useless), *Phalaris arundinacea* 'Picta', a plant only fit for public places except in its finer forms. *Glycera maxima* 'Variegata' is a very much better grass, with relatively long and broad leaves, almost rounded at the tips, and growing to about 1.3m (4ft). The leaves are brightly variegated creamy white in the early months of the year, fading to a merely outstanding white variegation later in the season. However, since it keeps throwing up new growths through most of the season, it always looks clean and bright. The new growths, as they emerge in spring, are bright pink. Although this grass is often associated with water and will, indeed, grow with its feet in water, it does not actually need to be grown in a wet situation. Some people believe that the colouring is better if it is grown in rather dry conditions.

The variegated griselinas are so fine that they are well worth growing, in spite of a suspicion of tenderness. The trouble is, of course, that just as your plants are getting to a good size and really starting to have impact, along comes the winter of the century and knocks them sideways. But they are so brilliant, and so easy to propagate, that they are well worth the gamble. *Griselina littoralis* itself is a beautiful evergreen shrub of compact and dense habit, with leaves of a unique light green always held somewhat upright on the stems of the shrub. The finest of the variegated forms is 'Dixon's Cream', with large, rounded leaves that are splashed and marked with a rich, creamy yellow. 'Variegata' is better known, but fractionally inferior, the variegation being pale creamy white though clearly marked and especially strong on the leaf margins. In time, both can make densely leafy shrubs up to 5m (16½ft) high – though they are seldom seen that large. Both are completely evergreen, and both thrive in any fertile soil.

Hebe is a genus about which a lot of people go overboard. For myself, I have never been able to see why, though it does contain a number of very beautiful plants. If you want to know all about hebes, Graham Hutchins at County Park Nurseries, Hornchurch, Essex, is the man to get in touch with. He seems to know more about them than most of the rest of us put together. There are two that are far too outstanding as variegated plants suited to massing to pass over merely because one does not like the hebes as a whole. The first is *Hebe andersonii* 'Variegata', a vigorous little hybrid between *Hebe salicifolia* and *speciosa*. The leaves are oval, pointed, about 10cm (4ins.) long and less than half as much across, deep green in the middle fading to violet mixed with cream, and surrounded by a broad creamy-white margin. It is a very fine variegation indeed. Given a sheltered position and a run of mild winters, it will grow up to about 2m (6½ft) tall, but is more usually seen at about half that height. The stems are technically woody, but if you look at them closely and squeeze them, you will find that they are more suffruticose. Indeed, this little shrub is most often treated as though it were herbaceous, being cut back almost if not quite to the ground in winter and covered with some light litter, bracken or something similar. Grown this way it is reasonably reliable, certainly reliable enough to mass, and it is very effective massed.

The second of the hebes is *H. franciscana* (used to be *lobelioides* until someone discovered it is actually *elliptica* x *speciosa*) 'Variegata'. It is a very popular plant, and you are probably familiar with it, if not by name, at least by acquaintance. It has an oval leaf, with a green centre and a very wide marginal band of creamy white. The leaves are opposite, and equally spaced all along the stems. It too, is a little tender. If you grow either of these hebes, do so in the knowledge that they are not entirely hardy, so it is always wise to keep a few young plants around in pots and to take a batch of cuttings in most seasons. You can always give them away if you do not need them.

The ivies are usually regarded as bone hardy, but in fact not all of them are. The Canary Isles ivy, *Hedera canariensis* is, as one might expect of a plant from the Canary Isles, a little on the tender side, though many people in total ignorance of this fact treat it as though it were hardy and get away with it. There is a variegated form, *H.c.* 'Gloire de Marengo' ('Variegata') which has leaves with a thin white margin and a few white streaks on what I can only describe as a grey background. The young leaves have a pleasing pink flush. I always find the variegation of the individual leaves disappointing, but the effect when massed is fine. It makes an excellent ground cover for large areas, especially under trees, which afford it some protection from frost. *H.c.* 'Margino-maculata' (a sport of 'Gloire de Marengo') is visually better, with heavily white-speckled leaves and the defect of reverting to 'Gloire de Marengo' unless you keep an eye on it. As a wall plant it is much more showy; as a ground cover, you might as well use 'Gloire de Marengo' to which it will revert in time in any case unless you can nip out reversions as they occur.

The variegated form of the Persian ivy has the showiest individual leaves of all the ivies. This is *Hedera colchica* (which has been both *amurensis* and *roegnerana* in the past) 'Dentata Variegata'. The leaves are of enormous size, as much as 20cm (8ins.) long and very nearly as wide (though they tend to roll themselves back on themselves so they never look that wide), very thick and leathery. The variegation is mainly marginal, creamy white in spring, fading to white later in the year, but much of the leaf is marked in varying degrees of whiteness or greyness. It is a far more dramatic plant than 'Gloire de Marengo' and far hardier. It is good for making large, bold areas of ground cover under trees. There is also an arborescent form, which has all the virtues of the trailing or climbing form, but is compact and shrubby.

The problem with *Hedera colchica* and its forms is that they are far too large for small gardens, unless you want to put the whole area down just to that one ivy. *Hedera helix*, the common English ivy, is smaller in all its parts and generally less vigorous, though it can cover quite large areas in time. There are so many excellent variegated forms that it is difficult to know which to commend and which to condemn. 'Adam' has small, white-variegated leaves that turn pink at the edges in cold weather, and a bushy, much-branched habit of growth. 'Ardingly', which again has a small leaf with a white variegation and turns pink at the edges in cold weather, has an even more dense and bushy habit of growth. The leaves are more rounded than those of 'Adam'. 'Cavendishii' (which used to be 'Sheen Silver') has leaves that are triangular in outline, with a fine, white variegation, but it is a slow grower. In time it will make a more leafy plant than the faster-growing forms. 'Chicago Variegated' has a leaf which is similar in outline to 'Harald', but is very much broader at its broadest point, and very much longer at its longest. The variegation is a rich, creamy white, with relatively little green appearing on the leaf. It is reasonably vigorous. 'Glacier' has been around for a long time: I find its variegation rather poor. The leaves are small and greyish, the greyishness being made up of a masking of thin white. On the other hand it is a strong grower, pretty tough and very easy to obtain. 'Harald' has the same vigour and hardiness but is richly variegated, the variegation being cream in spring, fading to white, on quite a large leaf, and there is just an occasional splash of green. 'Heise' is very like 'Adam', but has larger leaves and is a very vigorous, bushy grower. 'Little Diamond' has a diamond-shaped leaf, with a strong white variegation. What distinguishes it most from other white-variegated clones is its characteristic habit of growth: if you use it as a ground cover you will find that the stems branch outwards in a stiffly flat, circular fashion: if you grow it in a pot or hanging basket you will find that the stems arch stiffly outwards. It is always densely leafy, which is part of its charm: some varieties – and 'Adam' is one of them – are too sparsely leafy to be very effective as ground cover. 'Lutzii' is an old variety, but has lost none of its merits for all that. The leaf is small, blotched, spotted and marbled creamy white: quite distinct. When massed the overall effect is grey, and the contrast between this effect when seen from a distance and the detail of the leaves when seen at close quarters is one of the joys of this plant. 'Pedata Variegata' is very distinct: 'Pedata' is the bird's-foot ivy, with exceptionally narrow and elongated lobes. In the variegated form the leaves are splashed with white. It is not exceptional, but is useful if the area you need to cover is not too large. 'Saggitifolia Variegata' also has a leaf of a quite distinct shape: as its name suggests, the leaf is shaped like an arrow head, and in the variegated form is margined and marked white. If you see it pot-grown in a garden centre you are likely to fall for it: the combined effect of the leaf shape and the variegation is charming. But it is useless as ground cover, and in my experience not really hardy. 'Trinity' is so called because it always has leaves of three different colours on it. Some are dark green; some are mottled white and green; and some are creamy white with green veins. It creates an extraordinary effect which I rather like, but people who do not know it are inclined to start trying to pinch out the green leaves, thinking it is reverting, which it is not. There are several in this bunch that I would happily use for massing, but in the end you pays your money and takes your choice (and probably end up with whatever caught your eye at the garden centre).

Helxine soleirolii is a monotypic genus native to Corsica, which means that it is unfortunately slightly tender. It is one of those plants that impresses by the sheer number of its leaves, for each leaf is minute, smaller than that of a duckweed – a mere couple of millimetres long and across – produced on almost invisible thin stems, but produced in abundance. It is a low-growing little plant, creeping, crawling (almost grovelling) and just occasionally climbing up into any little shrub that offers it a chance to do so. It was at one time widely used as a ground cover under green house staging, but that vogue seems to have passed. There is a very lovely white-variegated form, *H.s.* 'Albo-variegata', whose tiny round leaves have a white marginal variegation on a grey ground, and it is a delightfully effective little plant. It will grow readily in a damp, shaded corner, especially if the atmosphere is very humid, and in such situations will spread surprisingly fast to make quite large carpets. It is very effective used as a carpeter in a damp, dark corner in a garden where you do not have to cover too large an area. It grows well beside a pond or stream, or under shrubs, provided that the soil never dries out. It is often blackened by frost in winter, but seldom killed outright. You only need a small piece or two, tucked away in a position that is slightly more sheltered than the rest, for the whole thing to grow away again strongly in spring. It is always a wise precaution, though, to detach a few pieces and pot them up in autumn.

Of all the variegated plants I have grown, none has given me so much joy at all seasons as a fascinatingly beautiful little saxifrage found by Stephen Taffler in a garden in Chester. He was driving around and he saw in a front garden a vast square island herbaceous border, wholly edged with London pride (*Heuchera sanguinea*). Being a man highly tuned to good variegated plants, he would no doubt never have given the garden a second glance except that he spotted half-way up one side something among the London pride that appeared to be variegated. The owner of the garden thought the variegated sport appalling, and was only too glad to be rid of it. Since then, almost everyone who has seen it or grown it has not only thought it quite outstandingly beautiful, but has also endorsed that opinion by wanting a piece. It is, unfortunately, slow to increase, but one or two people are gradually building up stocks of it. The whole leaf, which is typically London pride in size and shape, is densely speckled and spotted rich creamy white on a grey ground, the margin turning rich pink in winter and a proportion of the leaf becoming slightly pink. It is a plant of quite exceptional beauty, and it is because it is so outstanding that it has been named *Heuchera sanguinea* 'Taff's Joy', for Stephen Taffler's first wife. Unlike the ordinary London pride it grows best in a somewhat shaded position in a soil well enriched with leaf-mould. It is the perfect low-level plant for massing in a cool, shaded corner in a small garden.

Holcus mollis 'Variegatus' is often billed as the brightest white-variegated garden grass in existence. *Arrhenatherum elatius bulbosum* 'Variegatum' is actually brighter, but the *Holcus mollis* 'Variegatus' is the better garden plant. It is ideal for small gardens, growing to only about 20cm (8ins.) in height and spreading slowly to form patches of bright white. The individual leaves are only about 5cm (2ins.) long and about 6mm (¼in.) wide and are brightly margined white. Although related to couch grass, it only runs slowly – indeed often more slowly than required. Ideal for massing, both because of its bright variegation and because of its running habit, it is best in a sunny situation, but happy on almost any fertile soil. It is easily controlled by simply chopping it back to where you want it, and very readily increased by planting on detached pieces.

The hostas are very much in vogue at the moment, and there is little I can add to the songs of praise already lavished on them by others. They are adored by flower arrangers for their large leaves, by exponents of the art of ground cover for their weed-suppressing qualities and by landscape designers for their architectural qualities. Moreover, quite a number have extremely good variegation. Most have broad, striking foliage and all of them are strongly perennial, going on from year to year getting bigger and, by and large, better in the process. They are clump-forming plants, slowly building themselves up into magnificent mounds of foliage, but they are never fast to increase. It is always a shame to split up a large and well-established clump (though if you have to the way to do it is to take a slice out of the clump with a sharp spade in much the way that one would take a slice out of a cake). Otherwise a better policy is to buy young stock, and to lift it annually, dividing each time, either by cutting the crown into its subsections or by teasing the pieces patiently apart. In this way it is possible to build up quite substantial stocks for massing in a matter of a few seasons. If you want to mass a large area of hostas, you need them all to be as nearly identical as possible, in which case division is the only really reliable way of achieving your objective. Apart from *Hostas sieboldiana, sieboldiana elegans* and *ventricosa* which vary little from seed, the seedlings of most hostas show enormous variation. Which is not surprising. Our present ignorance concerning the members of the genus is still relatively profound. Many of the plants have been named not, as is usually the case, from plants collected in the wild, but from clones cultivated for centuries in Japanese gardens, and the true status of many of those, whether species or hybrids, is still not wholly understood. Furthermore, the hostas cross very readily. It would not really be true to say that you might get anything from seed, but you are unlikely to get even a close approximation to the original seed parent. As for cultivation, the hostas are relatively easy, hence, no doubt, their popularity. They will grow on acid or alkaline soils (though on chalk soils they benefit from liberal mulchings of leaf-mould or manure), in sun or in shade – even dense, dry shade – though in shade you will get more and more larger leaves than you do in sun, but fewer flowers, while in sun they definitely need more moisture at the roots than they do in shade. The huge, corrugated leaves of plants such as *H. sieboldiana* and *tokudama* can look quite dreadful when stained with the drip from overhanging trees, and in such positions it is wiser to avoid the glaucous and corrugated-leaved forms and grow instead those with shiny leaves, such as *ventricosa*, since these do not suffer in the same way. Hostas are greatly loved by slugs, which is a misfortune, since they put on their leaves only once in a season, and if these leaves are destroyed they will not produce any further leaves that season and will have been weakened for the following season.

All hostas are ideal for massing, and probably look better massed than grown as single plants dotted around the place. *Hosta albomarginata* is one of the least imposing of the species, growing to only about 45cm (18ins). It is, largely because of its relatively small stature, an ideal plant for massing in a small garden. The leaves are longer and narrower than those of most hostas, technically elliptic, with a narrow white margin. The rootstock is creeping, and plants quite readily form reasonably big clumps; furthermore, because of the creeping rootstock, clumps run into one another readily. This particular hosta has also been called *Hosta lancifolia* (a name which now belongs to a totally different plant), *Hosta lancifolia albomarginata* and *Funkia ovata albomarginata*. And, as if that were not enough to confuse anyone, I feel honour bound to tell you that this year its correct name is *Hosta sieboldii*, a name which, following the lead set by Graham Stuart Thomas and taken up by other eminent gardeners, I am not using because it causes such confusion with *Hosta sieboldiana*. There is also a form of *Hosta albomarginata* known as *Hosta albomarginata alba*, in which the leaves are bright green. The variegated form has the specific epithet because it was introduced first. *Hosta decorata* is also one of those specific names which denote a variegated plant (that having been the form first introduced), the normal green-leaved form being known as *forma normalis*. *Hosta decorata* is a much finer plant than *Hosta albomarginata*, growing to 60cm (2ft) and with much bigger, bolder and broader leaves. These are strongly marked with a wide, white margin, which extends not only round the blade of the leaf, but also down the sides of the deeply grooved leaf stalk. It is a free-spreading plant, making largish clumps relatively quickly. The flowers are rich lilac.

Much finer is *Hosta fortunei* 'Marginato-Alba' – indeed it is probably the finest of all the white-edged hostas, and a sumptuous plant. The leaves are, with good cultivation, 75cm (2½ft) long and almost as much across, sage green, broadly margined white, and grey beneath. It is magnificent when massed. Almost as good is a hosta known simply as 'Thomas Hogg': no one gives it a specific name any more, and it is fairly generally presumed that it is a hybrid. The leaves are smooth, dark green and pointed, with a broad creamy-white margin. Though not so fine as *Hosta fortunei* 'Marginato-Alba', it is probably a better general-purpose garden plant, having a smooth upper surface to the leaves and so not collecting the traffic dust of cities or the debris from tree-drip as do the leaves of hostas with corrugated leaves.

Hosta undulata is quite distinct among the hostas: the leaves are very undulate or at times even spirally twisted. They are dark green, pointed, and at the centre of each is a large area of creamy white occupying well over half the surface area of the leaf blade. It is a very effective plant, particularly when massed. Even better in every way is *Hosta univittata*, which is larger in all its parts and equally suitable for massing.

Finally there is *Hosta ventricosa* 'Variegata' which has typical hosta leaves – broad, dark green and strikingly margined creamy white.

Hollies are not among the first rank of plants that spring to mind during a discussion on plants with variegated leaves: perhaps most of us have relegated them to a rather utilitarian role, as hedging plants or for windbreaks or as the sort of thing you use to screen something unsightly. In fact, many have extremely fine variegations, both the individual leaves and the plants as a whole viewed from a distance. *Ilex x altaclarensis* 'Silver Sentinel', for example, has a very symmetrical, pointed, oval leaf with scarcely a spine on it, and a very symmetrical creamy-white marginal variegation that on any other plant would be considered outstanding. It is a tall, narrow grower, useful in relatively confined spaces, ultimately of rather pyramidal outline, and lushy foliaged. *Ilex aquifolium* 'Argentea Pendula' is even more lovely: it has the typical spiny leaves of the species, with a clearly marked margin of almost pure white, is densely leafy, and has a most pronounced habit of growth – it is as weeping as a weeping willow, with the branchlets hanging perpendicularly from the framework of branches. Its problem, of course, is that it takes ages to grow it up tall enough to gain the full impact of this weeping habit. Left to its own devices it makes a mound on the ground, never lifting itself very high but slowly building up a small framework of branches, with the branchlets running out across the ground. It is precisely this quality which makes it excellent for massing, since one plant will readily run into the next and so on. 'Silver Sentinel', by contrast, is of little use for massing, but makes an ideal dot plant among a massed group of something lower growing.

Ilex a. 'Ferox Argentea' is excellent for massing. This is the silver hedgehog holly, aptly named, for not only does it have marginal spines but it also has masses of smaller spines dotted about all over the upper surface of the leaf. It is quite the prickliest of all hollies. The green-leaved form *Ilex a.* 'Ferox' was, incidentally, the first holly clone to be brought into cultivation, and 'Ferox Argentea' is probably the earliest white-variegated holly to have been deliberately cultivated. It is a very slow-growing plant, very dense and very showy. Its habit is roughly rounded, so that you can either mass it or use it as a rounded accent plant among some prostrate colour band.

Ilex a. 'Silver Milkboy', also sold as 'Silver Milkmaid', differs from the hollies mentioned so far in that the variegation is in the centre of the leaf, whereas the variegation on all the others is marginal. It is a very striking plant with a typical holly leaf, dark green at the margin and pure, pure white in the centre. The habit of growth is rather open, which goes a little against it. It would make a good specimen plant. 'Somerset Cream' may appear to you to be identical, but it is not. It originated as a sport on a different plant, and therefore, under the rules which govern these things, had to be given a different name. The colouring, though just as bright, is slightly creamier, and the habit of growth is better: it is more dense and leafy.

The hollies are all easily propagated by hardwood cuttings taken in November and put in a frame under a north wall through the winter.

The genus *Iris* contains such a diversity of good garden plants that one can only suppose that the generation which devoted vast areas of its gardens to that abomination, the tall bearded iris, simply did not know the other species. Quite the most useful of the species is *Iris foetidissima*, a British native, known variously as the Gladwin iris, the stinking gladdon or the beaf-steak plant. It will thrive in sun or shade, even dry shade, and in any soil, even almost pure chalk. The evergreen foliage is excellent, a rich, dark green, and if you crush the leaves you will find that they emit a peculiar odour. The flowers, compared with those of the tall bearded irises, are insignificant – scarcely 13mm (½in.) across and pale violet with exquisite veining. The real glory of the plant comes in autumn, when the huge seed pods burst open to reveal their rich display of brilliant orange seeds. The variegated form, *Iris foetidissima* 'Variegata' has leaves brightly margined and striped white. Sadly, it seldom flowers and never seems to fruit. It is a plant that looks at its best massed and, since it is slow to increase, it may take time to build up sufficient stocks to do this, but it is well worth while. Once established, it is best left alone to go on increasing at its own rate.

Iris japonica has typical iris leaves, produced in typical fan-form, but on a short, semi-erect stem which in time keels over, roots, and produces further fans, while a new fan arises from the original growing-point. The flowers are also typically iris but small and, in 'Ledger's Variety' (the one most commonly grown), white with purple markings and an orange crest. It is pretty enough, but unremarkable. *Iris japonica* 'Variegata' by contrast is quite breathtaking. About half of each leaf is margined and vertically striped cream at first, fading to clear white, and the overall effect of the fan is brilliant. It is a little tender, the sort of plant you put in a well-drained spot in the shelter of a south wall. It would be lovely massed, if only one could find the right corner.

There is a white-variegated form of *Iris kaempferi*, whose leaves are striped white, but it is a singularly unexciting plant.

Iris pallida is similar in many ways to the bearded irises in the structure of the roots, the arrangement of the leaves and above all in the size and quality of the flower, which is a pleasing light blue and, according to Gerard, smells much like an orange flower. There are two variegated forms, one with leaves brilliantly margined white known as 'Variegata', and the other with leaves equally brilliantly variegated, but cream, and known misleadingly as 'Aurea-variegata'. Both are absolutely stunning plants, keeping their leaves much later in the year than most irises. They need good cultivation, and need to be lifted and divided every couple of years to maintain their vigour, but they are well worth the trouble. They look marvellous massed in association with one of the bergenias whose leaves colour in winter.

I have never understood why anyone would grow *Kerria japonica* in their garden. It seems to have nothing whatsoever to commend it. The flowers, which are small and produced so far one from another as to have little combined effect, are of a most distasteful shade of orange-yellow; the leaves are feeble things, with no positive qualities, and the habit of the plant has little to commend it, being a straggly thing and suckering about the place, usually where it is not wanted. It therefore never crossed my mind that *Kerria japonica* 'Variegata' could be a worthwhile plant – but I was so wrong. The variegated form grows to little more than 1m (3ft), less than half the height of the normal form, suckers slowly, and is of relatively dense habit; the variegation is not dramatic – rather it is elegant, a creamy-white marginal variegation, with some creamy white and grey on the leaves. It is not a particularly good variegation when you look at a single leaf, but when you come across a large patch of it, it is extremely effective. The shrub has also the merit of growing in shade, in any reasonable soil. It has some tendency to revert, and any green-leaved shoots should be cut out while they are in leaf.

The dead nettle is a common British native, revelling in moist woodland. It has no special qualities to attract the gardener, except that it does not sting. The variegated dead nettle, on the other hand, *Lamium galeobdolon (luteum)* 'Variegatum' has much to commend it provided you have a garden large enough to accommodate the plant. It is a rampageous ground cover producing pairs of opposite, dark green, white-marbled leaves on long trailing stems that run in all directions, rooting as they go. To accommodate it, you really need 0.2 hectares (½ acre) of beech woods where nothing else will grow: in such a situation it is both useful and decorative. If you try growing it among small shrubs it will quickly swamp them. The lesser dead nettle is *Lamium maculatum*, and it is one of those plants which are naturally variegated: it has a bold white stripe down the centre of the leaf. It is a much smaller, slower-growing plant than *Lamium galeobdolon* 'Variegatum' and can easily be kept under control in a small garden. It is excellent as a massed ground cover under rhododendrons, where it will trap the leaves and keep the weeds down. If you dislike the mauvish pink of the flowers, there are forms with white flowers ('Alba') and pink flowers ('Roseum'). Both of these dead nettles will grow just about anywhere, so long as it is reasonably moist, with very little trouble.

The genus *Liriope* produces its flowers late in the year, well into the autumn, and they are extremely long-lasting. Typically you first notice the unopened spikes in August or September, and the flowers are still effective at Christmas. The genus consists of rhizomatous liliaceous plants with strap-shaped leaves produced in whorls, a tufted habit, and spikes of normally purple flowers (though there are pink and white-flowered forms). It is sometimes confused with the genus *Ophiopogon*, and one American botanist has suggested merging the two genera and giving them the portmanteau name *Liriopogon*, which might seem at first glance a good idea but in fact would satisfy neither gardeners nor botanists. In practice you can usually tell which is which once you know the two genera. The main difference is that in *Liriope* the ovary is sub-inferior; in *Ophiopogon* it is superior. The Americans call the plants lily turf, and some of the species do have a turf-forming habit. They also call them mondo grass, which is misleading: they are not grasses at all and only superficially grass-like.

There are several variegated liriopes, but only two or three are worth growing. The finest is *Liriope platyphylla* 'John Burch', which has leaves margined with broad bands of a rather yellowish, creamy colour and slightly striped creamy white. The flowers are purple. This seems to be the most vigorous of the variegated forms, also the most frost-resistant and the most resistant to damage by sun. 'Silvery Midget' is useful as a rather dwarf plant – it grows to about half the height of 'John Burch' – but the variegation is less good though in much the same style. Quite the most exciting of the group is 'Silvery Sunproof', which is dramatically white-variegated both at the margins and in the centre of the leaves. Sadly, it seems to be the most tender form of *Liriope platyphylla* around. All the liriopes grow best in a light, well-drained deep soil and flower best in sun but produce the finest leaves in the shade. There you have a dilemma: I try growing them in half-shade, which seems a reasonable compromise.

While the liriopes are merely grass-like, *Miscanthus* is a genuine grass, known in America as Eulalia grass, a name particularly applied to *Miscanthus sinensis*. Don't close your mind to miscanthus merely because it is tall-growing. It is not a vigorously invasive plant, though many people seem to think so. It is slowly clump-forming, never invasive, and the stems are tall and wiry, very erect, and seldom broken by wind. The variegated form, *Miscanthus sinensis* 'Variegatus' ('Vittatus'), is less tall-growing than other varieties (which will grow up to nearly 2m (6½ft): if you are lucky, this will reach only about 1.5m (4½ft). The long, narrow leaves, produced at regular intervals up the stems, are boldly margined and striped white along the whole of their length. It is a most effective plant, and very dramatic when massed, as it might be in a colour band in front of a dark, evergreen band. It is not fussy as to soil and is readily increased by division.

A grass in quite a different style is *Molinia caerulea* 'Variegata', the variegated purple moor grass. It is a low-growing plant, slowly forming dense tufts up to about 60cm (2ft) of limp, thin leaves which are narrow and arch gracefully outwards, conspicuously striped creamy white, with some yellowish and pinkish touches. The flowers are borne on thin, wiry stems, high above the foliage; what you see of these are the purple stamens and stigmas, and when these are produced abundantly they greatly enhance the effect of a large planting of this grass. It is an ideal plant for massing, either in colour bands or in freehand patterns, and is readily increased by dividing the clumps in spring. Though the green-leaved form will tolerate extremely acid conditions, the variegated form seems to do best in good garden soil, preferably in light shade.

Ophiopogon is grass-like, but not a grass, and is often confused with liriope, to which it bears a close superficial resemblance. From a garden point of view, the flowers are generally less showy. The most dramatically variegated ophiopogon is *Ophiopogon jaburan* 'Variegatus'; whose strap-shaped leaves are boldly striped a good, clean white. It is not a particularly hardy plant, though it will succeed on light, sandy soils in a sheltered position under shrubs. Rather hardier is *Ophiopogon intermedius* 'Variegatus' which is a diminutive little thing, growing only about 12.5cm (5ins.) high, with a very narrow leaf about 6mm (¼in.) across, so narrow that it scarcely seems worth variegating, but in fact the variegation is strong and good, well over half the leaf being striped boldly white. It has a slowly running, turf-forming habit, but is much slower than the green-leaved form and also a little more tender. It is a plant to be treasured because it has such a delicate, refined appearance.

There is a number of plants that commend themselves on account of their usefulness, rather than any intrinsic beauty and the pachysandras fall into that category. *Pachysandra terminalis* is a low-growing evergreen ground cover with a long-stalked, three-parted leaf, toothed towards the tip. It is of a very average green: really, a plant of quite outstanding dullness. *Pachysandra terminalis* 'Variegata' has leaves that are blotched creamy white, more creamy in shade, more white in sun. If you came across it in a pot you would probably dismiss it as worthless. It is only when you see a big, bold patch of it at the edge of a shrubbery or in some similar situation that you start to see its potential, for in such situations it is really extremely effective. Spreading slowly by means of stolons which run just below the surface of the soil, it can readily be propagated by means of these, or by cuttings at any time so long as the growth is firm. It will grow in just about any soil, but enjoys a good top dressing of old leaves or peat from time to time to keep it vigorous.

It is a common fallacy that variegated plants are a modern interest, so it comes as something of a surprise to find that *Phalaris arundinacea* 'Picta' ('Elegantissima'), better known as gardener's garters or ribbon grass, has been in cultivation since 1596 and is recorded by Gerard in his herbal, along with a yellow-variegated form which we seem to have lost. It is an easily grown, spreading grass, straggling up to 1.5m (4½ft) with leaves longitudinally striped white. It is probably in fact the most commonly seen and grown of all ornamental grasses, but of some merit for all that. What is not perhaps appreciated about it is that while the leaves tend to fade and become tatty as summer wears on, if the plant is cut to the ground in July or August it will produce a new flush of stems and leaves every bit as bright as the first flush. In addition to the form normally seen, there is a much more strongly variegated and slower-spreading form known as 'Feesey's Form', and a dwarf form known as dwarf's garters which only grows to about half the usual height. All of these are ideal for quickly creating colour bands in new gardens, or large patches of white in large gardens.

It is a shame that such a great gardener as E. A. Bowles is remembered mainly for those plants which he relegated to that area of his garden which he called his lunatic asylum, such as the curly hazel and the curly thorn, when he was responsible for finding and distributing so many really first-rate garden plants. One of the finest of these is a variegated mock orange blossom, *Philadelphus coronarius* 'Variegatus', a form of the common mock orange with leaves brilliantly variegated with a bold white margin. A stunning plant, growing slowly to 2–2.5m (6 or 8ft), with a spread of about half its height, it is readily propagated by cuttings taken as soon as the wood is firm, so that it is very easy to produce enough of it to mass, when it is really seen at its best. Few white-variegated shrubs are so effective. There is a form around known as 'Bowles Form' which is reputed to be better than the ordinary 'Variegatus', though the authenticity of the name is dubious, and the claimed superiority of the form doubtful.

The garden phloxes are one of those groups of plants that went through a period of popularity, then waned, and seem now, with the advent of new, large flowered hybrids, to be making something of a comeback. There are two absolutely stunning variegated forms which are worth seeking out and taking the trouble to grow well. The better known of the two is *Phlox paniculata* 'Nora Leigh', the other is *Phlox paniculata* 'Harlequin'. I doubt whether you could tell them apart by the leaf alone. In both cases the leaf is margined and marked the most brilliant bright white, and in both cases the variegation is stunning both from a distance and at close quarters. 'Nora Leigh' is the older of the two clones, and has miserable pale lilac flowers. 'Harlequin', which has only been relatively recently introduced to the market, has vivid purple flowers which are such a shocking contrast to the leaves that you really have to admire their courage. I rather like the violence of the contrast between leaf and flower in 'Harlequin'. If you have the space, it is entertaining to grow both, a large block of one side by side with a large block of the other, preferably a continuous block: it is only when it flowers that you realize that there are two components, not one.

Phlox 'Nora Leigh' has a somewhat low reputation; it is said to be a miffy plant and almost inevitably this reputation has rubbed off on to 'Harlequin', presumably because most people cannot tell the one from the other. They are not miffy plants so long as you cultivate them well. They do not like heavy clay, and they do not like chalk: they do not like to be dry at the roots, but neither will they endure excessive wet at the roots. What they need is a well-nourished soil, with plenty of humus in it, and an annual top-dressing of humus – leaf-mould, compost, even manure: whatever is available. Give them that and they will thrive. If you want a lot of plants, the phloxes are reasonably easy to divide in spring or autumn, and they come readily from root cuttings (which is how the professionals increase them).

It must have been the flower arrangers who made the New Zealand flax – the phormiums – popular. Certainly there is now no sophisticated garden in Britain that would be seen dead without a phormium. It is a dramatic foliage plant with rather architectural overtones – great bold sword-shaped leaves sprouting almost erect from the ground: a good clump can be all of 2.5–3m (8 or 9ft) high, and 1–1.5m (3 or 4ft) across at ground level. We seem at the moment to be going through a passing fad for importing from New Zealand a variety of clones with brightly coloured leaves, some of them quite stunning. Fine in the conservatory, but in my experience of little worth in the garden. But if you have the money and don't mind trying these new clones, knowing you may lose some if not all of them, good luck to you. For my money I would rather stick with a handful of forms that have already been tried and tested sufficiently to be trusted. It is hopeless using unproven plants in multi-coloured bands or blocks. The typical green-leaved plant is both useful and lovely: there are some good purple forms, including some useful dwarfs. A proven favourite is the one known simply as *Phormium tenax* 'Variegatum'. The leaf, which measures over 3cm (1½ins.) on a mature plant, has a relatively thin white margin and is emphatically folded along the midrib. Though the width of the marginal variegation is small, it is quite unexpectedly effective – and it is effectiveness that matters. It is an excellent plant as a specimen, or as a group of dot plants, but definitely at its most stunning massed: have the courage to try it in a big, bold curve and you will find that for sheer effectiveness there is little that can compare with it. It is readily increased by lifting the clumps in spring and dividing the fans, each with an adequate amount of old root.

If you are a flower-arranging buff you will almost certainly know and be growing *Pittosporum tenuifolium*; if you are not, you will probably have been put off by being repeatedly told that this is a tender plant. Up to a point it is, but not disastrously so. The typical plant is a shapely shrub or small tree with bright, pale green leaves distinct on account of the undulate margins (a charm which is lacking in some degree from many of its cultivars). The flowers, which too many gardeners have never noticed, are dark chocolate maroon and have the most divine honey-scent, most noticeable in the evening.

There is a number of variegated forms of varying degrees of garden merit: 'Garnettii' has leaves flushed pink and white, and is scarcely worth garden room. 'Irene Patterson' has leaves spotted white and is very striking as a small plant, but when it gets larger its sheer size seems to diminish the effectiveness of the leaves. 'Silver Queen' has leaves suffused silvery grey: not perhaps sufficiently striking to bother with as a variegated plant, though if you did not expect it to be variegated you might find it quite charming. 'Variegatum' has leaves margined with a good creamy white and is a pleasing variegation. On the whole, however, I think the variegated pittosporums rather a disappointment.

If you are into variegated weeds you might take a fancy to a stunningly variegated form of that common weed of lawns and other grassy places, *Plantago lanceolata* 'Streaker'. It is just a common plantain, but the long narrow leaves are boldly and broadly margined brilliant white. It is a very striking plant, relatively slow to increase, but it can be multiplied by division and, if you could propagate enough of it, it would make a most dramatic low ground cover, more effective massed than as a specimen. It seems not to be fussy as to soil, but does need to be grown in full sun.

People always seem surprised when they learn that the common laurel (as in hedging) belongs to the same genus as the flowering cherry. The leaf is, perhaps, a little larger and it is evergreen, but the flowers and fruits are so similar that the surprise is rather that people do not recognize the similarity sooner. The great virtue of laurel, of course, is that you can grow it just about anywhere. While, like most plants, it grows best with good cultivation and in good light, it will grow better than most on poor soil in shade, even under the drip of trees and in situations where tree cover is such that the light is poor. What is more, even the variegated form will tolerate such abuse. The correct name of the variegated laurel is not entirely clear. The laurel itself is *Prunus laurocerasus*. The variegated form turns up variously as *Prunus laurocerasus* 'Variegata', *Prunus laurocerasus rotundifolia* 'Variegata' and *Prunus laurocerasus* 'Green Marble'. Under whatever name, it is a slower-growing plant than the typical laurel, with a more dense habit, the leaf more rounded at the tip, and heavily mottled bright creamy white, the mottling being spread thickly over the entire surface. It is not a beautiful variegation; it is curious. But the really important thing is that it is effective. A plant of good size will attract your attention from a great way off, while a massed planting is surprisingly attractive.

The variegated Portugal laurel, *Prunus lusitanica* 'Variegata', is a much more conventionally variegated plant, with pointed oval leaves and a bright white marginal variegation, with a little dirty white shading on the leaf. The petioles are bright red, and the leaves tend to flush pink in winter, which is an added attraction. Grown in full sun, this is a striking variegated plant; it is not quite so effective in shade. The Portugal laurel is reputed to be hardier than the cherry laurel. It will grow well on thin chalk soils, which the cherry laurel will not. Both laurels are easily increased by hardwood cuttings in a north light in winter.

Rhamnus alternata 'Variegata' is ultimately a quite large, densely leafy, well-furnished evergreen shrub or small tree, but slow-growing. The individual leaves, which are less than 2.5cm (1in.) long, are oval, marbled grey and margined with a clean, bright white. It is far more effective in the mass than as an individual, and a small plant in a pot gives little idea of the beauty of the mature plant. Young plants seem to be invariably lank, leggy and far more liable to damage by frost and wind than established plants. It is absolutely ideal for massing, as a high bank of greyishness in the background. It seems not to be fussy about soil, but definitely grows best in sun, and can be increased reasonably readily by cuttings taken from mid-summer onwards.

A variegated rose might strike you as something unspeakably hideous. But then, if you like variegated plants and appreciate the subtleties of foliage, you may well find the sort of roses that people grow for their flowers unspeakably hideous. The only truly, regularly and constantly variegated rose which I have met so far is sold in commerce under the name *Rosa wichuriana* 'Variegata', though no one seems quite certain whether that is what it actually is or not. Certainly it has every outward semblance of affinity. It is one of those roses which you can use as a ground cover or as a climber, or both. The leaves are blotched white, not an attractive variegation, but because it occurs on a plant of some vigour which can be used to cover large areas quickly, it is worth growing: the effect of the foliage massed is far greater than the sum of the variegated leaves. It remains, for all that, essentially a curiosity – a variegated plant in a genus singularly lacking variegated forms.

Rue, if I remember my Shakespeare rightly, is for remembrance, though one old boy I know always says rue is for regret, though he has never revealed what it is he regrets. Rue is a herb, and it seems to be currently enjoying some popularity among flower arrangers. The typical rue, *Ruta graveolens*, is technically a shrub though you or I would probably consider it herbaceous – suffruticose at most – and it suckers. It grows to about 60cm (2ft) in height and 1m (3ft) across, and produces a wealth of doubly-pinnate leaves which owe their peculiar charm not so much to their colour, a sort of steely blue, as to their shape, for the ultimate segments of leaves are all rounded (unusual in a leaf of this type). There is a variegated form, 'Variegata', which is cream and green, spotted, splashed and striped, the variegation being at the point where growth is occurring. I do not like the plant and I dislike the variegation even more, but if you want a variegated herb to mass on light sandy soil in full sun it can be very effective. You can increase it easily by seed, most of the seedlings reproducing the variegation: even those few that start green usually seem to develop it. The same goes for cuttings, which strike readily from midsummer on: a proportion of rooted cuttings will make a go of trying to turn green for a while, but they usually give up and end up as variegated as the rest. Rue is a Mediterranean plant, so it likes full sun and perfect drainage. It will not tolerate cold, wet soils, and will show this by dying if it is planted in them. To keep it in good vigour it is worth cutting it almost to the ground each spring.

The elders are really rather gawky, ungainly shrubs quite unsuited to civilized gardens. There is one, just one, which is breathtakingly beautiful, *Sambucus nigra* 'Pulverulenta'. 'Pulverulenta' means 'very beautiful', an apt epithet for this plant. It is far smaller-growing than the green-leaved common elder, probably about half the height, and the leaves are dramatically striped and mottled white. A lovely thing, both in the detail of the leaves and in overall effect, it needs well-cultivated soil and a position in full sun, then there are few garden shrubs that can outshine it. By comparison, *Sambucus nigra* 'Variegata' or 'Albo-Variegata' puts up a poor show, with a creamy-white marginal variegation on a very ordinary leaf. It looks quite bright in dense shade where little else will grow, but it does not justify much more praise than that. There is also a plant listed by some nurserymen as 'Aureomarginata'. I cannot tell the difference between this and the foregoing, nor can a lot of other people. All the elders come easily from cuttings taken at almost any time so long as the plant is in growth.

Scrophularia aquatica 'Variegata', the variegated water figwort, is closely related to the foxglove but, apart from the shape of the basal leaves, you will probably see little other resemblance. The leaves are long in proportion to their width, deeply corrugated, and very broadly margined creamy white, a colouring which persists all year. To keep it at its best, you need to grow it in damp, semi-shade in a deep, moist soil well enriched with leaf-mould. If it is variegation you want from the plant, it pays to remove the flower-spike as it begins to emerge: if you let it flower the whole plant looks tatty, and anyway there is a danger of it seeding, producing green-leaved seedlings. It is an excellent plant for massing, and a fine companion for *Ligularia* 'Desdemona', that lovely hybrid with large rounded leaves of a deep coppery purple. Both enjoy the same cultural conditions.

The green-leaved form of the plant, *Sisyrinchium striatum*, is a plant that few people nowadays would bother deliberately to cultivate. It looks, until you examine it closely, like an iris, producing a fan of mid-green leaves of quite exceptional ordinariness about 30cm (1ft) long. The most immediately noticeable way in which the plant differs from an iris is that the fans of leaves are all produced from a single rooting point, whereas in an iris the fan tends to be spread out along the rhizome.

The flowers are quite different from those of iris, straw-yellow, very small and produced on a long and rather unsightly spike. I suppose the plant has its uses: it will grow, for example, in the deepest, darkest parts of beech woods where nothing else will.

The variegated form, *Sisyrinchium striatum* 'Variegatum' (which is also known as *Sisyrinchium striatum* 'Aunt May') is as much one of the most brilliant of variegated plants as the green-leaved form is one of the dullest. It is slightly smaller-growing than the typical plant, and the leaves are brilliantly striped creamy white, about half the width of the leaf being taken up with this colour. To say that it is stunning is to understate its drama and appeal; it is breathtaking. It is, perhaps, all the more desirable in that it has a reputation for being difficult to grow. This is not to say that it *is* difficult to grow: it merely has that reputation. Perhaps it helps to understand its habits. The ultimate objective of each fan of leaves is to produce a flower. Having done that, the fan then dies. By that time there should be other fans to replace it. It is understandable that people seeing a fan dying after flowering might think that the whole plant is starting to die. But it isn't; all you need do is remove the dead fan. The plant will grow in any fertile soil, acid or alkaline, and you have the best chance of keeping it alive if you divide the clumps in late summer and keep the plants well fed with liberal mulchings of leaf-mould. If you find it grows particularly easily with you, it would be well worth massing, but it is not advisable to attempt massing it if you have difficulty keeping even a single clump going.

Should you ever come across a variegated symphytum offered for sale, grab it. Under whatever name, it is most certainly one of the world's top-ten best-dressed white-variegated plants. It is sold variously as *Symphytum asperum, Symphytum peregrinum, Symphytum officinale* and *Symphytum asperrimum*. The chances are that in fact it is *Symphytum x uplandicum* which is a hybrid, though no one seems too certain who the parents were. Whatever its true taxonomic status, it is a marvellous plant, with huge, typical comfrey leaves, broadly margined a deep, rich, creamy white, and a singularly symmetrical variegation. The leaves can be well over 30cm (1ft) in length, and half as wide, and a well-grown plant is just a great pile of these beautiful leaves. Clumps can spread to be as much as 1m (3ft) across, and when the plant is massed the effect is almost unbelievably good. It is easily grown, thriving in deep, fertile soil, with a little shade through some of the day. It enjoys a good mulch annually of leaf-mould or good garden compost. Though slow to increase, with careful division in early spring you can build up quite a number of plants over a year or two. Whatever you do, don't miss it merely because you think some nurseryman has it wrongly labelled. It is too good and too seldom offered to miss.

Thuja plicata 'Wansdyke Silver' is too newly introduced for anyone to draw much in the way of conclusions about its ultimate height or spread, or even its ultimate rate of growth. It is a delightful form of the western red cedar, whose sprays of fine, filigree foliage are speckled and splashed white, a striking contrast against the dark green of the rest of the foliage. It is one of those plants whose variegation delights when seen at close quarters, but I doubt if it would be effective from much distance. It is fairly slow-growing, and therefore would seem to be excellent for a hedge or for massing in a position where you need perhaps only five or six plants packed together. In such a situation you can keep it down to size if you need to. It is a good new conifer, useful in its way, but there are better white-variegated plants. The variegation is constant and reliable, which is more than can be said of some, it is easy to grow, and it comes readily from autumn cuttings.

The term 'hemlock' confuses people. To most it is the plant from which the potion was made by means of which Socrates so honourably took his own life. In America it is a tree of the largest size, an elegant and useful conifer. It is best known to gardeners through the innumerable forms it has produced, including some beautiful semi-dwarf weeping ones. There are one or two forms which are more or less variegated, and one that turns out to be really good. This is *Tsuga canadensis* 'Dwarf Whitetip'. It has the typical habit of *Tsuga canadensis*, but is very much slower-growing, forming, after many years, a broadly pyramidal bush of semi-pendulous habit. The new shoots in spring emerge a bright creamy white and are highly effective against the very dark foliage. What is more, the colouring is retained until well into the winter. It would be worth trying in a massed planting if you had the space, but its prime use in the multi-coloured garden is as a dot or linking plant.

Almost the last and about the lowliest of the creams and whites for massing are the periwinkles, most of which are probably too well known to need much description. The lesser periwinkle (*Vinca minor*) makes a more effectively weed-suppressing ground cover than does the larger one (*Vinca major*), even though that is the opposite of what one would expect. It is slower to spread, and it may be precisely for that reason that it is so much the better of the two. On the whole, the variegated forms of *Vinca major* are better, both as variegations and for massed effect. *Vinca major* 'Albo-reticulata' is not particularly stunning, though it sounds as though it ought to be. It has the typical large green leaf of the species, but every vein on the leaf is white, producing a curious reticulated effect which is beautiful on the individual leaf, but you really rather lose sight of it once you have walked a couple of strides away from it. *Vinca major* 'Variegata' ('Elegantissima'), on the other hand, is a bold plant with a bold variegation, effective in almost any setting. The large oval leaf is richly margined bright white, with some white marking inside the margin too. It is the most dramatic of all the variegated vincas. *Vinca minor* 'Variegata' is a miserable thing by comparison. The leaf is smaller and narrower and more pointed and the variegation consists of varying degrees of greyish whitishness all over the leaf. If you looked at a leaf close to, you would probably assume that the plant would scarcely show its variegation at all: in fact it is only when you have a large clump of it that you really start to appreciate just how well variegated it is. It looks much brighter from a distance than it does from close quarters, giving an overall silvery effect.

The yuccas in cultivation form a fairly homogenous group, either with stems or stemless and with relatively stiff, sword-shaped leaves presented in a rosette.

Probably the best known is *Yucca gloriosa*, with its stiff, dark green leaves with very fiercely pointed tips. More widely grown is *Yucca filamentosa*, in which the leaves are glaucous, of much flabbier texture, and the margins decorated with a disarray of fine white threads. There is a marvellous white-variegated yucca sold in nurseries and garden centres as *Y. filamentosa* 'Variegata', and a stunning plant it is, though it is very questionable whether it is actually a form of *filamentosa*. The leaves are too short, too broad and carry insufficient marginal threads for the species. Whatever it is, it is well worth obtaining, and that is the name under which you are likeliest to find it. It is a stemless, rosette-forming species of low growth with extraordinarily broad leaves and quite incredibly wide white marginal bands of variegation, touched and tinted pink. It is outstandingly decorative, and ideal for massing. It seems easy enough to grow, in full sun on a well-drained soil.

The variegated form of *Y. gloriosa* is among the most desirable of all variegated hardy plants. It is stem-forming, growing up to about 2m (6½ft), and the leaves, which may be over 60cm (2ft) long and 7.5cm (3ins.) wide at their widest point, are longitudinally striped green, white, pink and cream. Because of the vicious points at the tips of the leaves, it is far too eye-piercing a plant to risk massing. What it is ideal for is as a focal point on a ground of low, dark ground cover. The emphasis is even greater if, instead of using a single plant, you put in a group of five or seven but put them in each a few years apart, so that you get the effect of a pile of this magnificent plant – the tallest and oldest in the middle with smaller plants around it.

That, as you might expect, is not a complete or comprehensive survey of plants with cream- or white-variegated leaves; indeed, it scarcely scratches the surface of the rich diversity of such plants. What it does do is pull out a handful that are of particular value in the multi-coloured garden, either for massing or for use as specimens or linking plants.

CHAPTER FIVE

Yellows and Golds

You may very easily assume that there are more cream- or white-variegated plants than gold- or yellow-variegated ones, but that is merely because, on the whole, cream and white variegations are so dramatic that they tend to stick in the mind's eye. In fact, if you sit down and make lists of one against the other, there are actually considerably more of the golds and yellows, the great majority of them good garden plants.

One of the most desirable is *Acer japonicum* 'Aureum'. Like other Japanese maples, it slowly grows into a multi-stemmed small, elegant tree. The flowers, which appear before the leaves, are bright red, and quite showy in their way. But it is for the leaves that the tree is grown. They are rounded, slightly lobed, and of a soft, quiet, golden-yellow, a colour which is retained through the season. In autumn the leaves turn fiery scarlets and crimsons, but what is most intriguing is that there is an in-between stage in which the leaves are bi-coloured, the centres burning with fiery autumnal scarlet, encircled by the same rich golden-yellow the leaves have been all summer. It is not a difficult tree to grow, demanding only a neutral or acid soil, plenty of humus, and a little shade: but not too much. In deep shade the leaves remain green, but in too much sun they scorch. There you have a cultural problem, but solving such problems is much of what gardening is all about. It is too special a tree for massing and always at its best when used as a specimen, preferably with a dark background.

In the previous chapter we considered a brilliantly white-variegated ground elder. There is also a yellow-variegated one, *Aegopodium podogaria* 'Aurea Variegatum'. The variegation is not so fine as that of the white-variegated form, but it is still good and makes an interesting and useful plant in the multi-coloured garden, being completely unfussed as to soil.

There is a number of yellow- or golden-leaved grasses in cultivation, but the golden foxtail grass, *Alopecurus pratensis* 'Aureus', is unquestionably the most brilliant of them all. It is a densely tufted, slowly-spreading, deciduous perennial grass that grows to about 30cm (1ft) in height (the foxtail flowers overtop the leaves), bearing leaves that are the richest golden-yellow (with just a hint of orange) imaginable. They almost glow with the intensity of the colouring. It sounds like a rare exotic, but in fact is perfectly hardy and very easy to suit, needing only a reasonably fertile soil and a position in full sun. If you clip it down in spring and clear the previous season's growth out of the way, it will remain happily perennial, going from strength to strength on most soils, but on heavy clays it is better to lift and divide it every couple of years otherwise it is inclined to lose its vigour. It is very easily increased by division in spring (never autumn), and is just about the perfect grass for massing in colour bands since its colouring is exceptionally intense and it has no tendency to run out of line.

The next plant is neither tough nor wholly frost hardy, but if you can give it the conditions it requires, it provides a totally unexpected touch to the multi-coloured garden. It is, in fact, a succulent, and as such is usually and unnecessarily nurtured in greenhouses or on window-sills. The plant is *Aptenia (Mesembryanthemum) cordifolia*, and the form to use for massing is *A.c.* 'Variegata', whose rough, warty, thick, fleshy, succulent leaves, which are roughly diamond-shaped, about 1.5cm (3/5in.) long and less than 1cm (2/5in.) across, are, like the stems, the palest creamy yellow, but margined and marked with an overlay of rich yellow. The overall effect of a massed planting is a surprisingly rich yellow. The plant only grows about 5cm (2ins.) high, and will spread in time to 30cm (1ft) or so across, but roots as it spreads, gradually making a carpet. The one thing that lets it down are the flowers, which are the most frightful mauve and clash horribly with the colour of the leaves. Happily, the flowers are very small. Although a succulent, it is not nearly so tender as might be expected and will survive out of doors for years provided that it is planted in full sun in a sheltered place (such as a patio) and given perfect drainage in a gritty soil. If you can give it a light covering of newly fallen leaves to keep the edge of the frost off it through the winter, it will survive all but the most severe winters with little more than a rather tired look to it by spring. It is readily increased by cuttings rooted in sand.

In complete contrast, the golden bamboo, *Arundinaria viridistriata (auricoma)* is one of the toughest and most robust yellow-leafed plants around. It is a slowly-spreading, clump-forming bamboo, growing ultimately to about 2m (6ft) and spreading to about 1m (3ft) across in six or eight years. The leaves, which are about 15 or 20cm (6 or 8ins.) long and about 4cm (1½ins.) across, are brilliantly striped with the brightest, most intense golden-yellow, the area of golden-yellow normally being far greater than the green area in a leaf asymmetrically longitudinally divided, one half usually all golden-yellow, the other green richly striped golden-yellow. The colour remains strong throughout the year, though in exposed situations the leaves begin to look a little tatty by the end of winter. The densest and most brightly coloured plants are achieved by cutting the old canes down to ground level in late spring every year, just as the new canes break through the ground. There is a dwarf form, known as 'Feesey's Form', which grows to little more than 30cm (1ft) in height, with a proportionately lesser spread. Both forms need to be grown in full sun to show their colouring. When grown in shade they are merely an oddly ill-looking green. They will grow in any fertile soil and give of their best when regularly mulched. Both are among the finest of plants for making colour bands, since the growth is dense and weed-proof, the colouring quite stunning, and yet the spread of the plants is easily controlled (you just chop off any rhizomes that grow out of line, with a sharp spade).

The mere mention of *Aucuba japonica* conjures up in most people's minds images of drab Victorian plantings of dull evergreens in semi-basement city gardens. It is not an image the spotted laurels deserve. When well grown they are a joy to behold, with their glossy leaves and well-rounded habit of growth. Among the dozens of named clones is a small number with good yellow markings to the leaves. *A.j.* 'Crotonifolia', which has an exceptionally large leaf, is a form spotted and splashed with gold. 'Gold Dust' is similar, but better. The finest of all, however, is 'Gold Splash', which is being billed as though it were something new, when in fact the Victorians knew it and grew it. The centre of the leaf is wholly filled with a huge oval of the richest possible butter-yellow, leaving only a thin margin of green round the edge. It is a very dramatic leaf: and an even more dramatic plant, seen at its best massed in shade. All the spotted laurels are easily grown, tolerant of any soil, of sun or shade, but definitely performing best given a good fertile soil and regular mulch. All are readily increased by cuttings which seem to root at any time of year. They also root exceptionally quickly when layered.

There is a number of forms of *Calluna vulgaris* with more or less yellow foliage: 'Beoley Gold' is a particularly brilliant golden-yellow with white flowers, growing to about 30cm (1ft); 'Golden Carpet' is even better, rich gold all summer turning more nearly orange in winter, but growing to only 15cm (6ins.) – an excellent carpeting heather; 'Gold Haze' is taller-growing, to about 45cm, again bright golden-yellow but not such a clean colour as the previous two. 'Robert Chapman', however, is a little different: though usually billed as golden-yellow, the colour is far nearer orange, changing to a mixture of bronze, orange and red in winter; it has purple flowers, only grows to about 25cm (10ins.) and forms a very dense carpet. 'Sir John Charrington' again has orange-yellow foliage, but turns bright red in winter; it is stronger-growing, up to about 45cm (1½ft). 'Sunset' changes colour with the changing seasons, being orange-gold in spring and summer and decidedly bronze in winter; it grows to about 30cm (1ft), and is the least bright in colouring of all those mentioned. None of these heathers is lime-tolerant, and all enjoy a soil well enriched with humus. All colour best in full sun.

Carex stricta 'Aurea' is as much the most brilliantly golden-yellow sedge as *Alopecurus pratensis* 'Aureus' is the most brilliant golden grass. It is breath-taking, especially when used in large quantities. The leaves can be up to 60cm (2ft) long and about 13mm (½in.) across, of the deepest imaginable rich golden-yellow with just the narrowest though quite distinct thin margin of green. The almost black flowers, which are produced towards the tips of the long, thin wand-like stems, are wholly in keeping with the character of the plant. It is a useful and adaptable plant, probably happiest growing with its feet in water, when it will form large clumps of arching leaves; grown in drier conditions it is invariably smaller with the leaves more upright, but the colour is just as good. It is very easily increased by division, which is best done in spring. *C. reticulosa* 'Aurea' is generally very similar though the leaves are a little wider, but instead of being a rich golden-yellow, it is a pale lime-yellow. Its general behaviour is very similar to that of *C. stricta* 'Aurea', and the two are very effective when grown together, a massed planting of one beside a massed planting of the other. They are so alike in foliage and habit that the change in colour is quite unexpected.

Arguably the finest golden tree in existence is *Catalpa bignonioides* 'Aurea', the golden Indian bean tree – arguably, since some people do argue that *Robinia pseudoacacia* 'Frisia' is even better. The golden Indian bean tree has the same large, soft, floppy, elephant's-ear leaves as the green-leafed tree; the same white, scented, chestnut-like flower spikes; the same long, bean-like fruit pods; and the same bifurcating habit of growth. It differs only in that the leaves are rich, golden-yellow all summer long, and in that it is a little slower-growing. For some reason the green-leafed form is usually grown as a tree, on a single stem, while the golden one is usually grown on several stems, three or five, presumably because that way you get more leaves when it is younger. If you buy it from a nursery you will usually get a grafted plant, which will be expensive. It comes quite readily from soft cuttings taken from June onwards.

Chamaecyparis lawsoniana in some of its forms came up in the previous chapter: no doubt it will come up in the next one too. There are dozens of more or less yellow or golden forms, ranging in size from the really quite small to the very tall. The one you will probably come across most often is *C.l.* 'Erecta Aurea', a relatively slow-growing plant of broadly oval outline and of a good, rich yellow. Its main problem is that the foliage is presented in flattened sprays that are held vertically erect, and it is liable to fall apart under the weight of snow. Once the damage has been done, it never looks the same again. *C.l.* 'Hillieri' has somehow gained the reputation of being the most brilliant of the golden lawsons, though quality is something you must judge for yourself. It is certainly a very bright, clean yellow and, though not fast-growing, ultimately reaches 12m (40ft) or more, of narrowly pyramidal outline. *C.l.* 'Lanei' always seems to me a brighter colour, and is of even more narrowly pyramidal outline. *C.l.* 'Luteocompacta' is very much smaller, growing to about half the height, and of a very clear, clean yellow, though not so bright as either 'Hillieri' or 'Lanei'. *C.l.* 'Minima Aurea' is a real dwarf, a dense little bun of a bush, almost ball-shaped, of compact habit, made up of congested, golden-yellow foliage. It is useless for massing, unlike most of the lawsons, but excellent as a dot plant. *C.l.* 'Smithii' is another of the lawsons that ultimately makes a tall, conical tree, but it never seems to have gained popularity, perhaps because it looks so unpromising early in life. It starts off as a very untidy plant, with branches splaying out in all directions, and only after some years pulls itself together and forms a neat conical outline. The colour is a good yellow, but no advance on several others that are tidier when young. *C.l.* 'Stewartii' behaves in the opposite way: it starts life as a neatly conical bush, but is less regular in outline later in life. It does, however, have the bonus of the tips of the branches drooping in a manner that is almost pendulous; to my mind, it is the best colour of the lot.

Most of the lawsons are relatively large-growing plants, suitable for hedging or screening, or for massing in gardens where there is plenty of space. For smaller gardens it is clones of *Chamaecyparis obtusa* which offer most scope for multi-coloured massing. *C.o.* 'Nana Aurea' is of a good, deep two-tone yellow, quite a small, tight little grower, that presents its foliage in intriguing whorls. It will reach 3m (10ft) in its old age, but if you keep the growing tips pinched out you can keep it down to much less with no harm to the plant. It will even stand a light clipping. *C.o.* 'Tetragona Aurea' is one of the most brilliantly golden-yellow conifers in existence, but its habit of growth is so appalling that it scarcely warrants garden space (unless you are collecting plants that should have been smothered at birth). However, you can beat its dreadful habit of growth (it just throws out odd limbs in all directions) by massing it and then clipping it. If you do that, you get the benefit of the colour without the untidiness of the habit.

There are more good small conifers for massing among the forms of *Chamaecyparis pisifera*. *C.p.* 'Filifera Aurea' is ideal for the purpose. It slowly forms a dome-shaped bush of golden-yellow thread-like branchlets and foliage which, if the plants are massed, flow together in a series of humps and hollows. Though slow-growing, it will ultimately reach 3m (10ft). *C.p.* 'Gold Spangle' is an even better, brighter colour, and the habit similarly low and mounded. The foliage is less thread-like than that of 'Filifera Aurea', and probably all the more effective for that. It will grow to about 60cm (2ft) in height with a spread of 1m (3ft) in ten years. *C.p.* 'Strathmore' is quite different. Indeed, from the foliage you would probably think that it was a lawson, but the roughness of it to the touch asserts its *pisifera* allegiance. The broad sprays are lemon-yellow – a much lighter colour than the other two. The habit is spreading on a small plant, but it gathers itself together as it grows and eventually makes a symmetrically conical plant. Its rate of growth is a little faster than that of the other two *pisifera* forms mentioned here, but it is a plant that happily stands clipping. All the *Chamaecyparis* species and forms are readily increased by cuttings taken at almost any time during the growing season and rooted in sand (not a sand-peat mix). They are quite unfussed about soil, and colour most brightly in full sun.

The genus *Cornus* abounds in good white-variegated woody perennials to such an extent that the yellow- or gold-variegated plants in the genus tend to be overlooked. Probably the most widely grown, and certainly the most generally useful, is the golden-variegated form of the red-stemmed dogwood, *Cornus alba* 'Spaethii', which is similar in idiom to the white-variegated 'Elegantissima' and 'Variegata' but the variegation is rich golden-yellow. It is just as outstanding in its colour, especially when used in bold, massed plantings. It is always a mistake to plant the gold-variegated form of *Cornus alba* next to the white-variegated forms: that way, far from producing the best of both worlds, neither variegation shows up particularly well. It is far better to plant either a green-leaved (and perhaps green-stemmed) dogwood or else something completely different, like *Osmanthus decorus*.

There is an even more desirable cornus that seems to be scarcely known at all –
Cornus mas 'Aurea', the golden Cornelian cherry. It is a far more subtle and
appealing plant: whereas *C.a.* 'Spaethii' screams its colouring at you, *C.m.* 'Aurea'
just quietly sits there and glows. It is just like the common Cornelian cherry, except
that the leaves are a soft golden-yellow all summer. Marginally slower-growing than
the green-leafed plant, and every bit as good in flower, it is excellent for massing
against a background of some dark-leafed plant such as *Coryllus maxima* 'Purpurea'.
Both of these cornels grow well in any fertile soil, and are reasonably easily increased
by winter cuttings.

The gold-variegated pampas grass is one of the most desirable variegated plants in
existence, always at its best when massed. It is sold variously as *Cortaderia sellowana*
'Gold Banded' and 'Aureo-marginata', but both are the same thing. It is basically just
an ordinary pampas grass, in size and habit more nearly resembling the form 'Pumila'
than the typical plant, and with a broad stripe of rich golden-yellow along the edges
of the leaf. It is a stunning plant, both at close quarters and seen at a distance massed.
The flowers are typical pampas-grass plumes, but not so freely produced as on
green-leafed plants. Like the other pampas grasses, it needs regular grooming every
spring, which is just a matter of pulling out dead leaves, a task for which it is
imperative to wear leather gauntlets to avoid injury, as mentioned previously. It used
to be fashionable to set fire to a clump of pampas grass every spring, but that really is
one of the quickest ways of killing it. It is easily increased by division in spring. While
it seems to grow well enough in almost any fertile soil, it quite definitely does best in a
light, sandy soil and in a sheltered position.

There are a couple of good golden cypresses worth knowing about, and a couple
worth avoiding. *Cupressus macrocarpa* 'Aurea' is one of the most frightful golden
plants around. It is just a Monterery cypress, but with golden foliage and a hideous
habit of growth. If you stand about 3 kilometres (a couple of miles) from it, you get
the impression of an erect tree of pyramidal outline. Close to, you find that it is
actually made up of a series of disarrayed branches that stick out at all angles. If you
want a fine rich gold with a good pyramidal habit, the one to go for is *C.m.* 'Donard
Gold', which not only has a singularly clean colouring, but is also symmetrically the
shape of a candle flame. 'Goldcrest' is similar, the habit being a little tighter, but the
colour slightly paler. The plant sold variously as 'Horizantalis Aurea', 'Gold Spread'
or 'Golden Spreader' is quite different. It is virtually the same colour as 'Donard
Gold', but is low-growing and wide-spreading. It is the perfect plant for massing in
colour blocks and bands, while the flame-shaped forms are excellent as linking
vertical accents.

Cupressus sempervirens is the Italian cypress, sometimes known as the pencil pine,
and there is a marvellous golden form of it known as 'Swane's Gold'. It is not quite so
upright as the typical Italian cypress, and it is very much slow-growing, but it is a
stunningly strong gold, colouring best in full sun. It will reach about 2m (6½ft) in ten
years, compared with about 5m for the typical form. Like the typical plant, there is a

suspicion of tenderness, so it is better not planted in very cold, bleak spots. With its upright habit, it is an ideal linking plant.

Eleagnus pungens 'Maculata' is one of the most garishly variegated plants in existence, with grey-green leaves splashed the most bilious two-tone orange-yellow imaginable. It is very tough, hardy and ugly, and its only use in a multi-coloured garden would be in a position too cold for anything else to grow. Its one redeeming virtue is that it has a strong tendency to revert, and in time, if you are lucky and have the sense to allow the reversions to take over, you will finish up with a quietly unassuming but very charming grey-leaved shrub. Rather better is *Eleagnus* x *ebbingei* (x *submacrophylla*) 'Gilt Edge' in which the greyish leaves are margined pale yellow. It seems to have little merit when seen close to, but from a distance the effect is extremely good. Both will grow in just about any soil almost anywhere.

Heathers are in many ways the perfect plants for massing, and they are ideal for making low-level colour bands. *Erica carnea* is not merely lime-tolerant, it will actually grow well on chalky soils, provided that you give it plenty of humus. There is an ever-increasing number of good forms with coloured leaves. *E.c.* 'Aurea', whose foliage is a rich golden-yellow (somewhat spoiled by purplish-pink flowers), grows to about 30cm (1ft); *E.c.* 'Anne Sparkes' is more nearly orange than gold and grows to about 25cm (10ins.). Both keep their colour and form best grown in full sun and given a light clip over with shears every spring. That treatment also helps to keep them compact and spreading.

Erica cineraria is not lime-tolerant but it does have the merit of growing in much drier conditions than any of the other heathers. 'Rock Pool' is a particularly colourful form, of a very deep golden-yellow, and is extremely low-growing – virtually prostrate. It turns a coppery orange in winter. 'Windlebroke' has light yellow foliage which turns a deeper colour in winter, but is taller-growing, up to about 25cm (10ins.).

Erica x *darleyensis* inherits the lime-tolerant qualities of its *E. carnea* parents, but there is, so far as I have been able to trace, only one yellow form of it, 'Jack H. Brummage', whose foliage is a soft mid-yellow: the colouring shows most strongly on alkaline soils.

Erica erigena used to be *E. mediterranea*, by which name it is still generally known. It is popularly called a tree heather. If it actually were a tree, it might be a very exciting plant, but it isn't; it is merely a very large floppy bush with little to commend it unless you are besotted by heathers. There is one bright golden-yellow form, 'Golden Lady', a sport of the compact 'W. T. Ratcliff' and itself a compact plant growing to about 1m (3ft). It is useful for making colour bands, and particularly useful for giving height in a scheme of coloured heathers.

Erica vagans is another of the calcifuge heathers. One of its forms, 'Valerie Proudly', is probably the brightest of all the yellow heathers, the colour being singularly clean and penetrating. It grows to about 20cm (8ins.), and is definitely brightest if clipped over lightly each spring.

Euonymus radicans 'Emerald 'n Gold' is one of the brightest, daintiest and most useful plants in the multi-coloured repertory. In size, shape and character it is a typical *Euonymus radicans*, except that the leaf is dramatically variegated brilliant golden-yellow, a singularly strong colour, especially in sun. In shade it is just as good, but the colouring is more subdued. It will creep or climb as you wish, will grow almost anywhere, and very readily makes very dense and colourful ground cover. Furthermore few plants are easier to increase: it comes very easily from cuttings taken at almost any time. *Euonymus japonicus* 'Ovatus Aureus' is just as good in colour, if anything even richer, but it has never gained the popularity that 'Emerald 'n Gold' has. It lacks the creeping habit and is in many ways a rather stiff, ungainly bush, its branches all growing upwards so that it tends to look bare at the base. However, if you have enough of it and can pack it in closely, a massed planting of it is extremely effective. It comes very easily from cuttings, so there is no problem in obtaining large quantities. Its one failing is that occasional twigs revert, but these can easily be removed.

Meadowsweet or queen-of-the-meadow is really not a particularly ornamental garden plant, but its golden form, *Filipendula ulmaria* 'Aurea' is absolutely stunning. The leaves are pinnate, toothed and deeply veined, and coloured a marvellous, even, vivid, smouldering gold. Because the colouring is so even, it is exceptionally effective when massed. Planted by water and grown in full sun, the whole plant seems to be pure gold. It is always at its best in deep, rich, moist soil in full sun. If it does not have a damp enough situation, it will simply fade away. The flowers are drab, and most people cut them off before they have a chance to show themselves. In fact, if you allow the plant to flower, the leaves become greener. By keeping the flowers chopped off, you retain the colouring better. It is quite easily increased by division in spring or autumn.

Most of the fuchsias with coloured leaves are too tender to be left out through winter, but *Fuchsia* 'Golden Treasure' will come through most winters unharmed. It is just a typical fuchsia in leaf, habit and flower, but the leaves are evenly suffused a warm golden-yellow. It is quite a small grower, reaching only 30cm (1ft) or at most 45cm (18 ins.) so you need a large number of plants to create an effect with it. It is as easy to increase as other fuchsias, and is singularly effective in the garden grown next to the little blue grass, *Festuca caesia*.

What a pity that *Hakonechloa macra* 'Albo-aurea' does not yet have a popular name. I'm sure that if it did it would be much more widely known and grown, as it deserves to be. It is one of the most delicately beautiful of all grasses, and absolutely perfect for use in colour bands. Whereas *Alopecurus pratensis* 'Aureus' is merely brilliantly colourful, the hakonechloa, while having every bit as much brilliance of colouring, is stylish with it. It looks delicate, growing from a thin, red, slowly-creeping rhizome, and the leaves, which are held on slender red stalks, are thin-textured, about 15cm (6ins.) long and little more than 6mm (¼in.) wide, brilliantly striped gold with just a little green. Late in the season the leaves become stained with crimson. It is always delightful, but never more so than when it is massed. It is, however, slow to spread, and you need a lot of plants to make a good effect. It grows best in a dampish soil, in sun or semi-shade, and appreciates plenty of peat or leaf-mould mixed into the soil and a good top-dressing of one or other every year. It can be increased by division in spring.

The ivies, as you might expect of a genus that has sported in almost every imaginable direction, have produced one or two good yellows, though not as many or as good as you might hope for. Probably the most outstanding is *Hedera colchica* 'Sulphur Heart' ('Paddy's Pride'). This is a large-leaved ivy whose leaves are splashed rich golden-yellow with markings of a lighter yellow as well as green. If you grow it in shade the colouring virtually disappears. Grown in sun, it makes an excellent ground cover, but it is strong-growing and will cover a substantial area.

There are only two yellow-variegated forms of the English ivy worth growing for their colour. Both need to be grown in good light otherwise they become merely green. The more popular is *Hedera helix* 'Jubilee' ('Gold Heart'), which has a rather saggitate leaf with a triangle of rich golden-yellow in the centre and a dark green margin. It is a strangely symmetrical grower, the leaves being produced symmetrically on the stems, and the branches being produced symmetrically in relation to each other. The other is *H.h.* 'Buttercup', whose leaves are evenly gold-yellow all over – but only if it is grown in full sun. It is an excellent ground cover, the better of the two, and could well be used to make a colour band, just being trimmed back to line once a year.

I sang the praises of the white-variegated form of *Helxine soleirolii* in the last chapter. The golden variegated form, *H.s.* 'Aureus', is, if anything, even better. The leaves are just as tiny, produced in just the same abundance, and evenly suffused deep, rich yellow. It needs the same damp, shaded conditions as its white-leafed sister.

Hostas are probably just about perfect companions for the helxines. I would use the golden helxine with yellow- or gold-variegated hostas, but you may prefer to mix them. Two of the finest yellow-variegated hostas are forms of *Hosta fortunei*. The first is misleadingly called 'Albopicta': why, I don't know. It doesn't have a hint of white anywhere. The leaf blade is about 30cm (1ft) long and half as wide and it unfurls in spring to an almost unrivalled richness of colouring. The centre of the blade is bright butter-yellow, fading to a paler yellow-green along the margin. The brilliance of the display lasts about a month, and then starts fading. The yellow-green margin turns to dark green, and the bright yellow to pale yellow-green; still later the leaf is merely two not very distinct shades of green. But while it lasts, that spring colour display is unrivalled. Flower arrangers adore the foliage, and rightly, so long as you do not let them pick so much that they kill the plant. In time a mature plant will build itself up into a great pile of luxuriant leaves, and a massed planting is a marvellous sight. *Hosta fortunei* 'Aurea' is better for my purpose, but on the whole not quite such an impressive individual. The leaves are evenly suffused soft yellow, but fade to a light green later in the summer. It is a plant of exceptional beauty when massed, but it is not such a strong grower as *Hosta fortunei* or even as 'Albopicta', so you do need a lot of it to achieve impact.

A plant that is far more dramatic as an individual, and correspondingly less effective when massed, is *Hosta sieboldiana* 'Frances Williams'. It is a big grower, like nearly all forms of *Hosta sieboldiana*, differing only in that the edge of the leaf has a broad marginal band that is creamy yellow at first but deepens to a rich gold as the season advances. It is a stunning plant. I have never tried massing it, but it does look singularly eye-catching when a single plant is placed amid a massed planting of *Hosta fortunei* 'Aurea'. It was originally sold in Britain under the name 'Gold Edge', and a plant called 'Gold Circles' appears to be the same thing.

Yet a further variation of the theme of yellow variegation is to be found in *Hosta tokudama* 'Aurea-nebulosa' (also sold as 'Variegata'). This has typical *tokudama* leaves – big, bold, very thick, very deeply corrugated (the most deeply corrugated of all the species) and a good glaucous blue with a sort of nebulous clouding of yellow all over. The result could not be described as particularly beautiful but it is curious, and the plant is effective, especially when massed. It will grow to about 30cm (1ft) in height, and is definitely slower to increase than most other hostas.

Hosta 'Wogan Giboshi' is the smallest of the all-yellow hostas. The leaf is little more than 15cm (6ins.) long, little over 1in. wide, very short-stalked and a rich, even yellow all over, the depth of colour increasing as the year advances. It is one of the most desirable of all hostas. In spite of its smallness it increases relatively fast, and it is ideal for massing in a small garden. It is, however, one of those frustrating plants that colour best in full sun, but also tend to scorch in this position, though are never such a good colour in shade.

The golden hollies by and large are totally unsuitable for massing but there is one – just one – that is perfect for the purpose. This is *Ilex crenata* 'Golden Gem'. *Ilex crenata* is the tiny-leaved Japanese holly, the leaves in this particular form being little more than 6mm (¼in.) long and scarcely as much across, of an intense bright yellow all over. The plant slowly forms a compact bush wider than it is high – about 60cm (2ft) high and 1m (3ft) across in old age. It is a very eye-catching plant, but does need to be grown in sun to colour well and then it is stunningly bright. It is ideal for massing in a small garden, not fussy about soil, and readily increased by winter cuttings. There are one or two other clones of *Ilex crenata* gradually starting to come on the market which are well worth watching for.

The summer-flowering jasmine, *Jasminum officinale*, is without question one of the most marvellously perfumed of all hardy garden plants. The smell of the relatively large white flowers, borne in terminal trusses, can fill a whole garden. Most of us are so used to seeing it confined to the wall of a small suburban house that we tend to overlook the fact that it can actually make a very large plant: given its head, it will scramble over a medium-sized tree reaching a height of 9m (30ft) with no trouble. The golden-variegated form, *J.o.* 'Aureum' ('Aureo-variegatum'), is one of those plants that when small look as though it is going to be a disaster: it has a messy yellow variegation, the leaves being spotted and speckled with yellow. A large plant covering an old tree, however, is a surprisingly good yellow, and both dramatic and unexpected, though it seems to turn to a pale yellow when in flower. It is not fussy about soil but is never happy in a cold, exposed situation.

Juniperus chinensis 'Aurea' is one of the finest of all tall, narrow, golden conifers. It is exceptionally narrow and the foliage (it bears both adult and juvenile foliage) is of a quite unique colour, a curiously platinum sort of gold. In fact, part of the fascination of its colouring arises from the fact that foliage of different ages is different colours: the young foliage is a very light, silvery yellow; the second-year foliage a little darker; and the third-year foliage a really rich yellow. It is very slow-growing, especially when young, and will make about 2 × 0.75m (6½ × 2½ft) in ten years. In the second ten it grows faster, more than doubling its height but increasing very little in girth. If it were just a little faster it would be among the most desirable of gold upright conifers for use as linking plants: it still is, provided that you do not want too much height too fast. It comes fairly readily from winter cuttings.

Most of the other golden junipers are low-growing, rather spreading plants, and ideal for making colour bands. *Juniperus communis* 'Depressa Aurea' has prickly foliage which changes colour through the season – but that is true to a degree with most of the spreading golden junipers. In this one the foliage starts into growth in spring bright butter-yellow, gradually changes to a bronze-yellow for summer, then becomes a decidedly copper colour in winter. It is very low-growing, with the branches held almost horizontal, just above the ground, and slightly down-curved at the very tips. In ten years it will make about 30cm (1ft) in height with a spread of about 1.3m (4ft.). *Juniperus* x *media* 'Gold Coast' has the most nearly true gold foliage of any of the yellow-gold junipers. It is relatively newly introduced but once it is better known will probably largely supplant the other spreading junipers in the same colour range. It has fine, lacy foliage that looks soft but isn't, produces its branches in horizontal tiers (but not too strongly differentiated) and grows to about 0.45 × 1.3m (1½ × 4ft.) in ten years. *Juniperus* x *media* 'Plumosa Aurea' differs from the others in that the branches, instead of being virtually horizontal, are borne at a slight upward and outward angle. The foliage, very fine and scaly and rather pricklier than it looks, is of a good golden-yellow, though perhaps a little on the green side in winter. It is not a plant that grows evenly when young, having an irritating habit of throwing a great, strong growth out to one side, in a manner calculated to make you take the pruning shears to chop it off to force it to grow more evenly. Provided you leave well alone, though, it will equally unexpectedly throw up a strong growth on the opposite side, and so gradually balance itself. It is very much a quality plant, almost too good to use in colour bands. The branches, heavily draped with foliage, look for all the world like great plumes of pampas grass that have been dipped in gold paint and allowed to hang to dry one-sided.

Lamium maculatum 'Aureum' is a plant whose colouring is outstanding. The leaves are a rich golden-yellow, and where on the normal forms there is a central band of white on the leaf, in the golden form this is replaced by a band of light yellow on a yellow-green ground. The colour is definitely at its best in spring, but it is good all the year through. If you find the deeper summer colouring not to your taste, you can always freshen the plant up by cutting it down: it will then produce another flush of leaves of the same intensity of colouring as the spring leaves. It is not an invasive, ground-covering, weed-suppressing plant; on the whole it grows rather too slowly. Besides, it is definitely a plant that needs the benefits of your cultural skills. It is happiest in light shade, and it needs a gritty, well-drained soil that is always moist. It roots as it spreads, and proles detached in spring or summer can be planted where you want them to grow.

The thing for which liquidambers are famous is their autumn colour, which is brilliant. There is, however, one absolutely marvellous gold-variegated form. This is *Liquidambar styraciflua* 'Golden Treasure'. The leaf is the same maple-leaf shape as that of the typical plant, but the centre is bright golden-yellow (perhaps more yellow than gold) with a pale lime-lemon-green edging before the green margin. The variegation is beautiful, and so is a whole tree. The autumn colouring is every bit as good as the typical tree, and like the typical tree, 'Golden Treasure' tends to have a rather tall, narrow habit of growth. It is far too hard to come by to even think of massing (though it might be effective), but is ideal as a dot or linking plant in a relatively large landscape.

The most consistent and useful of the gold-variegated forms of liriope or lily-turf is *Liriope platyphylla* 'Gold Banded'. It is a typical liriope in every respect, including the flowers, except that the strap-shaped leaves have a broad golden-yellow band running down each side, with only a relatively thin green band down the centre. An excellent subject for massing in sun or shade, it is tolerant of quite dry conditions at the roots.

Lonicera nitida 'Baggesen's Gold' is one of those shrubs that seem, when examined at close quarters, to be promising; it is when it is seen from a distance or massed that it fulfils that promise. It is a singularly bright golden-yellow, a colour which has a curiously penetrating quality: you feel that it is so bright you would see it through a solid laurel hedge. It does, however, depend a little on the time of year at which you see it – if in the dead of January or February (always the cruellest months, whatever Eliot may say) it is a wan and anaemic thing, its colouring bleached and half its leaves gone (it is semi-deciduous, like the common hedging honeysuckle). But by March or April, once the buds have swelled and new leaves started to appear, it seems that there is hope for the thing, and once it is fully clothed in its new season's foliage it is back to the very best of its beauty in which state it will stay till late November. It is this brilliance of colouring that makes it so effective for massing, but only effective in its season: another equally bright plant is needed to distract your attention from it in winter when it looks so poorly. *L.n.* 'Baggesen's Gold' benefits from a regular haircut, mainly to encourage vigorous, leafy shoots, but also because it has a straggly, untidy habit of growth, throwing careless branches this way or that. It is readily increased by cuttings, and even trimmings thrown on the rubbish heap usually root.

The golden creeping Jenny, *Lysimachia nummularia* 'Aurea' is a good thing, useful rather than beautiful. It has trailing stems with round leaves, about 1cm (2/5in.) long and across, produced in opposite pairs, and it roots as it runs. The leaves are a good golden-yellow, brighter in full sun, greener in shade, and it produces little yellow flowers that you probably won't notice against the foliage during July. It is particularly useful as a temporary, eventually self-effacing ground cover to plant under golden-leaved shrubs while they are building themselves up into a colour band. By using the golden creeping Jenny this way you may get a two-tone colour-band for a while, but at least it will be all yellow, and a yellow ground cover at this stage is better than weeds.

Melissa needs mention, but not by way of praise. *Melissa officinalis* is not an ornamental plant, merely a culinary herb, and the same goes for the so-called yellow form, 'Aurea'. It is easily grown, reaching about 45cm (18 ins.) each way, with the leaves supposedly yellow-variegated: at best it is an anaemic yellow, and the colour tends to be confined to the edges of the leaves in very much the way that many nutrient deficiencies show themselves. Its real problem is that it seeds itself like fury in all directions, and the seedlings will almost all be green-leaved. Mass it in a 12.5cm (5ins.) flower pot if you must, but that should be enough for anyone.

By contrast, Bowles' golden grass, *Milium effusum* 'Aureum' is one of those plants to which it is difficult to do adequate credit. Milium is the wood millet, a grass that is dainty enough in its way, but nothing you would rush to plant. The golden form is breathtakingly brilliant in spring when the new leaves emerge a marvellous matt yellow. It is a curious yellow, for it is a colour that plainly masks green – very similar to that of the so-called yellow tobacco plant flower. The depth of colour is most intense in spring, but the grass remains yellow the whole year through. One of the most extraordinary things about it is that it is all yellow: the flower stem, the flowers and even the seed heads as they ripen. It is at its best in light shade, but will grow well and remain yellow even in dense shade, where it can lighten the darkness. A clump-forming grass, growing to only about 30cm (1ft) in height, perhaps a little more, and taking some time to get to 1ft across at ground level, it can be divided very easily in spring and seeds itself slowly – certainly never freely enough to be a nuisance. It is definitely happiest in a soil that has been enriched with, and which is regularly dressed with leaf-mould.

Origanum vulgare is a culinary herb but has its uses in the multi-coloured garden since it is a low-growing, carpeting plant, reaching about 45cm (18 ins.), with masses of small, dark green leaves which in summer disappear under a mass of flowers. The golden form, *O.v.* Aureum', has leaves of a good bright yellow gradually fading as summer wears on, till by autumn they are almost the same colour as the leaves of the typical plant. The flowers impair the colouring slightly, but they do not last too long. It has the merit of being very easy to grow, though definitely happiest in sun, and it looks lovely when grown with heucheras, being of just the right proportion in every way.

Even more useful in the multi-coloured garden than the white-variegated mock orange mentioned in the previous chapter is a gold-leafed form, *Philadelphus coronarius* 'Aureus'. It is in every respect (except the colouring of its leaves) just a typical mock orange. In spring the leaves are the most brilliant yellow, the colour gradually fading, though never completely, so that even in autumn the plant is still plainly recognizable as the golden-leafed form. It is an excellent plant for massing – indeed that is the best way to use it – is very easy to grow in any soil, and will increase readily from cuttings in summer or winter or by layering.

A similarly evenly coloured shrub is *Ribes sanguineum* 'Brocklebankii', the golden-flowering currant. It is just like any other flowering currant except that the leaves are deep yellow, the colouring being singularly evenly spread across them. It is smaller-growing than most flowering currants, usually reaching only about 1m (3ft), and you need a lot of it for it to look really effective, when it will make an excellent colour band. It comes easily from winter cuttings, and the great majority of the seedlings are of almost the original colour. It is happy in just about any soil, but only colours well in sun.

So many people have praised *Robinia pseudoacacia* 'Frisia' so lavishly and it has become so popular in consequence that, trends being as fickle as they are, it is now becoming almost fashionable to denigrate it. It is, in fact, probably the most outstandingly colourful tree in leaf ever introduced, and it is absolutely indispensable in the multi-coloured garden, either used as a series of specimens or massed as a background. It forms an elegant, small tree with pinnate leaves, each leaflet being rounded, and every leaf and leaflet is the same penetrating bright gold from the moment the leaves break in spring until the moment they fall in autumn. It is stunning. If you find it too bright, there is another yellow-leafed form of the same tree, *R.p.* 'Aurea', which is similar except that the leaves, instead of being a strident yellow, are a soft, gentle version of the same colour which slowly fades to very light green as summer advances. 'Aurea', incidentally, won an FCC (First Class Certificate), the highest award a plant can receive; 'Frisia', by contrast, has only won itself an AM (Award of Merit), and an AGM (Award of Garden Merit). Both grow well in any fertile soil and both colour best in full sun. They are usually increased by grafting.

Another plant much in the same size and colour-range as *Ribes sanguineum* 'Brocklebankii' is *Rubus idaeus* 'Aureus'. It may never have occurred to you to plant a raspberry as an ornamental, but then you may never have known that there is one whose leaves are evenly suffused a bright golden yellow. It is an excellent little plant with few vices. The leaves are identical in shape to those of the fruiting raspberries, but the whole plant grows to only about 0.5m (a couple of feet), and the foliage is much more densely presented than on the fruiting forms; further, while it spreads by suckers, the suckers appear close to the original plant, so that a plant left to its own

1 A dramatic bedding scheme at the Royal Botanic Gardens, Kew, containing *Chlorophytum elatum* 'Medio-pictus' and the purple-leaved, red-flowered *Begonia* 'Red Devil'. Such a planting is arresting because unexpected. What one expects of bedding is the same plant used *en masse*: here equal numbers of two plants are symmetrically mixed.

2 Carpet bedding in classic style at the Royal Botanic Gardens, Kew. The composition is made up of a purple-leaved, red-flowered busy Lizzie with *Helichrysum petiolatum* used both as semi-standards in the centre of the planting and as a low surround at the perimeter. The plants in the centre of the bed provide a vertical relief from an otherwise extremely flat planting.

3 The black-leaved *Ophiopogon planiscarpus* 'Nigrescens' against the golden *Carex morrowii* 'Aurea Variegata'. Black and gold, black and bronze and black and blue are always good combinations.

4 Perhaps the most dramatically variegated of all the larger grasses, *Miscanthus sinensis* 'Variegata', useful either as a series of accent plants striding over two or three dark colour bands, or massed in its own right in front of a dark backdrop.

5 Grasses and sedges used in a multi-coloured manner. The blue is *Festuca caesia*, the bronze *Carex buchanani* and the creamy yellow at the back *Carex morrowii* 'Aurea Variegata'.

6 The brilliant blue rosettes of *Yucca whipplei* make a dramatic feature in a carpet of *Setcreasea purpurea*.

7 *Setcreasea purpurea*, one of the few plants whose leaves are a true purple, used as permanent ground cover in a sub-tropical grouping of yuccas and *Griselina littoralis* 'Variegata'.

8 A *Dicentra oregana* hybrid with the typical blue foliage of the group. Plants will thrive in sun or shade.

9 An example of a brilliantly multi-coloured plant: *Pelargonium* 'Mrs Henry Cox'. The individual leaves – indeed single plants – can be stunning, but massed it is merely a mess.

10 *Cotinus coggygria* 'Royal Purple', a slow-growing but ultimately large purple-leaved shrub that has brilliantly fiery autumn colouring. It makes a good companion for grey- and silver-leaved trees and shrubs.

11   The most desirable of all the elders, *Sambucus nigra* 'Pulverulenta', a marvellous plant for massing. This specimen is growing in the famous variegated border at Oxford University Botanic Garden; the plant to the left is *Tovara virginiana* 'Painter's Palette', and the purple-leaved plant in front is *Berberis thunbergii* 'Atropurpurea Nana'.

12   If you think of coleus as colourful to the point of garishness, the black-leaved *Coleus* 'Roi des Noires' is positively subdued. The problem in placing it in the garden is always to find companions of a sufficient density of colouring.

13-16 Multi-coloured gardening: the raw materials. The drama of massed colour at the container unit at Hillier Nurseries (Winchester) Ltd.

17 *Iris pallida* 'Variegata' has a singularly symmetrical variegation and retains its leaves in better form than most irises for an exceptionally long period. The flowers are a clean, clear blue. This iris is at its most dramatic when used in large, bold plantings.

18 Multi-coloured plant materials used with a fine sense of definition of curves and contours. Notice how the bronze planting leads the eye to the foot of the golden lawson and enfolds the blue conifer, and how that in itself helps draw the eye on to the golden yellow beyond.

19 The willow-leafed silver beauty, *Artemesia ludoviciana* 'Valerie' with *Heuchera americana* 'Purple Form'. Both plants are brilliant when massed, but the heuchera is really not of a sufficiently deep purple to combine with such a bright silver.

20 The large, lush leaves of *Symphytum peregrinum* 'Variegatum' are at their most effective when massed at the edge of a shrub border or in the fringes of woodland. An established clump can be as much as a metre across.

21 Both form and colour matter in the multi-coloured garden. *Yucca filamentosa* 'Bright Edge' combines good foliage with good colouring. It is an excellent plant for massing.

22 *Centaurea gymnocarpa*, one of the most glorious of all silver-leafed plants, positively opulent in the luxuriousness of its foliage.

23 The variegated horseradish is dramatic, in spite of the irregularity of the variegation. It tends to become a very permanent plant in heavy soils and is at its best massed in a more or less wild garden.

24 *Cornus florida* 'Tricolor', with its multi-coloured leaves, is better used as a specimen, when the beauty of the individual leaves can be appreciated, rather than massed so that their charm is lost.

25 The most brilliant of all the mahonias in leaf colour, *M. fremontii*, growing against the wall at the Savill Garden. The steely blue leaves are extremely prickly.

26 *Centaurea candidissima* is a brilliant and adaptable silver-leafed plant that should be more widely used to replace the ubiquitous *Cineraria maritima*.

27 *Phlox paniculata* 'Nora Leigh', a shocking combination of leaf colour and flower colour. In foliage it is superlative, especially when used in vast quantities. The background plant is *Buddleia davidii* 'Harlequin'.

28 Ground elder is only an obnoxious weed because it is such a perfect ground-cover plant. The variegated ground elder, *Aegopodium podagaria* 'Variegatum', is stunningly variegated and far less invasive than the typical plant. It is important to remove the flowers as soon as they are over since seedlings would almost certainly be green-leafed.

29 *Aptenia cordifolia* 'Variegata' making a veritable carpet of yellow-variegated succulent leaves in front of bold clumps of *Phormium tenax* 'Purpureum'. The big-leaved plant is the background is *Fatsia japonica*.

30 Looking at the leaves, you'd probably pass this off as an iris; in fact it is *Acorus calamus* 'Variegatus', a member of the *Araceae*, a marvellous plant for massing beside water or in boggy ground.

31 Dramatic and desirable *Ricinus communis* 'Gibsonii' is a plant that combines the best of foliage form and colour.

32 Multi-coloured materials, massed and giving a hint of the excitement of the multi-coloured garden. The multi-coloured concept demands greater clarity of definition of the curves and contours.

33-4 Two views of a multi-coloured scheme designed by the author and created with the kind co-operation of Hillier Nurseries (Winchester) Ltd. Part of the fascination of such schemes is how different they appear when seen from different angles.

devices slowly forms a compact clump. Like so many plants whose leaves are evenly yellow, it tends to scorch in full sun, though it needs some sun to colour well. It is an ideal colour-band plant provided you can use it where it will get a little shade.

The golden elder, *Sambucus nigra* 'Aurea', by contrast, does not seem to scorch at all, even in the fullest blazing sun. It is just like the common European elder in every way, except that the leaves are golden yellow, the colour increasing in depth and intensity as the season goes on. It has a lot going for it: its colouring, its size, and most of all the fact that it is tolerant of almost any soil conditions. The poor plant really only has one thing against it: it is totally lacking in beauty. The same cannot be said of the currently fashionable yellow cut-leaved red-berried elder, *Sambucus racemosa* 'Plumosa Aurea' (formerly 'Serratifolia Aurea' until it became popular). You would scarcely recognize it as an elder – the leaves are so cut, so plumose, that any resemblance to elder has disappeared; and the colouring is marvellous, a rich red and orange in spring as the leaves unfurl, maturing to a rich golden yellow. It needs to be cut back to the ground every couple of years to keep it vigorous. Left alone, it straggles up into a quite tall semi-tree of ungainly and unbalanced stance. It is one of those plants that are equally adapted to use as a colour band or as a spot plant. Perhaps the best way to use it is to have a colour band of it in one part of the garden, and a number of plants of it used as dot plants, the dotting being most dense closest to the colour band, becoming thinner further away. Although it will grow in any fertile soil, it is a plant that rewards good cultivation by being more lush in leaf and richer in its colouring.

Saxifraga 'Cloth of Gold' looks so good when you see a well-filled pot of it at a nursery, with its finely cut filigree of leaves of the deepest, richest gold – quite the deepest all-gold leaf of any plant I have mentioned so far – that you might think it would make a good colour band. It won't: it is far too tricky to cultivate.

Spartina pectinata 'Aureo-marginata' comes as a bit of a disappointment, but it has quality and character to make up for what it lacks in brilliancy of colouring. It is a graceful grass with long, narrow, arching leaves (up to about 1.3m (4ft) at the highest point of the arch) narrowly margined with old straw-gold. The flower spikes, which are borne in autumn, are narrow and draped with bright purple stamens much in the manner of *Molinia caerulea*, only more so. It is at its most effective in big, bold groups, with the ribbon-like leaves restless in the wind and it grows best in deep, rich, moist soil and is excellent by water. The root system is said to be invasive, but seems not inconveniently so: it forms dense clumps rather in the manner of pampas grass.

Spirea x *bumalda* 'Goldflame' is a quite different colour from any of the gold or yellow plants we have looked at so far. The leaf is evenly golden yet has in it both pink and orange with a hint of russet. It is a unique colour and would be valuable for that reason alone, but it has still more to commend it. It is a dense, dwarf shrublet, growing, if you are lucky, 30cm (1ft) or so in height, with a spread of about as much or a little more, and the virtue of rooting itself as it grows. This of course makes it absolutely ideal for a colour band, since however densely you plant in the first place, the plant will continue to make the planting ever more and more dense. It needs full sun and a fertile soil, but beyond that is not choosy. The flowers are a crimson that clashes horribly with the foliage: just look the other way till they are over.

There are so many good golden yews that you really need to be well acquainted with them, both in youth and age, to know which ones to use where. Probably the commonest of the golden yews is *Taxus baccata* 'Aurea' which slowly grows into a large yet oddly compact bush densely packed with foliage, the leaves being broadly margined with gold in the first year but turning green in the second. It is the golden yew that you are likely to see most often, and it is an excellent plant, of good colour. As with all the yews, the colour is only good in full sun: even the sunny side is more golden than the other side. *T.b.* 'Adpressa Aurea' (which should probably properly be 'Adpressa Variegata') looks marvellous when you have a tray full of young propagules: the leaves unfurl old gold, then change to yellow, then a green stripe gradually appears on the middle of the leaf pushing, as it were, the yellow back to the margins of the leaves. The problem that you do not realize when you see only a small plant is that in time it will become leggy, with a few straggly branches thrown in random fashion in any old direction, and with surprisingly sparse foliage. Seeing it in that state, at 1.3–1.6m (4 or 5ft) in height and spread, could put you off it for ever. However, if you have the sort of garden in which you could make a colour band of it and keep it clipped over the top (flat, like a table) you would find it one of the most effective golden yews for the purpose. It could be kept down to 30cm (1ft) or thereabouts, since it is very slow-growing. *T.b.* 'Dovestoniana Aurea', by contrast, is enormous – at least, in the scale of a small garden. It forms a large shrub or small tree with tiers of long, horizontal branches, and long weeping branchlets, the leaves brilliantly margined rich gold, giving the plant an overall golden effect. If the leader is removed when the plant is young, instead of making a semi-pendulous tree it forms a wide-spreading, shallowly vase-shaped shrub of vast spread in relation to its height. It could be used very effectively in bold colour bands in gardens where it could be given enough space to grow to maturity.

T.b. 'Elegantissima' is now the most popular of the golden yews: the habit is semi-erect and very dense; the colouring bright, light gold on the new leaves, passing to a more golden-yellow later and again being pushed out to the margins of the leaves. 'Golden Gem' is probably the best of the golden yews for small gardens: a large plant is about 1.3 × 1.3m (4 × 4ft), very compact and densely filled with foliage of a deep, rich orange-yellow – it looks almost burnished. It is probably the best of the golden yews for making colour bands in gardens of less than 0.4 hectares (1 acre) since the plants can be packed close together and left to form a colour band even without clipping. 'Fastigiata Aurea' is the golden Irish yew. The Irish yew is the one with ascending branches and a vast quantity of red berries in autumn; the golden form has a similar habit but is less narrow. It is lovely when young, slim and elegant, but becomes obese with age. 'Repens Aurea' is not a particularly brilliant plant as far as its colouring goes, but the habit is useful, low and spreading, with reasonably dense foliage. The colour is pale yellow fading to almost cream. 'Semperaurea' is highly praised by almost everyone. It is supposed to have the deepest colouring of all the golden yews, the leaves starting old gold, then gradually turning a tawny orange. It has somewhat upward- and outward-pointing branches, but stiff, not relaxed. It is essentially a larger-growing version of 'Golden Gem' (though it is still a slow-growing plant) whose colouring is a little less good. 'Standishii' is a female clone of the golden Irish yew, and quite the best of its colour and habit; the colour is bright yellow, and the habit narrowly upright.

All the yews are easy to grow, good on chalk, tolerant of soils that are a little on the wet side or a little on the dry side and well able to withstand the severity of winter. They can readily be increased by cuttings taken in autumn or spring, rooted with or without heat.

There is a number of forms of thuja which are more or less yellow or gold. Of the *Thuja occidentalis* forms, 'Colombia' looks promising, but I have only seen young plants. The foliage is of the adult type, presented in flattened sprays tipped bright yellow. It is reputed to grow to about 2.4m (8ft) in ten years and to develop a broadly pyramidal habit. Then we come to one or two that have become household names. The first of these is *Thuja occidentalis* 'Ellwangeriana Aurea'. The colour of the foliage is a rich golden-bronze that becomes deeper and deeper as winter goes on, a marvellous glowing colour. It is slow-growing, usually throwing several leaders and reaching about 4m (13ft) each way at maturity. The foliage is almost entirely adult, though on young plants there is usually a high proportion of juvenile foliage. *Thuja occidentalis* 'Rheingold' differs in that, while the colouring and the foliage are just about the same, 'Rheingold' has a high proportion of juvenile foliage and in time grows into a bush with a single leader, wider than it is high. 'Rheingold' (just to confuse the issue) received an AM under the name 'Ellwangerana Pygmaea Aurea'. *Thuja occidentalis* 'Lutea' is a plant in a totally different colour spectrum: it is a bright clear yellow, turning light bronze in winter. It eventually grows into a tall, narrowly pyramidal tree, and you could expect it to make about 2.4m (8ft) in ten years, with a thickness of a little under 1m (3ft) at the base. It is sometimes sold as *Thuja occidentalis* 'Elegantissima', which is a totally different plant – like an anaemic and straggly version of 'Columbia'. *Thuja occidentalis* 'Wareana Lutescens' is distinct among the Siberian *arbores vitae* in the lightness of its colouring: it is a very pale yellow, almost creamy, turning to a correspondingly light bronze colour in winter. It is useful because the colour is so distinct: you can use it as a colour band, or as a linking dot plant among conifers of other colours.

Thuja orientalis is often confused in the abstract with *Thuja occidentalis*, but they are in fact quite distinct – so much so that *Thuja orientalis* was at one time accorded generic rank, as *Biota*. The quickest way of telling this thuja from the others is that the foliage is held in flattened, vertical sprays radiating from the centre of the plant. There are several good golden forms: 'Beverlyensis' is a most intense golden-yellow in spring and early summer, fading to green in late summer; 'Elegantissima' is similar but of a lighter colour; 'Semperaurea' is a very compact little globe of a plant growing to only about 1.6 × 1m (5 × 3ft) in ten years and very tidy at that, of a good bright yellow; 'Westmont' is similar but grows to about half the height and spread of 'Semperaurea' in the same time and is a far more intense colour. These globe-shaped conifers make excellent linking subjects, but are useless for massing.

Thuja plicata 'Cuprea' is distinct in its colour – the background is bronze-green, and the tips of the foliage sprays golden yellow. It is a beautiful colour combination on a beautifully proportioned dwarf conifer. It seldom grows to more than about 1m (3ft), is roughly pyramidal, with soft sprays of foliage which nod slightly at the tips. 'Old Gold' and 'Irish Gold' are both larger-growing, eventually making 3m (10ft) or so but slow to get there, and of erect, pyramidal shape. 'Old Gold' is a bright deep yellow, 'Irish Gold' a much lighter, brighter colour. 'Stoneham Gold' is orange-yellow on a dark green background, and very effective; 'Zebrina' is a bi-colour variegation, the foliage sprays being transversely banded deep yellow and light yellow giving the plant a pale lemon-yellow appearance at a distance. It is not the most effective yellow in its species, but probably the most widely available and generally planted. All are excellent plants for making colour bands.

The garden pickaback plant is an amusing little thing with rich green, ivy-shaped leaves, slightly hairy on top, producing small plantlets at the point at which leaf-stalk and leaf-blade meet. Each of these plantlets in time grows big enough to weigh the leaf down to the ground, where the plantlet roots and grows into another plant. In this way a single plant can gradually colonize quite a large area. Its only demerit is that it is an exceedingly dull colour. There is, by contrast, an outstandingly bright form with a brilliant yellow variegation. This is *Tolmeia menzeisii* 'Taff's Gold', in which the leaves are marbled and splashed brightest yellow. It grows best in a reasonably sunny position, though it likes a woodland-type soil (easily provided by the addition of plenty of leaf-mould), and is very readily increased by detaching leaves (with their stalks) on which plantlets have started to form. Pot these up carefully, with the stalk planted as one would plant roots, and the leaf-blade resting on the soil where the plantlet can root. You can very quickly build up large quantities by this method of increase.

We mentioned the white-variegated form of the tsuga in the previous chapter. The yellow-leafed equivalent is *Tsuga canadensis* 'Aurea', in which the leaves are solid gold, a marvellous rich colour at all seasons. The habit is broadly conical, and it is a relatively slow-growing small tree. It could be good massed as a background, but is probably better used in threes or fours as a linking plant. It will grow in any fertile soil, but needs sun to keep the colour bright. It is usually increased by grafting.

The gold or yellow periwinkles are, by comparison, undramatic plants. In *Vinca major* 'Aureo-maculata' the centre of the leaf is mottled three different shades of greenish yellow and margined dark green. The interest is all in the detail: the overall effect of the plant is quite unremarkable. The lesser periwinkle, *Vinca minor* has a yellow variegated form – 'Aureovariegata' – in which the relative merits of leaf detail and overall effect are reversed. The leaf is a muddled mess of cream and yellow suffusions: the overall effect is of a mat of light yellow. It is the more effective of the two for providing colour and also the more efficient weed suppressor. Both plants are happy in most soils in sun or shade, but the colouring is stronger in good light.

Weigela florida 'Variegata' is a somewhat garish shrub whose leaves are brightly variegated creamy yellow. The variegation is almost entirely marginal. It adds brightness to the garden, but little else. Of far more value in the multi-coloured garden is the little-known *Weigela japonica* 'Looymansii Aurea' whose leaves are evenly suffused a pale golden yellow, the colouring being best in a semi-shaded position. In spite of its somewhat straggly habit, it is a good plant for massing at the edge of woodland where its distinctive colour makes it quite eye-catching.

The yuccas, with their rosettes of sword-shaped leaves, always add a touch of the exotic to a garden, and the two yellow-variegated forms of *Yucca filamentosa* are excellent for making colour bands at the edge of a patio or in some similar position. In *Yucca filamentosa* the rosette is stemless, gradually increasing by producing offsets at ground level close to the original rosette. 'Bright Edge' has a bright, rich, yellow marginal variegation, while 'Variegata' has leaves banded bright yellow. Both are somewhat variable: you will never find the pattern of the variegation identical on any two rosettes. I have my doubts as to whether the two clones really are distinct, since some plants of 'Bright Edge' fail to produce their marginal variegation, while some plants of 'Variegata' have the variegation confined only to the edge, and if you grow sufficient of either you will finish up by not really knowing which is which. Both make beautiful and unexpected colour bands: the leaf form is so unlike anything else that one normally grows out of doors. They need full sun and the best drainage you can give them.

It is important to remember, particularly with the golds and yellows, that it is not necessarily the brightest colour on the individual leaf that will be most telling in the garden as a whole: you need both the brilliant and the quieter colours to give a garden that rich sensuality which foliage can provide, and you need contrast in the shape of leaf and the form of the plant too.

CHAPTER SIX

Greys and Silvers

Grey- and silver-leafed plants differ from most of the other plants in this book in that their colouring is normally an adaptation to an extreme climatic situation, whereas the colouring in the leaves of the majority of variegated plants is either virus-induced or mere eccentricity. Grey- and silver-leafed plants have taken on their colouring as protection against hot, strong sun and drying conditions. The greyness and silveriness reflects the light away from the leaves and prevents them being scorched. This does, of course, create the problem that if you want to cultivate these plants you need to give them hot, dry conditions: certainly that is true for the great majority. Happily there are exceptions – even grey- and silver-leafed plants that need damp shade.

The New Zealand burrs have been called poor relations of the rose. Relations of the rose they are, but poor they very definitely are not. They are diminutive plants, usually prostrate, with minute pinnate leaves, each of which is individually very similar to that of a rose, but much smaller, and coloured grey or silver. The burrs are produced on long stalks, held high above the foliage, and are usually coloured bright bronze or red, in striking contrast to the matt of leaves. The most popular of the New Zealand burrs is *Acaena* 'Blue Haze', which grows to about 15cm (6ins.) in height, has intensely blue-grey foliage, and produces a wealth of bright crimson burrs regularly every year. Like all the acaenas, it will spread almost indefinitely, rooting as it goes. *Acaena buchananii* grows to only about 7.5cm (3ins.) and makes vigorous dense mats of glaucous foliage, perhaps a little nearer blue than grey, and again produces an excellent show of burrs. *A. microphylla* is even more lowly, growing to only about 5cm (a couple of ins.) at most, with tiny leaves of an intense grey and very showy bright red burrs. *A. saccaticupula* is similar but has leaves of the most extraordinary brownish-grey: in certain lights they seem to be the colour of strong coffee, but in others the silveriness shows up; its burrs are orange. All acaenas are perfectly hardy, but grow best in a gritty soil in full sun. They are readily increased by proles.

The agaves are unexpected in the garden, bizarre, even outlandish, but such qualities are necessary in any interesting garden. And they do have the most marvellous grey leaves. The finest and probably the hardiest of the agaves is *Agave gracillima* which slowly forms a rosette of broad, silvery-grey leaves, strongly toothed, with a clearly defined margin of very dark purple – almost black – and a very long terminal spine of the same colour. A mature rosette is about 45cm (1½ft) across. It is one of the species that produces an abundance of pups, by means of which it can very readily be propagated. It is stunning when massed. *A. parryi* is generally similar, though the leaf lacks the black marginal marking and is perhaps a little narrower. *A. shawii* and *A. schottii* are similar but usually a little smaller. *A. utahensis* is diminutive by comparison, a large plant being about 15cm (6 ins.) across. The typical plant is *A. utahensis* var. *utahensis*, whose leaves, very narrow in relation to their length, are edged with a creamy-white, horny, undulating margin, with hooked spines and a very long terminal spine of the same colour and substance. *A. utahensis* var. *nevadensis* differs in having even narrower leaves and an even longer, more fearsome terminal spine, but the colouring is the same. *A. utahensis* var. *eborispina* is the most dramatic of all: the leaves are edged and tipped with black. There is a further variety, var. *kaibabensis*, which is quite distinct on account of its size: it will grow to over 1m (3ft) across. All the species mentioned here are relatively hardy, and all have been grown out of doors by various people at various times, often for very long periods, and if they no longer have them it is usually because they have flowered, not because the frost killed them. Agaves need to be grown in the sunniest place you can find for them, in a perfectly drained soil, preferably topped off with a layer of grit about 10cm (4ins.) deep both to suppress weeds efficiently and to help prevent collar rot.

The beauty of Lady's mantle, *Alchemilla mollis*, in the garden should not be underestimated merely because it lacks the bizarre qualities of the agaves. The leaves, which are rounded and gently scalloped, are covered in fine, silver hairs which give the leaves a fascinating sheen as they move in the wind. Moreover, the hairs hold any drops of moisture, and these droplets catch the sun in an intriguing way. The plant grows about 30cm (1ft) high and across, but taller in flower, the flowers being yellow and tiny but effective because of the sheer quantities in which they are produced. It seeds itself freely in all directions, which makes it an effective ground cover where you have large areas to cover relatively quickly. Seed is produced without the benefit of any sort of sexual performance. *A. erythropoda* is similar but tiny, the leaves less than 2.5cm (1in.) across and the whole plant growing to scarcely 7.5cm (3ins.). It is very similar to the better-known Lady's mantle, except in size, which makes it ideal for massing in small gardens where the other would be much too vigorous in all respects. Both will grow well on any fertile soil, in sun or shade.

By comparison the wormwoods are coarse and vulgar plants, though by comparison with almost anything else they number among themselves some of the finest of all grey or silver plants. The wormwoods are *Artemesia*, and they all have vigorous and invasive root systems. On the positive side they all have beautiful ferny silver foliage, and range from tiny creeping mats to spreading herbaceous plants to woody shrubs. They all need reasonable drainage, and the mat-forming species appreciate a grit-covered surface to crawl upon. They are reasonably hardy, though they do tend to look rather bedraggled in winter. *A. absinthium* is the familiar wormwood or absinth, a plant of waste ground in the eastern Mediterranean. It has finely divided, grey-green foliage, and is semi-woody. It gradually forms a woody base, but the long growths are merely suffruticose. The wild plant has largely been superseded in cultivation by the form 'Lambrook Silver', a superb foliage plant with good silvery leaves and stems. *A. arborescens* is immensely desirable, making a shrub about 1.3 × 1.3m (4 × 4ft) of the finest filigree silver foliage imaginable, but is sadly almost impossible to cultivate satisfactorily. It is a native of the hot sand dunes of the south-western Mediterranean, and unless you can provide it with similar growing conditions, you will see it off in a couple of years: a pity. *A. canescens* (of gardens, which is probably also *A. discolor* and *A. splendens*, no one seems quite sure) is a smaller shrub than *A. absinthium* 'Lambrook Silver', but it is an awful sprawler (which is all right if you have been forewarned). It grows to about 45cm (18ins.) but spreads 1.3–1.6m (4 or 5 ft), throwing out long shoots of the finest filigree foliage and the brightest whitest silver in the genus, the colour being at its best from late summer towards autumn. *A. ludoviciana* is my own favourite, a spreading, sprawling herbaceous wormwood, with simple, willowy leaves of a true silver: the form 'Valerie' is even more silver. It grows about 60cm (a couple of ft) tall with a spread of about 1.3m (4ft) – but much more if you let it get away. It is excellent for massing, and this can easily be done merely by replanting any root pieces you have to trim off to keep it in check. *A. ludoviciana* is probably the same thing as *A. palmeri*, but even experts don't agree about that. Certainly for garden purposes they appear to be the same thing. *A. purshiana* is definitely distinct, though a plant in the same idiom as *ludoviciana*: it grows to about 60cm (2ft), spreads less than *ludoviciana* and the willowy leaves are rather broader and very much whiter. *A. nutans* deserves a special mention, not for outstanding merit, but because it is one of a relatively small number of silver-leaved plants that actually do better on heavy clay than on light sandy soils. The foliage is the finest and laciest in the whole genus, a mere pattern of threads, of a good silver, with a light and airy quality. It is not a strong grower, throwing up its flimsy stems to about 45cm (18ins.), but they flop over on the way up, so it seldom seems as tall as it really is. You need a lot of plants of it in one place for it to be effective, and massing it really is the best way to show it off. *A. schmidtiana* is one of the crawling species, growing to only about 10cm (4ins.) and slowly spreading and rooting, to form low hummocks of fine silvery foliage. It needs absolutely perfect drainage in a good, gritty soil. Grown in that way, it is ideal for a low colour band. The leaves of *A. stelleriana* are so similar to those of *Senecio maritima* that the two are sometimes confused. Occasionally when you see what you think is the senecio overwintering outside, what you are looking at is really *A. stelleriana*. The leaves are white-felted in just the same way as in the senecio, and very similar in shape. It is more herbaceous than woody, and throws up long, lax stems that spread on the ground to make an effective carpet about 20cm (8ins.) high and about 60cm (a couple of ft) across. Again, its habit makes it ideal for a silver colour band near the front of a border.

If you should ever be in search of a grey or silver plant to grow in shade, the plant to go for is the Japanese painted fern, *Athyrium goeringianum* 'Pictum', now properly *Athyrium nipponicum* 'Metallicum'. It is a low-growing, slow-spreading fern whose triangular fronds, growing to about 23cm (9ins.) long and 10cm (4ins.) across, are basically silver-grey flushed with pink at the centre. The effect of a large patch of it is definitely silver, but it is one of those plants that is so beautiful that it will stand the close scrutiny usually bestowed on outstanding individuals, as well as the broader view of a massed planting. It needs a soil containing plenty of humus, a reasonably damp situation and adequate shade: it simply scorches in sun. It is equally at home on acid or alkaline soils, though it dislikes shallow chalk soils.

About as unexpected among the grasses as the Japanese painted fern is among the ferns is the giant provencal reed, *Arundo donax*. Its sheer size is staggering – it towers over even those grasses which are normally considered to be big growers. *Miscanthus sacchariflorus* looks small beside it. Given good cultivation and an abundance of moisture at the roots, you can get *A. donax* up to 4.5m (15ft), with the tall culms arching outwards to give a spread almost as wide. It is a magnificent grass with very thick culms, bearing alternate huge grey leaves over 45cm (18ins.) long and more than 5cm (2ins.) across. The colour is a rich, deep grey. It is made more conspicuous by the showy ligules, which are horny and almost transparent. You get the tallest culms and the largest leaves if you cut the plants to the ground every spring, and mulch it liberally with manure. The form 'Macrophylla' has broader leaves, but otherwise requires the same cultivation. It is excellent for massing but it does need to be in a large garden. Though slow to increase left to its own devices, it can easily be propagated by cuttings of the main stem or better still the side-shoots, taken in summer and rooted in a moist sand, preferably with a little heat.

Astelia nervosa is so grass-like that unless it is in fruit it is often mistaken for a grass. It is in fact a rare New Zealand member of the *Liliaceae*, though this would probably only become obvious to most people with the appearance of the red berries in autumn – just like those of asparagus. The leaves are like long, thin, evenly tapering rapiers, deeply keeled, and the plant forms an enormous tussock. It grows about 60cm (2ft) tall and 1.6m (5ft) across. The leaves are a brilliant silvery colour; they have a silver patina on them. *A. nervosa* is probably the same plant as *A. cockaynei* and *A. montana*, but *A. petriei* is distinct. The leaves are grey-green on the top, but a brilliant silvery white beneath. An established tussock has a confusingly two-tone effect. Silveriest of all is *A. chatamica*, a large grower, still little known, though probably hardiest of all. The leaves are of the most brilliant silver. These plants will grow in any ordinary garden soil and seem to prefer plenty of sun: they also seem happiest backed up by shrubs – presumably since these afford them some degree of frost protection. They would be ideal for a colour band at the edge of a band of some colour-leaved shrub, and would probably look more effective used like that than in a free-standing group in the open. They are not perhaps as hardy as one would wish, but nothing from New Zealand ever is.

The heathers or lings are reliably hardy and in time forming dense, weed-suppressing ground cover. There are two forms of *Calluna vulgaris* which are outstandingly silver. One is 'Silver Knight' which is quite a compact grower, reaching only 30cm (1ft), and a reasonably tidy plant. The other is 'Silver Queen', which is a smaller grower, but not of quite such a tidy habit: it will reach 25cm (10ins.). Both are silver, but the second is probably the more silver of the two. The first has appalling pink flowers, the second purple flowers which somehow don't look quite so frightful against the foliage. There are a number of other good silver callunas: 'Silver Rose' is grey rather than silver, grows to 40cm (1⅓ft) and has deep rose pink flowers which are awful. 'Sister Anne' has woolly greyish foliage and pink flowers, and is useful because she only grows to 10cm (4ins.). The callunas are happiest in full sun, but will not tolerate limy soils.

In the good old days it used to be called *Leucophyta brownii*; nowadays it is called *Calocephalus brownii*, which doesn't have quite the same silvery ring to it. *Calocephalus* means antler-headed, and the plant is just a bundle of silvery twiglets that branch very much like antlers. It is a curious plant: you are never quite sure whether it is alive, for it is just thick, curved twigs with no leaves, and the twigs look as though they have been splashed all over with silver glitter-paint. I find it very beautiful, but could imagine that other people might not think well of it. It makes a shrub to about 30cm (1ft) high and across. The rub is that it comes from Australia and has an intense aversion to cold, which means that it has to be regarded as a bedding plant. Used as such, it can create a bright silver highlight, but you do need many plants closely packed together. It comes readily from cuttings at just about any time of the year, but the cuttings seem reluctant to root unless you give them bottom heat.

The majority of centaureas are singularly unpleasing plants with nauseating, usually purplish, thistle-like flowers. The genus does, however, contain two of the most outstandingly beautiful silver-leaved plants. The more beautiful of the two is *Centaurea gymnocarpa*, whose leaves are of such an intense silver – almost white – that people always seem to want to touch them to feel what they are made of. The leaves are nearly 30cm (1ft) long, about 9cm (3½ins.) across, doubly pinnate, and are presented like a small fountain, thrown up from the centre of a rosette to arch outwards and flow back. Young plants grown from seed seldom have the chance to show their habit. You need plants in their second year to see the full beauty: by then the rosette has risen a little on its stem (rather in the manner of a feather-palm), and the leaves can fall outwards and downwards to show off their full character. Grown like this, it produces an effect quite extraordinarily light, lacy and delicate, and quite the silveriest thing in the garden. Be warned, though, that the plant does have a couple of bad habits. Seedlings have an inclination to run to flower rather rapidly. You must ruthlessly pinch out any incipient flower-shoots. If you keep at it, the plant will give up trying to flower, and settle down happily to life as a foliage plant. Cuttings are less inclined to run to flower. Its other bad habit is catching cold in the frost, and dying of it. It will scrape through the occasional winter, but really you are better off bedding it out in its pots, and lifting it in its pots for the winter; it only needs frost-free conditions if you keep it rather on the dry side. Cuttings of side-shoots taken in July will root readily and be large enough to go out the following year, if you think that that is less time-and-energy consuming. It is stunning both as an individual and massed, but is certainly much better massed than used as parks' departments tend to use it – as a dot plant among a garish display of scarlet salvias. On the whole, it is well worth the little trouble it requires. Far easier, and only a little less lovely, is *C. rutifolia*, which is usually sold as *C. candidissima*. The leaf is of just about as pure a silver-white as that of *C. gymnocarpa*, but less finely divided – rather more like that of a refined dandelion – and the plant is altogether smaller, growing to only about 23cm (9ins.): you can get the other one to go up to 60cm (2ft). *C. rutifolia* seems to have little inclination to run to flower, and is also surprisingly hardy, not sufficiently to be relied upon, but it will survive two or three winters in a row out of doors on a light soil.

There are two chrysanthemums whose leaves are so grey that they are grown for that quality alone. The first is *Chrysanthemum foeniculaceum*, also known as *C. anethifolium* and *C. frutescens*. It is a sub-shrub, growing anything from 60cm (2ft) to 1.6m (5ft) in a season, depending how soon you start it, and densely grey-leaved. Each leaf is about 10cm (4ins.) long and 6cm (2½ins.) across, very deeply pinnately cut, the segments linear, acutely lobed. It is of much the same colouring as *Ruta graveolens*, a blue-grey rather than a grey-grey, and the dense foliage is topped by numerous long-stalked chrysanthemum flowers, white with a yellow centre, in perfect character with the rest of the plant. Indeed, the whiteness of the flowers (which are exceptionally long-lasting) rather adds to the greyness of the leaves. *C. ptarmiciflorum* (which used to be *Pyrethrum ptarmiciflorum*) is even lovelier, silver rather than grey, with very finely cut leaves similar to those of *Tanacetum densum* but even finer, and borne on a semi-shrubby plant that will grow up to 60cm (2ft), though rather leggy in appearance. It can be kept dense and rounded if you continue pinching out the shoots to make it branch and flatly refuse to allow it to flower. Some authorities rate it as hardy, but they must be either pushing their luck or pulling your leg. In my experience it takes most of the average winter to kill it, but die it invariably does. Happily it roots readily from 5cm (2in.) cuttings taken between July and October, and rooted in a very sandy mix.

If you want something that is both grey and massive, you can't do better than to get a cardoon. In the old days cardoons were grown for their edible stems and shoots, which had to be blanched in the same way as celery. Nowadays no one seems to bother to do that – it is very time-consuming – but the flower-arrangers, bless them, rescued it from oblivion, and, while some people still howl in disgust to see flowering cabbages in your borders, the cardoon is regarded as quite acceptable. It is quite the grandest of all silver-leaved plants, producing great clumps of massive leaves – 1.3m (4ft) or more in length and 60cm (2ft) wide – deeply cut and as silvery as they come. It is a tall-growing plant – the flowering stem will go up to all of 2m (6ft), which can be inconvenient, and is really far finer if the flowering stem is removed as soon as it shows itself: you then get just massive clumps of foliage. Plants can be raised from seed sown under glass, and should be put in a nursery bed for a year before planting out. It takes a plant about three years to reach flowering size, and it is particularly important during that time that no foliage is cut (flower arrangers tend to be impatient) because this can kill young plants. When moved to their permanent quarters they need to be planted into deeply dug and richly manured ground, and the ground should thereafter be manured annually. The plants are at their happiest once they get their roots right down into sub-soil. In theory you can increase the plants by dividing them, but you try lifting one to divide it once it has got its roots right down into the subsoil!

The cardoon is *Cynara cardunculus*; the globe artichoke is *C. scolymus*. I much prefer it as a garden plant to the cardoon, though silver-foliage fanatics would not agree: though magnificent, it is deep, rich grey – not silver. It is a finer plant, with great arching leaves produced in luxuriant piles, 1.3–1.6m (4–5ft) long on plants at least as much across. Ultimately the choice of which you plant depends mainly on whether you want silver or grey. If you have room for both, grow both. The globe artichoke is most usually increased by removing offsets in early spring. I have found plants establish much more reliably if you leave them till May or June. They need a deeply dug soil enriched with plenty of old manure, and an annual dressing of manure. Both the artichoke and the cardoon benefit from having the old growth removed in the autumn – October is about the time – and benefit from a winter covering of straw or bracken. As colour bands they are superlative, but so massive that the only suitable backdrops for them are tall shrubs. One point worth remembering about both cardoon and globe artichoke is that they do not need the light, sandy soil demanded by so many grey- and silver-leaved plants. They are happiest in quite heavy soil, and so are excellent greys and silvers for clay.

There are not a great many grey-leaved plants that one thinks of first and foremost as woodlanders, but *Dicentra oregana* and some of its hybrids are superlative examples that luxuriate in lightly shaded positions. The leaves are very finely cut and much divided, of a bluish grey, but a strong, bright colour. *D. oregana* itself grows about 45cm (18ins.) tall, though some of its hybrids are a little taller. It has a fleshy root system that spreads slowly – never fast enough to be invasive – and in a criss-cross fashion so that the plant never becomes bald in the middle. The dense piles of lush foliage (described as ferny, but only presumably by people who do not know their ferns) are overtopped by arching stems carrying little dangling flowers like lady's lockets, of a pale, rosy mauve which is perfectly in keeping with the colour of the foliage. It is difficult to mass in most gardens, because of its need for a semi-shaded position, but if you have the scope for it, and many town gardens are suitable, it is lovely in bulk. It can be readily increased by removing sections of the root when dormant.

The spurges or milkweeds are in the first rank of grey foliage plants. The biggest growing is *Euphorbia characias*, a perennial with stems up to 1.3m (4ft) tall, each clump achieving a width of 1m (3ft) across, with deep grey leaves, in rows of narrow spikes up the sides of the stems. The flowers are tiny, but surrounded by big greenish-yellow bracts that give them great charm: *E. wulfenii* (which is in fact a subspecies of *characias*) is similar, but has a much bigger, broader head of flowers.

Both tend to seed themselves freely when happy. *E. myrsinites* is a low-growing plant, throwing out in summer 30cm (1ft) stems with grey perfoliate leaves. It is a trailing plant of great character, needing a sunny, well-drained soil. *E. rigida* is in effect an upright version of the same thing, but a little tender. Probably only the first two are of much use for colour bands on any scale, but *myrsinites* is a useful plant for a colour band at the front of a border.

If you think agaves are odd, you should try *Fascicularia*. It is a member of the *Bromeliaceae*, a pineapple relative, and looks it. There are two species, and both make stemless rosettes of narrow, prickly leaves, just like those of the pineapple. Having said that, it is actually questionable whether the two species are in fact two species. If you sow seed of either you will get the full range of variation from one species to the other. But I am being heretical. The accepted formula is that *Fascicularia bicolor* grows to 45cm (18ins.) with a spread of about 60cm (2ft), and has rather broad leaves, while *F. pitcairniifolia* has very much longer and narrower leaves, brown beneath (those of *bicolor* are grey beneath). Both are plants that slowly form hummocks of congested foliage. Their beauty lies in the grey leaves and the form of the foliage, but they are at their most stunning when they flower. The flowers are totally insignificant, like tiny, abortive pineapples tucked away at the centre of the rosette. What is unexpected is that the base of the leaves at the centre of the rosette and surrounding the flower turn an incredible bright pink (in *F. bicolor*) and bright red (in *F. pitcairniifolia*). There is nothing to compare with them that you can grow out of doors, but just how you do this is a little more of a problem. What they seem to need is a deep, well-drained but moisture-retentive soil full of small stones, either in sun or shade. They are worth every effort to grow: a colour band of either would be out of this world.

While we are on the subject, the genus used to be known as *Rhodostachys*, but plants of that genus are now taken as having a lateral, not central, flower, which means that they do not produce the dramatic colouring at the centre of the rosette. The species in cultivation, *R. alpina*, now properly *Ochagavia lindleyana*, certainly adds a stunning touch of the unexpected. The foliage is even more like that of a pineapple, but of an indifferent grey, though grey enough for most people. It is certainly worth growing if you can find it.

The gazanias are usually grown for their brilliantly coloured yellow, orange, pink or red daisy-like flowers; but they nearly all have more or less grey foliage (although there is a good variegated one, with creamy-yellow markings on the leaves), but in one form the grey is so outstanding that it is for that that it is grown. This is *Gazania* 'Silver Beauty'. It is technically a perennial, but since it has little tolerance of frost has to be treated as a bedding plant. You may get occasional plants to endure a passing winter or two, but cannot rely on it. 'Silver Beauty' grows to about 23cm (9ins.), with a spread of about 30cm (1ft) in a single season. You need a lot of it to make a really effective carpet. It will grow in ordinary soil but is better in a well-drained one. The flowers, which close at sunset, are typically yellow and black, but not outstanding among gazania flowers. The foliage is finely shaped and a brilliant white-silver.

Cuttings taken in August are ready to plant out the following May. Some people lift mature plants and overwinter them under glass, but I have never found this so satisfactory as taking cuttings.

There are two hebes which have good grey foliage: but probably others almost as good. *Hebe pinguifolia* 'Pagei' is a virtually prostrate little plant with soft, trailing stems densely packed with small oval grey leaves. Massed, it makes a carpet of grey. The flowers are white and unshowy. It is an easy plant to grow, happy in any good soil in sun and seemingly unaffected even by cold winters. It is excellent for a colour band, or for large blocks among colour-leafed heathers, and is very easily propagated by layers or cuttings taken almost any time. *H. albicans* 'Prostrata' is similar, but larger in all its parts.

The genus *Helichrysum* abounds in good grey and silver plants. *H. angustifolium* is often known as the curry plant on account of the strong curry smell emitted by the leaves when crushed, very noticeable in this species, but present in most species to a greater or lesser degree. It is a slow-growing shrub ultimately making about 60cm (2ft) each way with 2.5cm (1in.) needle-like leaves densely packed round the shoots. Both leaves and shoots are bright white-grey. It may not be the world's most stunning silver, but you have got to give it top marks for good behaviour. A plant that always looks good, is neat and always a clean silver, even in winter, it is relatively sturdy and reliable, and therefore excellent for a colour band. It can be kept down to size and shape by clipping over with shears, and is very easy to increase from cuttings taken at any time of year if you have heat, but taken in July if you haven't.

H. fontanesii is a far more delicate-looking plant, a sub-shrub growing to about 1.3m (4ft) but only about 1m (3ft) across, with the finest of soft, needle-like leaves, curling slightly upwards, which are produced in rosettes up the stems. The leaves and stems are both a stunning silver-white – till winter, anyway; then they should be cut down. The young growth is always the most brilliantly silvered, and some gardeners cut their plants down just before they flower and so get a second flush of new growth. The plant layers itself quite readily, and cuttings taken in July also root easily. I had already sung the praises of *H. petiolatum* when we came across the so-called yellow form. The best way of describing *H. microphyllum* is to say that it is in effect a tiny-leaved version of *H. petiolatum*. In *H. petiolatum* the leaves are about 13mm (½in.) long and nearly as wide: in *H. microphyllum* they are less than half that size. Both are charming and extremely useful grey- to silver-leaved plants for bedding, excellent in urns, tubs and window-boxes, but best of all in borders. They are too tender to be used or even attempted as permanent plants, but ideal grown as one grows bedding plants, taking cuttings in October and putting them out in May. Both can be allowed to spread sideways over the ground, or to trail out of urns and churns, or trained up canes to make little symmetrical grey trees. It is surprising just how much growth they will put on in a single season.

There is only one conifer I think brilliant enough to include among the greys and silvers (which is surprising, when you think about it), and that is *Juniperus squamata*

'Chinese Silver' – if in fact it is a form of *J. squamata* at all. It is a Chinese species, and was originally sold merely as *Juniperus* sp. Yu 7881. Whatever its true taxonomic status, from a garden point of view it is both beautiful and brilliant. It is quite the brightest, cleanest silver among the conifers. There is nothing to compare with it. The habit of growth is bushy, the plant throwing its branches upwards and outwards, the tips of the twigs being positively pendulous. Young plants look as though they are going to spread in the manner of *Juniperus* 'Grey Owl', but older plants are generally taller than wide. It needs full sun to be at its best, and is readily propagated from winter cuttings.

Kniphofia caulescens is really not in the first rank of grey plants, but grey it is, with rosettes of broad, strap-shaped leaves over 30cm (1ft) long. In time, a single crown will multiply to form an extensive colony. The effect of it massed has to be seen to be properly appreciated: it looks far greyer in quantity than it does when you look at a single leaf, or even a single plant. The flowers are typical red-hot pokers, but rather less showy than those of most species. Happy in any good soil in full sun, and easily propagated by division in spring, it is ideal for a grey colour band in a subdued idiom.

The genus *Leptospermum* is one that is usually grown for its flowers, and very fine they are too, small and starry and quite delightful. The majority of the plants most often grown are rather tall, leggy shrubs, but there are two absolutely brilliant greys in the genus. The first is *L. cunninghamii*, an Australian species growing to about 2m (6ft) and perhaps 1m (3ft) across, with reddish stems and tiny rounded silver-grey leaves, giving an overall grey effect. The flowers are white, and add to rather than detract from the plant. It is surprisingly hardy, and makes a good colour band if you give it a sunny aspect and the backing of evergreen shrubs. *L. lanigerum* is a slightly taller shrub with even more silvery leaves which are longer and more pointed than those of *cunninghamii*, and tending to turn slightly bronzed towards winter. The flowers are again white, but produced in early autumn, while those of *cunninghamii* are produced in July. It seems as hardy as the other species, but it is reputed to be slightly less so. Both come readily from seed, or from cuttings taken from mid-summer onwards.

Lotus berthelottii (formerly *Lotus peliorrhychnus*) is a plant that, sadly, is hardly ever seen any more. Perhaps it just requires too much skill in cultivation. It is not, as you might expect, the sacred lotus, that fabulous water plant with huge rose or blue flowers held high above the water and magnificent architectural seed-heads borne on even taller stems – that is *Nelumbo*. The ancient botanists, Dioscorides and Theophrastus in particular, are to blame for this muddle: they used the name lotus for some of the pea family. *Lotus berthelottii* is a member of the *Leguminosae*, and its brilliant scarlet flowers are typical pea family: just like those of the lobster-claw (*Clianthus*) but smaller – tiny, to be more precise. What the plant is grown for is its foliage, which is soft and silky and silver; the leaves are needle-shaped, but soft as down, silver-hairy, and borne in luxuriant profusion on stems that are exactly the same grey. The plant forms a woody collar, but the long, trailing or scrambling growths are annual. Grown in a hanging basket or urn, it is a veritable fountain of irridescent silveryness, dotted with scarlet flashes of flowers. The annual growths on mature plants can trail 1–1.3m (3–4ft) in a season. It is excellent as a colour band if you can give it a position where it is tucked away under shrubs, but facing due south. It may even survive the odd winter grown that way, but it is more usual to lift it or propagate it annually – it comes easily from late summer cuttings. The cultural problem is winter: it needs just sufficient water to keep it alive, but one drop too much will kill it. However, it is worth every ounce of effort to succeed with.

Of the prickly pears (*Opuntia*) the hardiest is reputed to be *O. cantabrigiensis*, which has great oval pads over 30cm (1ft) long and about 20cm (8ins.) across, fiercely armed with vicious papery white spines. The pads are very grey. When happy, the plant will grow to about 1m (3ft) high and spread outwards almost indefinitely. You just hack it back when it spreads too far. *O. phaeacantha* has much smaller pads, almost round, and about half the size, but it is even more dramatically armed with white spines, the majority of which point back down the pad. There seems to be more than one form of *phaeacantha* in cultivation. The one I have described is the typical form, but I have also grown forms with rather pointed pads and a form that is virtually prostrate. *O. haematocarpa* (the name means that it has bloody fruits) is very similar to the typical *phaeacantha*, but the pads are slightly larger. You do occasionally get flowers in the garden, but it is as a foliage plant that it is grown. The prickly pears need perfect drainage and full sun, and seem to be happiest grown in very poor, gritty soil, covered with about 10cm (4ins.) of grit – grey in colour for preference, to go with the grey of the plants. They are very easy to increase: simply cut a pad off an established plant sometime during the summer, leave it on a windowsill for a couple of days till the cut has dried, then plunge it into a pot filled with equal parts of good garden soil and very sharp grit-sand. Spray the pad lightly to keep it alive; water draining off it will wet the soil. Plant out a year later. If you toss newly fallen leaves into the shrubs in autumn they will provide some protection against frost and will have either rotted down or faded away by spring. A few dried leaves will do little to detract from the overall drama of the planting.

There are one or two really superb silver plants that will only grow in shade. They just curl up and die in sun. One of the finest of these is *Pulmonaria saccharata* 'Silver Heart'. Pulmonaria is lungwort, both in English and Latin, and all the lungworts are rough, hairy perennial herbs making excellent ground cover. Most of them have more or less elliptic leaves more or less spotted with grey. In *Pulmonaria saccharata* – alias *picta* or *grandiflorum* – the leaves are up to 20cm (8ins.) long and about 10cm (4ins.) across, very heavily spotted with grey. In the form 'Silver Heart' the grey spots merge to make the whole centre of the leaf a good clean silver with just an edging of green. It needs full shade to grow well, though it will tolerate light shade, and given shade and a deep soil well enriched with leaf-mould, it forms lush piles of these exotic leaves. A slowly-spreading dense ground cover, at its most effective used boldly, it can easily be increased by division, but if you are impatient for more, root cuttings afford a ready means of building a large stock quickly.

By far the most decorative of the dead nettles is a diminutive dead nettle called *Lamium maculatum* 'Silver Beacon'. The leaves are about half the size of those of the common dead-nettle, perhaps a little less, heart-shaped and a rich bright silver all over (except for a narrow margin of green). It is a low-growing plant, up to a mere couple of inches, and much slower to spread than the common dead-nettle, a small plant from a pot covering perhaps 60cm (a couple of ft) each way in a season. You can safely allow it into small gardens with no fear of it taking everything over; in larger gardens the problem is to get enough of it. It is happier in semi-shade than in full sun, and the colouring just as good and probably better appreciated in shade or semi-shade. Readily increased by proles or cuttings.

Pyrus salicifolia is known as the willow-leaved pear, and has willowy leaves, very narrow and extremely silvery, covered in fine silky hairs. The form most usually grown is 'Pendula', which slowly forms a small, weeping tree, seldom above 4.5m (15ft). As such it makes a good specimen or accent plant. I prefer it grown as a shrub and allowed to spread out across the ground. If you grow it this way you can make a colour band of it in which one plant will run into the next. It will show its true colouring only in full sun. You can propagate it by semi-ripe cuttings in heat, or hardwood cuttings under a north light. Plants in commerce are usually grafted and tend to sucker inconveniently.

The great majority of the rhododendrons are notable, once their flowers are over, for the funereal gloom of their dark green foliage. So it may come as something of a surprise to find species with grey or silver foliage. But they exist, and they are good. The baby blues all have more or less grey foliage. *Rhododendron* x 'Blue Tit' seems, on the whole, to have rather more silvery foliage than 'Blue Diamond', but both are good and there is little to choose between them. Both will grow well fully exposed to sun and wind. *Rh. campanulatum* is a lovely thing, a large-growing plant of open habit with huge campanulate flowers of a beautiful purple. *Rh. campanulatum* var. *aeriginosum* is grown not for its flowers, which are far inferior to those of the typical plant, but for its leaves, which are a wonderful silvery-grey above and an incredible foxy red underneath. It is one of the choicest of all rhododendrons, and very hard to come by. It needs a semi-shaded position, and good cultivation. *Rh. concatenans* has brilliant electric silver-blue leaves, rather rounded. It is a twiggy plant, with dainty dangling bell-shaped flowers of apricot-yellow which go well with the foliage, but it is for its foliage that it is grown. It needs semi-shade and good cultivation to look really fine, but even with poor cultivation it still attracts attention. *Rh. impeditum* is one of the dwarf, grey-leaved rhododendrons with much affinity to the baby blues. It slowly forms a small bun, about 1m (3ft) high and across after years and years if you are lucky, but more usually only about half that size, with tiny scaly leaves of a glittering silver-grey. There is a dwarf form, tiny and congested, that grows to only about 10cm (4ins.) high and 30cm (1ft) across after ten years or so. *Rh. lepidostylum* has probably the brightest foliage of this group of rhododendrons, but is quite different from all the others in that the foliage is densely prickly-hairy. It is of an intense blue-grey in spring, fading to a mature grey for the rest of the season. The leaves are about 13mm (½in.) long and 6mm (¼in.) across, densely packed on the plant, which will grow up to about 15cm (6ins.) in height but trails outwards indefinitely, rooting as it goes. It is at its best pouring itself down a bank. The flowers, which are seldom produced, are dirty yellow and very small. *Rh. scintillans* is a tiny plant with brilliant silvery-grey recurved leaves, similar to those of *impeditum*, but smaller and brighter in colour. The oldest plant I have ever seen had reached an amazing 45cm (18ins.) with a spread of 1–1.3m (3–4ft). Young, compact plants are much finer. It needs to be grown in sun, and, though the leaves keep their colour in shade, the plant loses its character, becoming leggy and twiggy and bare in the centre. It is certainly possible to make effective colour bands of those small-leaved species which will grow in sun, and probably also of *concatenans*, but *campanulatum* var. *aerigonosum* is far too rare to treat in that way. It is finer by far as a specimen. Everyone will tell you that rhododendrons need an acid soil, and so most of them do. But the baby blues and *impeditum* will grow on alkaline soils provided that they have sufficient humus into which to put their roots.

The willows embrace both large-growing trees and tiny, creeping shrubs. Of the larger-growing ones the most silvery is *Salix alba* 'Sericea' which is a fairly coarse-growing tree but of value on account of its brilliant silveriness. At the other extreme is a diminutive little thing, *S. x boydii*, with small corrugated rounded leaves about 13mm (½in.) long, which slowly forms a gnarled miniature tree about 30cm (1ft) high, if you both live long enough. The leaf colour is a curiously metallic grey. *S. exigua* is a large erect shrub with bright, light brown twigs and long, slender silver leaves. *S. hastata* 'Wehrhanii' is a slow-growing wide-spreading shrub up to about 2m (6ft) each way (though it will layer itself and spread still further) with rather stout, unwillowly twigs and heart-shaped leaves of a deep dark grey: a very popular plant, and excellent in a colour band. *S. lanata* is known as the woolly willow, and slowly forms a rounded bush of corrugated leaves of an intense silver: the leaves of the form 'Stuartii' are even brighter, but it is a slower grower and ultimately a smaller plant. *S. lapponum* is a willowly willow throwing up long, slender twigs bearing very narrow leaves of the brightest silver in the genus. It is densely branched and brilliantly leafy: when you first put a plant in it looks as though it will only ever throw up a straggly shoot or two, but it soon thickens out. Many willows grow beside water in the wild, but in cultivation they will nearly all thrive given a good rich soil with plenty of humus. They are not plants that need any fussing. All come easily from hardwood cuttings rooted in a north light, or from cuttings taken during the growing season and rooted in water.

The lavender cotton, *Santolina chamaecyparissus*, is one of the most brilliantly silver-white of all shrubs, tough, hardy and very useful. It is a low-growing, hummock-forming shrub achieving a height of about 60cm (2ft) and a little less in spread, of very dense habit and covered with finely cut woolly-white foliage ideal for a colour band or block. There is a dwarf form in commerce, usually sold as 'Nana', which turns out to be a species after all, *S. corsica*: which grows about half as high. It is also questionable whether *S. neapolitanus* is in fact a species, or merely a form of *S. chamaecyparissus*: certainly its leaves are longer and more feathery, and its colouring slightly less intense, but it is very similar, both in appearance and in garden use. The santolinas all need to be clipped over after flowering to keep them compact (before flowering if you want to get rid of the horrid yellow flowers), and it is useless trying to reshape a bush that has grown too leggy by cutting back to old wood. It will shoot, but it won't be worth having. Cuttings taken in July root readily.

Senecio is one of those genera that embrace a vast variety of plants. Botanists keep splitting the genus up, and then lumping everything back into it again. Ligularia, which seems so distinct to gardeners, has apparently been lumped back with the senecios again. However, as it is now generally understood, the genus embraces a great number of good silver-leaved plants, indeed some of the best. *Senecio cineraria* (alias *maritima*) is probably the most popular of all silver bedding plants, and rightly so. If you want it in quantity it is usual to grow it from seed, the seedlings being planted out about 20cm (8ins.) apart, and stopped when they get to 15cm (6ins.) or so in height. In hot summers the odd side-shoot may try to flower, and that should be nipped in the bud. The species has finely-cut silver-felted leaves, but there are named forms which are finer than those you can grow from seed. 'White Diamond' has leaves a little less finely cut, but is intensely white-felted, probably the best colour of all.

If you leave senecios in the garden over winter, they will need a good grooming in spring: it is only a matter of tidying up dead leaves and cutting frost-damaged shoots back to sound wood – if wood is the word. There is a woody senecio which is very common in gardens, and much confusion over its naming. It is often sold as *Senecio laxifolius*, which is what most people seem to know it as, but *laxifolius* is actually rather a rare plant, seldom grown, with narrower, thinner leaves. Probably the most common name for this popular grey-leaved shrub is *S. greyi* (of gardens), now properly *S.* 'Sunshine'. It is a shrub with rounded leaves of a good silvery-grey on top, the colour fading as the season goes on, gradually building itself up into a mound about 1m (3ft) high and twice as much or more across. It tends to grow leggy in time, so needs a routine trim in spring. If you ever want to kill one, do the trimming just as winter is setting in: it usually sees it off. *S.* 'Sunshine' is a fine plant, and its beauty would be better appreciated if it were not quite so easy to grow. It would be ideal for a colour band, being relatively happy-go-lucky about soil, and not too bothered if it is in shade for part of the day, though its colouring is never so good when it is shaded. *S. compactus*, though a distinct species, is to all intents and purposes a dwarf version of 'Sunshine', growing to only about 60cm (2ft) and about the same on spread. It is highly desirable, and far preferable to the more common plant for making colour bands: it is also a fractionally better colour. The hybrid 'Leonard Cockayne' is much finer than either, having large leaves of the same shape but up to 10cm (4ins.) long and nearly 7.5cm (3ins.) across, felted an intense silvery white: the colour is as good as that of *S. cineraria:* it is a much more vigorous shrub, up to 1.6m (5ft) high, and with a considerable spread. *S. reynoldii,* alias *rotundifolius,* has large leaves, as much as 12–15cm (5–6ins.) long, appearing rounded but actually more oval, very leathery with most of the white felting on the underside. The tops of the leaves are greyish, so it just scrapes into this chapter. Its problem is that it tends to become leggy and therefore has to be hidden behind better-dressed plants. *S. monroi* is in effect a miniature of *reynoldii,* forming a tight, rounded, dome-shaped bush, wider than high, only 60cm (a couple of feet) tall, with small seemingly round leaves on a seemingly round bush. It is better as an accent plant than for massing. Charming, but not really grey enough.

Lamb's lugs must have been with us and popular for quite a long time to have acquired a name like that. Its proper name is *Stachys lanata.* It is a fine grey-leaved ground cover plant growing no more than 30cm (1ft) high in flower, much less when not in flower, with long, oval woolly grey leaves, at their silvery brightest in spring and early summer. It can look quite dreadful in winter if the old leaves are allowed to remain on the plant and rot away into a black mushy mess. With good grooming it is excellent. If you don't like the flowers go for a form called 'Silver Carpet' which is non-flowering: the leaves are slightly longer and slightly brighter in colour. It is a more dense growing ground cover, so even more prone to rotting away in winter if you do not groom it properly in autumn. Both the species and 'Silver Carpet' are very easily propagated by removing rooted pieces and planting them. It needs full sun to be really bright, but can stand a little shade.

Far choicer, and just about as easy (usually no trouble at all) is *Tanacetum densum,* which used to be a chrysanthemum – *Chrysanthemum haradjanii* and *Chrysanthemum poterifolium.* It is a singularly dense silver carpeting plant growing to about 15cm (6ins.) and spreading about 15cm each way in a season. The leaves, which are barely 5cm (2ins.) long, are like little feathers, so finely cut are they. It is quite a hardy plant and, provided you give it a good gritty soil, excellent for making colour blocks or bands at almost lawn level and it is very easily increased by detaching rooted pieces and planting them on. The flowers may surprise you: they are just like groundsel.

Most of the hardy yuccas are a bit on the grey or silver side, but *Yucca whipplei* has quite the most penetratingly silver foliage of all the yuccas which can be grown out of doors. It is also the most architecturally outstanding hardy species. The leaves are exceedingly long and narrow, 1m (3ft) long and only 2.5cm (1in.) wide at the base, evenly tapering to a viciously pointed tip that can cause a really nasty wound: it can go right through your hand. It forms a stemless rosette of almost perfectly hemispherical shape, and gradually gets larger and larger until it finally throws up its magnificent flower spike, a vast, densely packed panicle of white flowers some 4.5m (15ft) high, after which it dies. It takes many years to reach flowering size, and while on its way is one of the finest foliage plants you can grow. To succeed it needs perfect drainage and all the sun it can get: it is quite tolerant of frost, but what tends to kill it is wetness. It makes a stunning dot or linking plant, and is very easily raised from seed.

If you have ever had any doubts as to how distinct silver and grey plants are from blue ones, the blues are dealt with in the next chapter. They really are quite distinct.

CHAPTER SEVEN

The Blues

It is surprising just how few plants there are whose foliage is really blue. The great majority of supposedly blue-leafed plants are quite definitely grey. Furthermore, those few true blues which do exist are very limited not only in number, but also in style: the majority are conifers; and most of the rest are grasses.

As though to emphasize the point, we start with a conifer genus, *Abies*. *Abies concolor* 'Glauca' probably has longer needles than those of any other blue fir. The typical plant is a stately tree, growing to as much as 60m (200ft), and it is reasonably distinct (though you might confuse it with *Abies grandis*) in its tiered branching system and its very long and very broad needles presented in a distinctive V-formation on the twigs. All forms of *Abies concolor* are bluish, but those sold as *A.c.* 'Glauca' are very much bluer than usual. The form known as 'Candicans' has the brightest blue foliage of all. The trouble is that all of these tend to be rather large-growing for any but the largest gardens, though they make very fine specimen plants. For small gardens the most useful form is *A.c.* 'Glauca Prostrata' or 'Glauca Compacta' – apparently one and the same plant – which forms a leaderless little bush of compact, almost congested habit and irregular outline. It is of a good, intense blue. In ten years it will grow to about 1m (3ft) wide and high. It would be ideal for massing if only it was easier to obtain. Plants have to be grafted, which makes them both scarce and expensive.

Abies lasiocarpa, the Arizona cork-bark fir, is itself seldom seen in gardens. The form of it that is grown is *A.l.* 'Arizonica Compacta', a perfectly shaped blue miniature Christmas tree, a symmetrical pyramid and a marvellous blue. In ten years a plant will reach about 1.3m (4ft). It is useless for massing, but just about the finest imaginable blue conifer to use as a linking dot plant in beds of heathers or other low-growing coloured cover. It is propagated by grafting, which again makes it both scarce and expensive, but it is so beautiful that it seems to justify its cost.

Of a similar intensity of blue, but possibly an even better colour, is a blue grass, usually sold as *Agropyrum glaucum*, though the validity of that name is decidedly suspect, which is a shame: it is the brightest and most beautiful blue grass in existence. The leaves are very narrow, up to 30cm (1ft) long, slightly rough to the touch, held very erect, and of the most intense steely blue. It is a tightly clump-forming grass, though with age the clumps get a little loose and floppy. It seldom flowers, but the flower spikes are blue to begin with, turning brown only as the seed ripens. The colour is highly desirable, but the plant makes you work for it. It needs to be groomed every year, having all the old leaves dragged out of it, and it must be regularly lifted, divided and replanted to keep it looking its best. This is a lot more work than you have to give to most plants in the multi-coloured garden, but in the case of *Agropyrum glaucum* it is well worth while.

There are among the lawsons good blues, just as there are good greens, golds, yellows, creams and whites. The best of the blue lawsons are pretty good. 'Blom' is about the smallest of them, growing to about 2m (6½ft) in ten years, with a spread of 35–38cm (14–15ins.). It is a very symmetrical, upright little conifer, the shape of a candle flame, with adult foliage arranged in flattened, vertical sprays. It is a reasonably deep blue, erring a little on the side of grey, but valuable among the blue lawsons in its slow growth. 'Columnaris' sometimes sold as 'Columnaris Glauca' (as though there were any other) is very much the same blue, quite an intense colour, but bigger-growing, making about 2.5m (8ft) in ten years, with a spread of 80cm (2½ft). The foliage is again adult, presented in flattened sprays held upwards, but not nearly so stiffly erect: it is an altogether much more relaxed plant. 'Pembury Blue' is quite the bluest of the lawsons; indeed it is one of the bluest of all conifers, since its colour really is blue, not frosted with silver as is the case with the firs and spruces. The habit is more open than that of 'Columnaris', the foliage even more relaxed, and it is a strong grower reaching 3m (10ft) or more in its first ten years, with a spread of about 1m (3ft). The habit is pyramidal, not flame-shaped, and it is well clothed right down to the ground. None of these three is suitable for massing (except as a hedge) but they are excellent linking plants. Of just as good a blue as 'Pembury Blue', but of a much more pleasing foliage type and growth habit is *Chamaecyparis obtusa* 'Blue Surprise'. The foliage is of the feathery juvenile type (very like *Thuja orientalis* 'Juniperoides), soft to the touch, forming after ten years a rounded plant taller than wide, about 1 × 0.5m (3 × 1½ft), the soft blue colouring turning to purple in winter. It is an excellent colour-band plant, and very amenable to trimming.

Cham ob. 'Boulevard' deserves a mention, mainly because it is in commercial terms probably the fastest-selling blue conifer around: it is incredibly easy to propagate, and reasonably fast-growing, making about 2 × 1m (6 × 3ft) in ten years and forming a neat, well-clothed bush that is pleasant to look at at any time of year. The foliage is blue, but pale blue, and a touch on the grey side. The obverse of its relatively fast growth is that, though you can cut it back, it looks a fright if you do. *Chamaecyparis pisifera* 'Squarrosa Intermedia' has far more merits. It is slow-growing, forming an almost perfect half-sphere of dense blue foliage, very compact, almost congested – but with none of the distortion of growth one associates with the term. The foliage is of the juvenile type, very fine and prickly. In ten years a plant will grow to about 50cm (1⅔ft), with a spread only a little greater. The neat habit does need encouraging: it is best clipped over lightly each year to remove any growths that stick out from the mass of the foliage. So long as this is done, it makes an excellent plant for massing, the dome-shaped habit creating interesting hills and valleys as the plants grow together at the base.

There is a lovely blue cypress that we have all been growing in our gardens for years as *Cupressus arizonica*, which we now have to call *C. glabra*. The typical plant is extremely variable, and seedlings range in colour from a dirty grey to a mauvish-blue. The best blue forms are easily propagated by cuttings. Even then, they are still a rather grey-blue – but not grey enough to go in with the greys. A good blue form of the typical plant will grow to 4m with a spread of 2m (6½ft) in ten years, which is cracking along a bit, and forms a broadly pyramidal tree, the foliage presented in pyramidal twiglets on pyramidal branchlets. Several clones have been selected for their blueness, and the best I have seen is 'Blue Pyramid', though 'Hodginsii' which I have not seen may be better. My favourite among the Arizona cypresses is the midget in the group, 'Compacta', which is tiny and congested compared with the others, making an irregularly dome-shaped bun about 45cm (1½ft) high and across in ten years. It is perfect for massing, though it seems to be not quite so easy from cuttings as the type and the other clones.

Chances are you know *Elymus arenarius*, if not by that name. It is that rampantly-spreading, bright blue grass they use to bind coastal sand dunes. Seen in that setting, it is a marvellous plant, with its 60cm (2ft) long steely blue leaves, beloved of flower arrangers. But if you let it into your garden either put it behind bars in a bucket on a concrete or paved area from which it cannot escape, or face the fact that, if you plant it in open ground, you will have your work cut out keeping it down to size. It would be lovely as a colour band if you had all the time in the world to look after it; unless you have, keep clear of it. It is of course excellent on a vast, municipal scale where it can be allowed to cover large areas and be grown in thick concrete containers.

The blue fescues are, by contrast, plants you can welcome into your garden with open arms. They will never take you over, no matter how much love and admiration – even encouragement – you give them. They are small, clump-forming grasses of very neat, tidy appearance. There are several blue fescues around, of which *Festuca caesia* is the finest. It is a brilliant blue, far bluer than any other fescue, a metallic blue with just a hint of turquoise. The leaves grow to about 23cm (9ins.), and an established clump to 15cm (6 ins.) across (after that the clump starts deteriorating). The clumps are extremely tight – hence the neatness of the plant – and the leaves all tend to grow to the same length. Your problem will be, as was mine, in recognizing a *Festuca caesia* when you see one. It tends to turn up in commerce as *Festuca ovina glauca*, but apparently there is no such thing. It is readily confused with *Festuca amethystina*, which is a larger plant of looser habit, and of a reasonable blue but not nearly so fine. It is also sometimes sold as *Festuca rubra*, or rather *Festuca rubra* is often sold for it: they are very similar. *F. rubra* is very similar in size and habit, but inferior in colour. If you buy your plants in winter you will not be able to tell the two apart, unless you look at the sheaths: in *F. caesia* the sheaths are split; in *F. rubra* they are entire – and that is the most reliable diagnostic characteristic to look for. *F. caesia* is a marvellous plant for making a colour band, and looks particularly good with some of the foxy-red New Zealand sedges next to it.

Of quite a different character is *Festuca punctoria* (*acerosa*). Whereas *F. caesia, rubra* and *amethystina* have, in spite of their upright stance, a silky appearance and are soft to the touch, *F. punctoria* is quite the prickliest blue grass around. The leaves, which are not quite such a good blue as those of *F. caesia*, are curled upwards from a creeping stock and quite rigid, with sharply pointed tips. While you would happily sit for hours on *F. rubra, caesia* or *amethystina*, you would find *F. punctoria* makes as uncomfortable a seat as a thistle. The prickliness is presumably a protective adaptation: it is a grass of the dry, arid regions of Greece and Turkey where this quality could only discourage animals from eating it. It is a little more trouble to grow than the other fescues, demanding gritty soil and good drainage and needing to be divided and replanted every two or three years – the old parts brown and the plant spreads outwards, becoming bare in the middle. It is not recommended for a colour band, but it does make an excellent contrast to the silkier fescues.

If the specific epithet *punctoria* implies an affinity with a porcupine, the specific epithet *sempervirens*, which means evergreen, is an odd one to give to the very blue grass generally known as the hedgehog grass – *Helictotrichon sempervirens*. This is the most marvellous of all the medium-sized blue grasses, forming a rounded tussock of stiff and spiky narrow leaves which are overtopped and beautifully complemented by elegantly arching flower stems. The tussock grows to between 1 and 1.3m (3 and 4ft), with leaves 30cm (1ft) long giving a 60cm (2ft) spread. It is not a plant for massing – it is wasted massed. Each plant should be given sufficient space for it to show off its individual character. It looks good in a large area where all the plants are the same age and growing exactly the same distance apart, with a lowly carpeting plant beneath, preferably of the same or a very close colour. It should be groomed every spring, and the dead leaves removed; it is best divided every two or three years. Ants have the most infuriating habit of making their nest right in the middle of a clump—seemingly in some intimate interrelationship with the very centre of the plant.

The great majority of the hostas tend to have leaves that are grey rather than blue, but there are two which are quite definitely blue. The first of these is probably the most magnificent you can grow: it is *Hosta sieboldiana elegans* alias *Hosta glauca elegans* alias *Hosta fortunei robusta*. The leaves are the largest and finest in the genus, 30cm (1ft) wide and 30cm long, on stems that hold them well up, making a plant with a height of 75cm (2½ft) to nearly 1m (3ft) with a spread of about the same; the leaves are the most pronouncedly corrugated in the genus. The flowers are very pale lilac and only just overtop the leaves. The other is in many ways a smaller version of the same thing, and yet quite distinct in its own way. It is *Hosta tokudama*, which has probably the most substantial leaves in the genus, and which is very nearly allied to *H. sieboldiana* but smaller in all its parts. The deeply corrugated blue leaves are dished or spoon-shaped, a little more than half the size of those of *H. sieboldiana elegans*, and the whole plant is much slower-growing. It is much more useful in a small garden than *H. sieboldiana elegans*, but if you have the room for both, grow both. *H. tokudama* is extremely slow to increase, but so lovely that it is worth persevering with. Both hostas do best in dappled shade, and in a good, fertile soil, and enjoy an annual mulch of leaf-mould or well-rotted manure.

Juniperus horizantalis is nearly always a virtually prostrate plant and ideal for massing. It is a native of the mountains of North America, where some twenty different clones have been selected and named. Just about all of them have thin, flexuous branches that not only lie flat on the ground but also actually follow the contours. One of the finest forms is *J.h.* 'Bar Harbour' whose main branches lie flat along the ground, but the tips curve upwards and outwards, creating a curious deep-pile-carpet effect. The foliage, which is singularly dense and finely textured, is blue, changing to purple in winter. Even bluer is *J.h.* 'Douglasii', whose foliage also turns purplish in winter but a rather less intense shade than 'Bar Harbour'. It has the same tendency to turn the tips of its branches upwards and outwards. Both grow to about 30cm (1ft) high, and spread laterally about 38cm (15ins.) a year. They are excellent, dense ground-cover plants. Even lower-growing, up to only 15cm (6ins.), is *J.h.* 'Wiltonii', a relatively new introduction which is completely prostrate, with very dense, very blue foliage, turning a richer blue rather than purple in winter. *Juniperus* x *media* is supposed to be a cross between *J. chinensis* and *J. sabina*: certainly many of the hybrids have the strong aroma of the Savin juniper. Two are outstanding blue plants and these two are often confused since they are similar in habit and colour. The first is *J.* x *media* 'Hetzii', the second *J.* x *media* 'Pfitzeriana Glauca'. Both have beautiful feathery silver-blue foliage, and both throw their branches upwards and outwards, but 'Hetzii' is the bigger-grower of the two, reaching about 2m (6½ft) in ten years, with a more upright habit of growth; the foliage is also smoother and less prickly than that of 'Pfitzeriana Glauca', and the latter has a slightly pendulous droop to the tips of the growing shoots, which 'Hetzii' does not. Both are excellent for massing and neat enough for colour bands. *Juniperus scopulorum* is the Rocky Mountain juniper and as such it is exceedingly hardy. In America a large number of forms have been selected and named, the majority of them with more or less grey foliage. But there is one outstanding member of the genus, *J.s.* 'Blue Heaven', whose foliage is decidedly blue, as are even the vast quantities of fruits it carries. Left to its own devices it grows into a compact, pyramidal bush 1m (3ft) high and 30cm (1ft) wide in ten years. If you take the heart out of the plant when it is young, it will spread instead, throwing its branches out at forty-five degrees, and used in that way is an excellent colour-band plant. All the blue junipers need good light and full exposure to the elements to show their colouring at its best. Most come very easily from cuttings.

Those beautiful tall blue conifers that people tend to refer to as blue Christmas trees are in fact very closely related to the Christmas tree. The Christmas tree is *Picea abies*; the blue Christmas tree *Picea pungens*, or one of its forms. *Picea pungens* 'Glauca' is bluer than the typical plant, and most of the really large specimens of blue spruce you see around are this form. The term 'Glauca' embraces seedlings that are bluer than the rest, and less than a third of all the seedlings grown on are blue enough to be sold as

'Glauca'. But one of the reasons that there are better-named clones around is that the seedlings are grown on: the very finest have been selected over the years and are propagated by grafting. The first of the clones to gain wide distribution was 'Koster' or 'Kosteri', which is decidedly bluer than the general run of 'Glauca'. 'Moerheimii' was the next to be named and distributed, and really there is very little to choose between the two so far as blueness goes. On the whole 'Moerheimii' is probably the better garden plant, having longer needles (making it appear more densely clothed) and a more erect habit of growth. It always looks the more vigorous plant of the two, but in fact both grow at the same rate, reaching about 2m (7ft) in ten years, with a spread at ground level of about 1m (3ft). 'Thomsen' is a much newer introduction and about the finest blue spruce you could imagine, of a more intense blue than either 'Koster' or 'Moerheimii', with needles that are not only longer but also wider, giving the plant a very dense appearance. The habit is vigorous and erect. 'Hoopsii' is even newer, a good, vigorous plant, but of a silvery-blue, so that the colour seems less blue. All of these are trees that form tall, narrow, symmetrical pyramids, ideal for colour bands in the largest gardens and as linking plants near the perimeter of smaller ones.

There is a number of other odd and eccentric forms of *Picea pungens* of which one of the most fascinating is 'Glauca Pendula', which has never made up its mind whether it is trying to be a tree or not. The branches are weeping, clothed densely in prickly bright blue foliage and, if you leave the plant alone, it will slowly hump its back up into a mound and send all its pendulous branches trailing outwards over the ground, a manner of growth that can very readily be exploited in large colour bands. Given training in its early years, it can be persuaded to develop a leader, and this will slowly climb above the mound of sprawling basal branches to form a narrow spire of pendulous branchlets. Even then the leader never grows straight, but this is probably a good thing since its crookedness helps to show off the weeping branches to perfection. 'Glauca Prostrata', however, did make up its mind what to do: it decided to stay prostrate. It is a gem, with rich blue foliage and a compact, very slow habit of growth. In ten years it will make about 2m (6ft) in width and little more than 45cm (1½ft) in height. You need a lot of it to make a colour band and that could be expensive since it is a plant that has to be grafted. But if 'Glauca Prostrata' does what you want of a colour band, then 'Glauca Prostrata' is what you will have to settle for, since there is nothing else remotely like it.

You could easily mistake *Poa colensoi* for a blue fescue, and to all intents and purposes it is the New Zealand equivalent of a blue fescue and should be used in the same way. I like it because I think it keeps its colour better through the winter than the blue fescues. The most noticeable difference between a blue fescue and *Poa colensoi* is that the leaves of the poa are nearly straight, while those of the fescues tend to curl, so that they are nearly round in section, and are glossy. There is a highly desirable diminutive relative called *Poa tasmanica* which grows only 5cm (2ins.) high and slowly spreads to form a low and lovely carpet, but it is a slightly paler blue. It is the perfect carpeting grass for troughs or sinks, or in the open in the very smallest gardens.

The Douglas fir, *Pseudotsuga menziesii (= taxifolia = douglasii)* is a very large-growing conifer, looking very much like an overgrown fir tree, and usually somewhat glaucous. There is one very fine form in cultivation, *P.m.* 'Glauca' (= 'Caesia') which is slower- and smaller-growing and whose colouring rivals the very finest forms of *Picea pungens*, being an intense, metallic blue. Some botanists believe the blue form to be a separate species, which is why the only blue dwarf form (a seedling of the blue Douglas fir) is sometimes sold as *Pseudotsuga glauca* 'Fletcheri', though more often as *P.m.* 'Fletcheri'. It is an excellent blue leaderless dwarf conifer of congested growth, wider than high, and thickly set with relatively broad needles. In ten years it will grow to about 60cm (2ft) and a little more in width. It makes a marvellous, very dense colour band.

Finally – after a chapter in which we have see-sawed between conifers and grasses – something completely different: rue (*Ruta graveolens*), one of my least favourite plants, but useful for its colouring, which is a good blue. In the form 'Jackman's Blue' the colouring is even better: what you might call a dense blue. It has compound pinnate leaves that are unusual in being rounded at the tips and it builds itself up into piles of feathery foliage. It has a slowly-tillering habit, and seeds itself frantically all over the garden (the main reason why I don't like it). It needs to be grown in full sun, though it doesn't seem fussy about soil or drainage, and puts its best colour on if you cut it to ground level every spring, after which it will grow to about 60cm (2ft) in a season, and continue to tiller slowly. It is readily increased by cuttings.

So much for the blues. Treasure them and use them well, for they are few and far between, and have quite a different value in the garden from the greys or silvers.

CHAPTER EIGHT

Purples

Most of the other groups of colours we have looked at have been fairly homogenous in that each has covered a fairly clearly defined spectrum of colour. With the purples it is quite otherwise. The problem begins with the pseudo-latin epithet 'Purpureum', which is applied to all sorts of purplish colours. One could separate the plants under different headings and refer to those plants which are bronze, or foxy-red, or brown, or mahogany or mauve, but it would almost certainly create more problems than it would solve. At least the term purple has the merit of being in general usage and most of us understand, within ill-defined parameters, what we are talking about when we call a garden plant purple.

The popular name for *Atriplex hortensis* is orach, which has me puzzled, because I always thought the orach was an extinct precursor of the common cow; but maybe there is some oblique connection I have overlooked. What the vegetable orach looks like is a purple-leaved fat hen, which is virtually what it is. There are two forms around, though no one seems to have differentiated them by names: one has heavy purplish leaves, the other – far more desirable – has leaves, stems and even seed heads of a dark carmine. Its colouring is marvellous, and the quality of the fleshy, almost triangular leaves is first-rate, but there is just something about the carriage of the plant, about the disposition of the leaves on the stems, that is a little ungainly. It is one of those plants that comes readily from a handful of seeds and which, as soon as it comes up, rushes to a height of 2m (6ft), flowers, and then goes on seeding itself round your garden ever after. Provided that you are prepared to cut off all the seed heads except for a handful to take you over till next year, the plant is highly desirable. It will make a band of strong colour and will grow in any soil, preferably in sun.

Bugle, which in its wild form can be such a nuisance if you don't want it, has some beautiful cultivated forms which make dense carpets of ground cover. The most purple form *Ajuga reptans* 'Purpurea' has reddish-brown leaves that are very dark and glossy, of typical bugle shape, 2.5cm (1 in.) or so long and half as wide and rounded at the tip. The best colouring comes in autumn, the plant being greener and less noticeable in the summer. Many people grow bugle in shady woodland conditions, which is logical since it is a woodland wild plant, but in fact it grows into a more dense carpet, and colours better, if you grow it in sun.

The purple New Zealand sedges are not really purple at all but bronze, and if space permitted a separate chapter on the latter colour, no doubt that is where these would belong. A number of these sedges are carices, but not all sedges are carices. The tallest of the group is *Carex buchanani*, a marvellous plant with slender leaves that seem to be round in section. On young plants these stand very vertical: on older plants the outer ones arch outwards at the top, the tip of each leaf winding up in a little spiral curl like a pig's tail, only much more slender and elegant. The leaves are a brilliant foxy-red. The whole plant grows to about 60cm (2ft), and slowly forms a very dense clump. *C. comans* is the blonde weeping New Zealand sedge, and the 'Bronze Form' is identical in habit, but the leaves are a rather flat, heavy bronze colour. I like it for its flat heaviness in contrast to the brighter colours of the other New Zealand sedges: *C. flagellifera* is superficially rather similar to *C. comans* 'Bronze Form' but the leaves are longer and they are also flatter in section, especially on the upper surface. The colour is a rich chocolate brown, but bright, not flat and heavy. *C. petriei* is sometimes mistaken by the unobservant for *C. buchanani*, though really they are very different, *C. petriei* being a smaller, more spreading plant with broader leaves and a slightly less intense colour. It grows to about 30cm (1ft) in height and in time forms a dense clump about 30cm across at the base but spreading much wider because the outer leaves lie along the ground. It is an excellent colour-band plant, coming true to colour from seed, and seeding itself quite freely when well suited. The tiniest plant in the group is probably the finest if you can get it and, having got it, can keep it: not that it is particularly difficult to cultivate, but everyone else wants a piece of it too. This is *Carex uncinifolia*, a diminutive little sedge, with leaves no more than 5cm (2ins.) long, curling and twisting on the ground, scarcely making any height at all. The leaves are decidedly pink in spring, but then gradually turn to a pinkish-bronze as the season advances. It is the gem of the genus any day of the year, and is perfect in its miniature way for making a colour band next to some other miniature, such as *C. firma* 'Variegata' (try them together in a sink). All these sedges like a rich, fertile soil that never dries out, and are happiest in sun or semi-shade. Most of them come easily from seed, with only the slightest variation in colour, but you can very easily increase them by division in the spring: never divide them in the autumn.

The purple hazel, *Corylus maxima* 'Purpurea', was very popular a generation ago, but seems to have faded somewhat from favour. It is not a lovely plant, but it is an excellent colour; the leaves are just like those of the common hazel, very coarse, rounded, rough-toothed and rough to the touch, but larger and of a very intense deep purple – a colour similar to that of the darkest of purple beeches, though the leaf is matt, not glossy, which perhaps makes it look even darker. It will grow to 4.5–6.5m (15–20ft), with fairly erect stems and not too much spread, which makes it ideal for packing in in bold blocks of colour with other coarse-growing plants such as the colour-leaved elders. It is definitely not a plant to associate with others of greater refinement. You can keep its height in check by cutting it to ground level every couple of years (every year is too often) and some people claim that the leaf colour is more intense if you do this. It is useful in being a plant that will grow in any soil, fertile or infertile, well-drained or waterlogged, though it prefers a good fertile soil. It is readily increased by layering, or by division.

Cotinus coggygria (formerly *Rhus cotinus*) is a large shrub, growing as much as 4m (13ft) tall with an equal or even greater spread, rounded leaves that turn fiery scarlet and crimson flushed with yellow in autumn, and bearing, in mid-summer, huge open panicles of tiny flowers which stay on the bush, giving it the appearance of being wrapped in smoke. There are several purple-leaved forms. *C.c.* 'Atropurpureus' (now *purpureus*) has unexpectedly – in view of its name – green leaves. I mention it merely because you might buy it in winter expecting purple leaves. 'Foliis Purpureis' has plum-purple leaves, much the same colour as those of the purple plum, and not particularly attractive. 'Royal Purple' is a far better colour, probably the best in the group, the leaves being a rich, deep crimson-brown and seemingly almost lit from within. It is very similar to 'Notcutt's Variety': I can't tell the difference. 'Rubrifolius' is quite distinct with deep wine-red leaves, and again that quality of inner illumination, and is best planted so that it can be seen with the sun shining through rather than on the leaves. All have brilliant autumn colour, and all will grow in any fertile soil. They can be increased by summer cuttings or by layering.

The barberries are brilliant garden plants, good in leaf, flower and fruit. Several have fine purple leaves, but oddly enough they are all forms of *Berberis thunbergii*. The best-known of the purple-leaved forms is *B.t. atropurpurea*, a plant which grows about 1.6m (5ft) high and a little less across and has seemingly round leaves less than 2.5cm (1in.) long of a rich, reddish-purple which grows more and more intense as the season advances. *B.t.* 'Atropurpurea Nana' is a veritable dwarf of the same thing, growing to about 45cm (18ins.) high and very slow to get there. 'Rose Glow' differs in that the spring foliage is arrestingly mottled and splashed silver-pink and bright rose-pink, as are the young shoots, but the colouring fades and the plant settles down about mid-summer to looking almost indistinguishable from *B.t.* 'Atropurpurea'. All three are ideal for making deciduous colour bands, and 'Rose Glow' of course has the advantage of changing colour as the year goes by. All will stand clipping or trimming to keep them down to size and shapely, will grow in any fertile soil but will die very quickly if it becomes waterlogged. They come very readily from summer cuttings. If you do not enjoy weeding between the barberries, control the weeds with good thick mulches and a pre-emergent weed killer applied in December.

The cannas are among the most opulently lovely of all bedding plants, and there are very few other plants that have such large leaves of such good substance, texture and colour. *Canna indica* itself has huge oval banana-like leaves, deeply impressed with parallel veins. There are two purple forms: the better one is 'Egandale', whose leaves are a very rich deep bronze, a wonderfully strong colour; the other is 'Purpurea', whose leaves by comparison are merely tinted purple. 'Egandale' is so much the better of the two that it is well worth hunting down and treasuring. It looks lovely used with the softer-leaved grey or silver plants, and is always unexpected when used with plants with pale yellow foliage.

Heuchera americana is called alum root in America. Like so many of the *Saxifra-*

gaceae, these are plants with woody roots which slowly spread to form large clumps which then die out in the middle. It is really essential to split the clumps up every two or three years, this being simply a matter of lifting the plants, quite literally pulling them to pieces, and then replanting the pieces firmly and deeply (the stems should be put right in the ground with only the incipient rosette of leaves showing); this is more successfully done on one of those mild, muggy days one gets in autumn than in the biting, drying winds of spring. The leaves of all the species are beautifully marked, marbled and veined, so that they appear to be lightly variegated. The leaf of *Heuchera americana* is relatively large, a good 5cm (2ins.) across, very roughly shaped like the leaves of ivy, dark-green-flushed and veined coppery brown. With good cultivation in a deep, rich soil, well enriched with leaf-mould, new leaves are produced continuously throughout the year. The flowers are dainty spires of jade, but it is not for them that this plant is grown, though they do make the perfect match for the leaves. So good is the colouring of the leaves that the plant has sometimes been known and sold as *Heuchera rubescens* or as 'Purpurea', which makes a problem now that someone has come up with a real purple form, known merely as 'Purple Form' at the time of writing. The leaves, instead of being flushed and veined with coppery pink, are flushed and veined dark mahogany-red on a coppery-pink background. It is a far better colour than the typical plant, though I think you need to both appreciate either fully. Both make excellent dense leafy ground cover, and look particularly good grown with plants with glaucous foliage, especially spiky-leaved plants like pinks.

The iresines, for which I have never been able to trace a common or popular name, introduce a completely new colour to what gardeners call purple: it is nearer beetroot. In *Iresine herbstii* the leaves, which are about 7.5cm (3ins.) long, narrowly wedge-shaped, smooth and blunt-tipped, are what might be described as bright, light beetroot in colour. There is a form called 'Brilliantissima', which is indeed brilliant, in which the leaves are deep beetroot with bright red veins. There is a further species, *Iresine lindenii*, in which the leaves have pointed tips, and the colouring is deep beetroot. All three look excellent grown with grey-leaved plants. They are all tender foliage plants for bedding or dotting about the garden in groups, will grow about 60cm (2ft) high in a season, and come very readily from cuttings at almost any time in the growing season. Cuttings taken in October can be planted out the following May, when they will be about 13–15cm (5–6ins.) high. They need a little warmth to see them safely through winter. All are quite brilliant massed, either in bold blocks or broad colour bands. Some of the senecios, such as *Senecio maritima* would be an excellent foil.

The plants described below were called senecio till the botanists changed them to ligularia. They have changed it back again now, but if you want to buy one, stick to the name ligularia. Those senecios which have been moved into ligularia and back again all have showy yellow or orange daisy-like flowers, borne either in thin spikes or broad panicles. It is for their brilliant flowers, usually produced in mid-summer that they are mostly grown, but *Ligularia dentata* (= *clivorum*) is grown as much for its foliage. The leaves are huge, almost round, nearly 30cm (1ft) across with good cultivation, not purple but of a distinctly purple hue. It is at its most effective grown in bulk, by the hundred if you can, and, grown in that way, the huge leaves suppress any errant weeds that try to come between the plants. The flowers are held on stout stems (they need to be) which branch into large heads of vivid orange flowers in July and August. It is really a bog plant: grown in those conditions it achieves its greatest size, but it will grow well in any really deep, rich soil into which barrow-loads of manure have been worked, so long as it is in shade or semi-shade. The foot of a north wall, provided that you do not plant in the rain shadow, would be an excellent place for it. It is readily increased by division.

Perilla is one of those plants that have been around for years: the Victorians grew it, so did the Edwardians, and you can still find it today in seed lists, yet no one seems to be sure what its specific name is – though most people give it one. It is a tender foliage plant with large leaves, borne very densely. The leaves are deeply grooved and toothed, of a deep brownish-purple, and the same shape as (though more opulent than) those of the nettle to which it is closely related. It is one of those infuriating plants that you have to grow from seed every year, since it will not grow from cuttings. The seed is notoriously unreliable, and the plants are tricky to nurse through the seedling stage. But if you can get the seedlings to thrive, it is well worth the trouble. The plants will grow to between 60cm and 1m (2 and 3ft) in a season. The name now generally accepted is *Perilla atropurpurea*, usually qualified by some epithet such as 'Laciniata' or 'Nankinensis'. Don't worry: if you are offered seed of any perilla it will be purple.

The New Zealand flaxes are indispensable plants in the modern garden, with their fine architectural appearance and long, dramatic sword-shaped leaves. The typical plant, *Phormium tenax* will grow to 2.5m (8ft) or more, but none of the purple forms is so tall-growing, the biggest I have ever seen being about 1.6m (5ft) tall. There are in fact several purple forms, but *P.t.* 'Purpureum' is probably the best known. The leaves are the same sword shape, but a rich, glowing red-mahogany, the colouring being exceptionally even on all the leaves. There is a similar form, sometimes sold under the same name, with leaves about twice as wide but the colouring is less strong, a rather greyish purple. Since purple phormiums can be raised from seed, some variation in colour is inevitable. If you see a good colour form buy it: if it is growing in someone else's garden, try to obtain propagating material.

There are also some dwarf purple phormiums. The finest so far is an unnamed hybrid between *P.t.* 'Purpureum' and *Phormium colensoi*, a dwarf species. It grows to about 60cm (2ft), and the colouring is very similar to that of *P.t.* 'Purpureum'. 'Bronze Baby' is a real miniature, growing only about 30cm (1ft) high, with very narrow leaves and if anything a brighter colour. It is excellent for massing. I would never mass the larger-growing varieties, but only use them as accent plants rising out of a low carpet of some contrasting colour. There are several relatively recently introduced variants on the purple theme, including 'Dazzler', which is rich, deep bronze-purple overlaid with bands of bright crimson: it is very exciting. 'Maori Chief' has greenish-purple leaves with a brilliant red margin, while 'Maori Sunrise' has almost pinkish bands overlying the basic bronze colouring. I have not grown any of these recent introductions long enough to make any meaningful comment on their hardiness. All are easily increased by division.

There is really only one truly ever-purple shrub, and that is *Pittosporum tenuifolium* 'Purpureum'. It is just like the typical green-leaved *Pittosporum tenuifolium* in every way – its wavy-edged leaves, its habit of growth and its rate of growth – except that it is an exceedingly deep purple: much the same shade as *Fagus sylvatica* 'Riversii', only the colouring is deeper and the leaves are extremely shiny. It is breathtakingly beautiful. You need to give it a sheltered position in full sun, preferably with good drainage, and even then you will probably not manage to keep it very long: it is quite definitely more tender than the typical plant. I kept one for about eight years, and have heard of people here and there who have managed to keep them a little longer, but not much. It comes easily from cuttings, so it is always worth having a few coming on in case an extra bad winter carries yours away with it.

Of a completely different purple from anything else so far, but probably nearer the iresines than anything else, is an extraordinary purple-leaved plantain, *Plantago major rubrifolia*. It really is just a common little plantain with extremely broad leaves of a colour that I can only describe as a sort of beetroot-tinted violet-mauve. I don't know that I particularly like it, but it is worth knowing because it is such a unique colour. It comes very readily from seed, and if you only want a plant or two you simply pick the seedlings with the best colouring. If you want a mass of it you have to lower your standards a little, but you should still weed out the seedlings of inferior colour. It seems to grow quite happily in any soil, but definitely colours best in sun.

The purple plums are, on the whole, rather a dreary lot, their colouring being heavy, their overall appearance drab, their habit nothing exciting and their flowers of fleeting insignificance. But one or two are worse than the rest. The cherry plum is *Prunus cerasifera*, and the purple form usually seen around is the one that is still sometimes sold as 'Atropurpurea' (now correctly 'Pissardii'). The young foliage is dark red, gradually turning to plum-purple, and it is one of the few forms whose flowers are worthy of comment: they are pink in bud, opening white, and borne in extraordinary profusion in March and April. It makes a small, densely twiggy tree. Surprisingly, it earned itself an FCC, but that was in 1884, and there is a far wider variety of good coloured foliage plants available today: I doubt if it would get the same award now. It was discovered, in case the information in any way compensates for the drabness of the tree, some time before 1880 by a Monsieur Pissard, who was gardener to the Shah of Persia. *P.c.* 'Diversifolia' (= 'Aspleniifolia') is a sport of 'Pissardii', and a slightly inferior colour, but has leaves that vary from broadly oval to narrowly lance-shaped, and from almost toothless to roughly toothed or even lobed. It is curious, but little advance on 'Pissardii'. 'Nigra' is the clone with the deepest colouring, both leaves and stems being of the deepest vinous purple – almost black – but matt, and a very heavy, dead colour. It is exceptionally free-flowering, though still not sufficiently free to be accounted a good flowering tree. 'Vesuvius' is so similar that most people now think it the same clone. 'Rosea' is a disappointment: the leaves start out purplish and, just when you are expecting the colour to deepen, it fades to green. 'Trailblazer' also fades to green as the season advances, but it has the most brilliant foliage early in the year of any of the cherry plums, like good port held up to the light. Stunning, especially if kept clipped hard back every year or two so that it throws up long, vigorous growths. So far as I know all of these will grow just about anywhere. They make a good backdrop for other plants, so if you can use one your neighbour is growing, you can keep your own space for more exciting things.

Prunus x *cistena*, the purple-leaf sand cherry, is a shrub in much the same idiom, but rather better. It is a shrub, not a tree, growing slowly up to about 2m (6½ft) with rich red leaves (more like madeira in colour than port), the colour lasting right through the year – much brighter than any of the cherry plums, and a much better garden plant. You may find it being sold as *P.* 'Cistena', or even as *P. cerasifera* 'Cistena', but so long as it is shrubby you can be sure it is the same thing.

There are two purple-leaved rhododendrons, and the first of them, *Rhododendron* x 'Elizabeth Lockhart', is already proving popular. It is a branch sport of one of the *williamsianum* hybrids and has a leaf that owes much to *williamsianum*, being an elongated-heart shape and of a rich, vinous purple-bronze: the colour is very dark. It is the perfect purple rhododendron for massing in a small garden, though I have never seen anyone use it this way. Most often it is seen growing as a singleton, and as such it looks merely an oddity. Massed, you could see at once that the colouring and effect were deliberate. It tends to throw green reversions if you grow it in too much shade – what it needs is semi-shade. The other purple-leaved rhododendron is *R. ponticum*, and at present it seems to be known only as 'Purple Form' a wholly misleading name to those who think of plant colours as pertaining only to the flowers. It is a typical *ponticum* in every way – in leaf, in habit, in its freedom of seeding and in its vile purple flowers. The leaf is always more or less purple, but the colouring is at its richest in winter when it is a strong reddish-brownish mahogany colour. The colour is best if the plant is grown so that it gets rather too much than too little sun. It is as easy to grow as any other rhododendron, but do remember to take off the flowers otherwise you will have an abundance of green-leaved seedlings (and possibly poisonous honey as well).

The castor oil plant always looks so impressive when one sees well-grown specimens in public places that people are often tempted to try it in their own gardens. The green-leaved typical plant is *Ricinus communis*, and the purple-leaved form is 'Gibsonii'. The leaves are very large, about 30cm (1ft) across, and palmate (that is, in general outline rather like a maple leaf), architecturally very dramatic. It comes readily from seed, but do be careful when handling the plant: it is exceedingly poisonous in all its parts, which is one reason most people tend to steer clear of it.

The roses contain just one plant of outstanding foliage quality: *Rosa rubrifolia* (formerly known as *R. glauca* and *R. ferruginea*). It is a marvellous shrub, growing to about 2.5m (8ft) up and across, of dense, well-furnished habit, with reddish-violet shoots and leaves of the most beautiful dusky purple, a colour which it holds well through the whole season. Grown in shade, the colour is still good though paler, more a mixture of grey and mauve. It grows well in any fertile soil. The flowers are of a beautiful clear pink, and the large red fruits very showy.

Salvia is the sage, a culinary herb cultivated since times of the greatest antiquity. It is a low-growing, more or less shrubby semi-evergreen plant growing to about 60cm (2ft) in height and slowly spreading to perhaps 2m (6ft) across if given time. It needs to be grown in full sun, and will not tolerate poor drainage, though it should succeed on any fertile soil without extra fuss. The purple form, *Salvia officinalis* 'Purpurascens', has leaves and young shoots suffused a rich, mauvish purple, a quite distinct colour. It is a plant that tends to get tatty in time, and needs clipping across the top every now and again to keep it tidy. Provided that this is done, it is excellent in colour bands or blocks.

The purple elder, *Sambucus nigra* 'Purpurea', is by contrast a most unexciting plant whose colouring is not distinctive at all: it is somehow merely dark. In fact, when you look closely, the leaves are quite a good purple in spring, and the darkness is what is left on the leaf as the intensity of the colouring fades during summer. It is useful as a dark backdrop to something showy, but scarcely a plant that one would go out of one's way to use on its own. It resembles the common elder in every way except for the darkness of the leaves.

There are two or three little saxifrages around with purplish leaves, and the best of them are among the finest of all purple-leaved plants. The one for which I have a great weakness is *Saxifraga cuscutiformis*, which is very similar in general appearance and habit to *S. stolonifera* with evergreen, rounded leaves about 5cm (a couple of inches) across, of a reddish purple with green veins and bright red undersides. It throws out bright red thread-like runners in all directions, producing little plantlets at their tips. It is from these threads that it gets its name since they are very similar in appearance to the stems of the dodder, *Cuscuta*, a malingering parasite of the worst sort. It is a charming little saxifrage to run about under evergreen shrubs where it will happily make a carpet. It is not wholly frost hardy, and in severe winters tends to get killed back to those plants that are best sheltered by overhead shrubs.

Saxifraga fortunei is in quite a different class. It is a first-rate garden plant, both in foliage and flower. It is a clump-forming deciduous perennial with big, bold, rounded leaves as much as 7.5cm (3ins.) across, of a rich green on top and bright red underneath. 'Wada's Form', which I would consider the finest, has rich mahogany leaves, redder on the underside than on top, and red flower stalks. The flowers, like those of the typical plant, are pure white, and make a stunning contrast with the foliage. It is one of the last plants to flower, and one of the most sumptuous. There is also a form in commerce called simply *Saxifraga fortunei rubra*, whose leaves are not quite so dark as those of 'Wada's Form' but are still of a very good reddish mahogany. All these saxifrages are plants for cool, moist woodland conditions (which you can with skill, reproduce at the foot of a north wall), and grow most vigorously given a soil well-enriched with leaf-mould and top-dressed annually with the same.

Setcreasea purpurea is one of the few plants that really is true purple, not horticultural purple, and it creates the most stunning effects when massed among yuccas or agaves needing the same cultural conditions. It has thick, fleshy, purple leaves, usually 10–13 cm (4–5ins.) long, purple stems and a prostrate habit. In general it is rather like a tradescantia, but finer. You probably know it well as a house plant (it is often seen on windowsills) but have probably never thought of using it in the garden. It is not so frost tender as you might expect and, since it is very easily propagated from cuttings taken at almost any time, is something you can readily try in the garden. It needs to be grown in full sun with perfect drainage, and a scattering of freshly-fallen leaves should be put over it in autumn. Given a start of a couple of mild winters, it should romp away, and if it does it will make about the most stunningly coloured patch in the garden. The colour is so unique that, if you really want a multi-coloured garden, it is worth any amount of effort to get established.

After that you might expect almost anything else to come as something of a let-down. In fact, *Tellima grandflora* 'Purpurea' (= 'Rubra') is so different that it is not a disappointment at all. This is a tufted, more or less evergreen perennial that makes excellent ground cover in semi-shade. The leaves are about 6cm (2½ins.) long and rather squarely heart-shaped with green veins and bronze-brown patches between the veins. The colour is at its best in late summer and through the autumn. The plant usually grown as the type is similarly coloured, but less so, and in botanical collections you will find a form grown which is completely green-leaved: it is this, rather than the bronze-leaved form, that is the rare one. The flowers are jade, borne on a slender spike, and quite pretty. It is at its most effective massed and, though it will endure in poor conditions, thrives in good soils.

The genus *Uncinia* contains two of the most brightly coloured New Zealand sedges imaginable. *Uncinia unciniata* is usually the easier to get hold of, and might well be confused with *Carex petriei*: it is very similar in leaf, habit and colouring, being a bright foxy red – but it is rather more tender. Far more brilliant is *Uncinia egmontiana*, which is quite the most richly coloured of all the New Zealand sedges. This is a rich red-brown, the red being most noticeable in winter, while the summer colour is similar to that of *Uncinia unciniata* but very much more chocolate-brown. Both come easily from seed and just as easily from division, and enjoy a deep, rich and somewhat moist soil, a position in full sun, and shelter from surrounding or even overhanging shrubs. They are excellent plants for colour bands, and reliable provided that you meet their cultural requirements.

Weigela florida 'Purpurea' (along with *Sambucus nigra* 'Purpurea') is among the dullest of purple plants, of use only as a background for it is of little merit in itself. The colour is a dusky, smoky-brownish shade on a matt leaf, and the plant forms a dense, well-rounded and well-furnished bush up to about 2.5m (8ft) high and across. It will grow in any fertile soil but preferably in sun or what little colour it has will fade. It is a useful plant in a rather negative way: if you can put something brighter in front of it, it is worth having. It is certainly not worth growing in its own right.

Viola labradorica is a name that tells you nothing about what the plant looks like. It comes from Labrador, which makes it very hardy. What it is grown for is the rich, vinous purple of its leaves, so dark that they are almost black, but of typical violet size and shape (the flowers are typical violet flowers too). It is a marvellous colour for massing, completely evergreen and demanding only a little leaf-mould mixed in with the soil. I have always used it in semi-shade, but it seems only slightly unhappy with a lot more sun. It spreads by overground as well as underground stems, and seeds itself freely. It is excellent under deciduous shrubs or as a ground cover in a belt or band of strong-growing ferns.

The last of my purples is the first to be a climber, though I much prefer to use it sprawling flat on the ground. It is a purple form of the grape vine, *Vitis vinifera* 'Purpurea', and a typical grape vine in every way except for the leaf colour. The leaves come through in spring a rich claret colour and from then on become an ever deeper purple as summer advances. It looks lovely as a carpet beneath the weeping silver pear, *Pyrus salicifolius* 'Pendula', being just the right shade to complement it, and also with the great majority of those silver-leaved plants that are not too white a silver. It colours best in full sun and, perhaps surprisingly, does not seem too fussy about soil. It is very readily increased by layering, or by internodal cuttings.

The purples, as you can now judge for yourself, are not purples at all but browns and bronzes, with the odd violet or deep mauve here and there. This may seem misleading, but it is the accepted horticultural convention. If you want anything darker than the purples, the only colour left is black.

CHAPTER NINE

Black

There are two plants which, to all intents and purposes, appear to be black, and a knowledge of both is indispensable to anyone with designs on a multi-coloured garden. They can be used in ways no other plant could be used: for example, you can use them in thin, black lines to separate two colour bands, or to ring round a singularly interesting or special colour grouping; or you can use them planted in egg-shaped patches to give the illusion of permanent shadows under trees (with the thin end of the egg pierced by the trunk); or you can use them to make a dark corner even darker.

The first of these seemingly black plants is a coleus, *C.* 'Roi des Noires', and as coleus go, it is a very good garden plant. The coleus with which most of us are familiar are the *C.* x *blumei* hybrids with large leaves somewhat resembling in shape and texture, and the toothing of their margins, the leaves of common stinging nettles, but brilliantly coloured in reds, yellows and oranges often splotched and splashed but with subtle touches too – the marginal teeth are often a different colour from the rest of the leaf or marked with a curious sort of hem-stitching. 'Roi des Noires' has a smaller leaf than most of these, and makes a good bushy plant without one's having to spend a lot of time pinching it out to make it assume this habit: it also seems less inclined to run to flower than its more garish brethren. It is very readily propagated from cuttings at almost any time in the growing season, but if you take your cuttings about the end of August, they will make plants of sufficient size and vigour to put on a good show once you set them out the following July. In the appropriate conditions they can be relied upon to make neat plants about 50cm (1⅔ft) each way in a season. Your problem, of course, is getting your first plant of 'Roi des Noires' from which to take the cuttings to produce the plants to mass. It is in commerce, and with patience and perseverance you will find it if you really want it.

The other black-leaved plant is a hardy perennial, which makes it even more useful in the multi-coloured garden. This is *Ophiopogon planiscarpus* 'Kogurka' (usually sold as *O.p.* 'Nigrescens'), a tufted grass-like plant (in fact a member of the *Liliaceae*), with leaves about 15cm (6ins.) long and 6mm (¼in.) wide, all springing from a central point and splaying out in the same vertical plane. It spreads steadily (at times one could wish it spread faster) by means of stolons, so that a single plant in time builds up into a dense clump of black leaves, and groups of plants readily intermingle making a thick, dense turf. The leaves are the blackest that I know of on any plant – far blacker than those of *C.* 'Roi des Noires' which only seem that colour until you compare them with this ophiopogon, when you realize that the leaves of 'Roi des Noires' are really only an extremely deep mauve. The leaves of the ophiopogon are at their blackest when slightly damp and shining with the moisture on them. It is a plant that grows best in deep, rich soil with plenty of humus and preferably a little shade, and can readily be increased by detaching proles and either planting these where needed or potting them up first. The curious black seeds also afford a means of propagation, though only about 40 per cent of the seedlings come black.

The odd thing about black-leaved plants is that, desirable though they may seem, they can be difficult to place in the garden: the colouring is just so strong. Large areas of black have a tendency to draw the eye to them, and a solution to this problem is to place them close to other plants of strong colouring, so that what the eye takes in is not just the blackness but the whole combination of colours. Black always looks good with greys, and with the stronger blues, but is probably at its best when growing next to the foxier reds in the spectrum, *Uncinia egmontiana*, for example.

So there you have it. I have surveyed plants with coloured leaves, if not from A to Z at least from white through creams and yellows to blues, browns, purples and blacks. But they are only my own selection of those that I know to be well suited to multi-coloured gardening. There are more, far more that I have not mentioned which you can find if you diligently seek them out, not forgetting the end purpose of the multi-coloured garden.

CHAPTER TEN

Working Plans

If you are not in the habit of planning gardens, the thought of sitting down in front of a blank sheet of paper and planning your own must be pretty daunting. Where do you begin? Do you start by just sketching in a curl or curve, and then working that into a series of interlocking patterns, for which you then have to find plants? Or do you start with a list of plants that you would like to grow, and then try to find shapes to contain them? Or do you start with some abstract idea that it is all going to be beautiful and get stuck there?

After all, most people's gardens are not planned at all: they just happen. Someone gives you a rooted cutting of chaenomeles, and someone else gives you some hypericum, and a neighbour gives you some old lupins he was going to throw away anyway, but giving them to you saves him the trouble. Inevitably the result is a promiscuous muddle: innate good taste may guide you to achieve some felicitous effects, but really you are leaving too much to chance.

On the whole the most practical way of approaching the planning of a garden is to look on the garden as a problem that has to be solved. Your first problems are your climate, the type of soil you have, whether it is acid or alkaline, waterlogged or pure sand. Your second group of problems are the things you need to accommodate in the garden. Do you need a shed in which to keep the mower? Are you going to have a compost area, a bonfire area, a propagating area? Are you going to have a greenhouse? What about the clothes line? Will you have a patio, a pond, a rock garden, or all three?

If you make a list of those practical necessities that must be included in your garden, you are already starting to plan it. You are beginning to impose order on chaos, which is what design is all about. Your greenhouse will have to be in full sun. Which almost certainly means that there are certain parts of the garden which would be unsuitable. So you can scribble a rough rectangle to represent your garden, and draw a little rectangle where you think the greenhouse might be placed. If you need a propagating area, it is best near the greenhouse, so you can draw that in. You don't want the compost area too near the house, nor too far from it, so that limits where you can put that. Already, you see, the garden is starting to take on some shape, because having determined where you are going to put, for example, the compost area, you can decide how you are going to screen it. So you can draw a bold circle round that, and colour it yellow: there are about fifty different yellow conifers you could use as a screen. Having planned a yellow colour patch, you need something blue in front of it and perhaps orange or brown would look good in front of that, and so on. Gradually a plan evolves: perhaps not *the* plan, but one which you can revise and redraw till you feel it is right.

If you work on tracing paper, it is no problem redrawing plan after plan. Always date your plans, so that you know which is the most recent, or number them.

At this stage one is usually working merely in blocks of colour – making patterns. But it is useful even at this juncture to write in not merely the colour, but also the height to which you want the plant to grow. Round the compost area perhaps you want a band of yellow growing to 1.6m (5ft) and in front of that an area of blue to 1m (3ft). If you then start listing those plants which are blue and grow to 1m, you will find that there is only a limited number which fills the bill. Should you switch from thinking about colour to considering contrasts in foliage type, you will find that that will probably exclude at least half of the plants you have already listed. If, for example, you have a band of yellow conifers round the compost area, and you have specified an area of blue 1m in front of it, you want the blue plants to have a different type of foliage from the yellow conifer. Rue, *Ruta graveolens* 'Jackman's Blue', would fit the bill, both for blueness and for contrast in foliage type.

So you need to think not only of contrasting or complementary colours, but also of contrasting or complementary foliage types. If you have a large leaf (for example, *Magnolia grandiflora*), put something with a small leaf next to it (such as *Azara microphylla*); if you have a glossy leaf (say, *Camellia japonica*), put a plant with a matt leaf next to it (perhaps *Trachystemon orientale*); if you have a spiky leaf (*Yucca filamentosa*), put a plant with a rounded leaf (*Bergenia cordifolia*) next to that. Contrast the ferniness of a fern such as *Polystichum setiferum* 'Divisilobum' with the texture of a grass. By the time you have run through the various permutations of matt and glossy, large and small, spiky or rounded, feather or fluffy, as well as the variations in colour, you will find that you have eliminated even more plants and your choice for a particular colour may be down to a mere handful.

All this may seem at first to be a matter of multiplying problems. But planning any garden is a matter of solving problems, and the way in which those problems are solved is by the elimination of possibilities. The fact that you adore that yellow conifer (1.6m/5ft) with which you are going to hide your compost area limits the choice of colours and size you can put in front of it (blue, 1m/3ft). The fact that the yellow conifer will shade the blue plant limits the choice of plants for that position: and so on.

If you use a grey- or silver-leafed plant you will very probably have to improve the drainage, and having done that you cannot then grow a bog plant next to it (though there are grey- and silver-leafed plants that can be grown in a boggy position).

In a way you may see this planning by elimination as negative. What you are doing is saying, 'I can't grow this because the climate is too cold; I can't grow that because my soil is too alkaline; I can't grow that because it doesn't like heavy clay; I can't grow that because it is too tall; I can't grow that because the leaf is too large (or too round or too pointed).' The positive side of planning by elimination is that at the end of the day you finish up with a list of perhaps five or ten plants that not only grow to the right height, have the right spread, the right type of leaf and so on, but also can be relied on to grow well where you want them.

Then again, looking at the garden as a whole, it helps to avoid filling it with shrub-shaped shrubs. It is far better deliberately to use a mound-shaped plant, like a weeping willow, with a vertical accent, such as a Lombardy poplar, behind it. Always be aware of the form of the plants you are using, as well as their colour and texture and leaf size and shape, and remember the importance of avoiding sameness. A garden that has too many vertical accents is unrestful; but so is a garden full of horizontal emphasis. You need, to satisfy the senses, the upright and the prostrate, the rounded and the vase-shaped, plants of soft as well as of well-defined outline. They all have their place. It is merely a matter of balance and personal taste.

However, you could understand all these principles, and follow them, and still not come up with a design for a wholly satisfactory garden. Some underlying concept is essential to give the design cohesion, and that must in some way relate to what you expect from your garden. To reach such an understanding you need to define to yourself what a garden is and what you expect from it. Basically a garden is that piece or parcel of land that surrounds your house and goes with it, and you grow plants in it, don't you? But why do you grow them? Because other people do? Or is a garden merely there so that you have somewhere to dry the washing, sunbathe or have a barbecue?

The purpose of a garden is to rest the mind and please the senses. Design with that in mind and you will not go far wrong.

Let's now work through an example or two. Take the back garden of a house standing on just over 0.2 hectares (½ acre) of ground (Fig. 5). The site is level and featureless – just as the builder left it. The soil can be acid or alkaline, the choice is yours. Since most back gardens are about three-quarters of the land area available, this is just over three-quarters of ½ acre. Let's keep the open centre: most people like their gardens designed that way, and really none of the other options has much to commend it. In this case, rather than having the usual painter's palette-shaped green lawn in the open centre, we have a rather longer one, snaking through the multi-coloured conifers, its shape contributing to the overall pattern of curves and contours.

The first move is to pick the high points of the garden: we will have one on the left, one in the top right-hand corner, and one about a third of the way down from the top right-hand corner. Since blue firs are always popular, let's have a group of *Picea pungens* 'Thomsen' as the high point on the left. This fir seems to me to have the clearest, cleanest blue of the bunch; 'Koster' is an older and more familiar variety; and 'Moerhemii', a similarly well-tried and tested variety. All are good. Now, with a

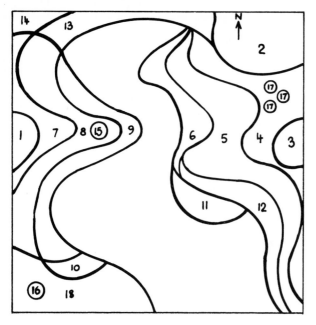

FIGURE 5
Key
1 *Picea pungens* 'Thomsen'
2 *Chamaecyparis lawsoniana* 'Winston Churchill'
3 *Cupressus macrocarpa* 'Donard Gold'
4 *Cryptomeria japonica* 'Elegans'
5 *Juniperus scopulorum* 'Blue Heaven'
6 *Microbiota decussata*
7 *Pinus sylvestris* 'Aurea'
8 *Juniperus communis* 'Depressa Aurea'
9 *Juniperus horizantalis* 'Bar Harbour'
10 *Thuja orientalis* 'Juniperoides'
11 *Thujopsis dolabrata* 'Nana'
12 *Cham. laws.* 'Albovariegata'
13 *Thuja occidentalis* 'Rheingold'
14 *Abies concolor* 'Compacta'
15 *Juniperus chinensis* 'Aurea'
16 *Cham. laws.* 'Silver Queen'
17 *Cupressus sempervirens* 'Cost of Living'
18 *Pseudotsuga menziesii* 'Fletcheri'

blue as brilliant as 'Thomsen' we need something in complete contrast in front of it – a contrast of both foliage and colour. *Pinus sylvestris* 'Aurea' provides both. It is a pale green throughout summer, but as the weather turns cold it gradually becomes a brilliant rich yellow, which lasts through into spring. We do not need height here, so instead of letting it grow up on a single leader, let's pinch out the terminal bud and keep pinching out terminal buds until we get a spreading bush. This conifer is far more effective grown this way: the habit is compact and the colour much more apparent.

To balance this block of colour we need to plant something fairly substantial in the top right-hand corner. I would go for *Chamaecyparis lawsoniana* 'Winston Churchill', to my mind quite the best of the golden lawsons. Do not be put off if the plants you buy arrive a less brilliant yellow than you were hoping for: this often happens when they have grown in polytunnels or other shaded structures. 'Winston Churchill' is a plant that needs full sun to show its golden paces at their best, and the planting needs to be thick and dense. It is a very clear gold; we therefore need a contrasting yellow in the group one-third of the way down on the right. I would suggest *Cupressus macrocarpa* 'Donard Gold'. This is a complete contrast in habit and foliage: instead of the flattened spreading sprays of 'Winston Churchill', 'Donard Gold' has spiky little twiglets of foliage and a relatively narrow and upright habit – not so upright as 'Gold Crest', which is an inferior colour (but popular with nurserymen because it is easier to propagate) – but still much more upright than

'Winston Churchill'. Again, the plants need to be packed in fairly tightly to make a dense mass of golden foliage.

Having assembled two of the finest yellow conifers commerce can offer, we again need something to show them off. Let's try *Cryptomeria japonica* 'Elegans', which is a soft green in summer, with non-prickly foliage which turns purplish-bronze in winter, but it really is too big a grower in comparison with the plants which it is supposed to complement. One has to prune it judiciously from time to time to keep it to size, but it responds well to such treatment.

A point worth noting in passing is that, although we have only discussed four plants so far, two of these four change colour from summer to winter. From the point of view of the multi-coloured concept, such plants are doubly valuable and at their most exciting when planted so that the eye can see both colours at both seasons. Each does the work of two plants while occupying the space of one.

We now need to put a colour band in front of an area that is going to be a relatively light green in summer and a rich bronze in winter. Blue is not only the obvious contrast for bronze; it is also one of the best. Blue and green are not so dramatic, but if the blue is chosen with care, the combination can be quiet and restful. One also needs a fairly spreading conifer here; one is, after all, beginning to come down towards the lawn. That factor would make the choice of something like *Juniperus virginiana* 'Grey Owl' the obvious one. But there is a more exciting possibility, though it means a little more work for the gardener, and that is to use a juniper with a much richer colour, such as *Juniperus scopulorum* 'Blue Heaven'. The problem is that, like all the scopulorums, it wants to go up: we want it to go out. In fact it will, and quite readily, provided you take the heart out of it while it is still a young plant, and do not subsequently allow it go up. You may have to work on it for a year or two, but it is well worth the trouble.

'Blue Heaven' remains a fairly constant colour all year through. One could therefore contrast it either with another plant that is constant in colour the whole year through, or with something that changes from summer to winter, sandwiching it in, as it were. In fact, the best bet is to take both options, planting one constant-colour conifer along one part of the colour band and a vari-coloured conifer along the other part. For the vari-coloured conifer I would go for *Microbiota decussata*. It is strange that a conifer as desirable as this should have been unknown to us and neglected for so long, especially as it is not merely hardy but fully capable of withstanding the very worst that our winters can do to it. It is, after all, a native of Siberia. It is slow-growing, never more than 30cm (1ft) high, spreading out over the ground and producing fans of rich green ferny foliage which changes to a burning orange-bronze in winter. And it is at its best when massed, one plant readily flowing into the next, making a continuous carpet that looks as though it were all one plant.

The other half of the colour band to go in front of 'Blue Heaven' is something of a problem. We are going to use a white-variegated conifer, and that in itself presents difficulties. The reason for using a white-variegated conifer is quite simply to extend the range of colours in the garden. But there are very few conifers indeed which are an even white in the way in which the golds or the blues are an even colour. The one or two that are, like *Chamaecyparis pisifera* 'Snow' and *Cryptomeria japonica* 'Knaptonensis', are none too easy to grow satisfactorily, which of course renders them useless for massing, and, to make matters worse, they tend to scorch in sun, burn in wind and wither in cold weather. This leaves those conifers which are flecked or blotched with white, though even they can present problems. Few are particularly constant in their variegation: all too often you will find that one part of the plant is heavily variegated and the rest of it bears relatively little variegation, or else you get the odd branch that will go completely white, while the rest are only lightly flecked. The one I would go for, quite one of the best of the bunch, is *Chamaecyparis lawsoniana* 'Albovariegata'. It is quite exceptionally evenly variegated, about half the total area being white-variegated, and it seems not to scorch or burn. Moreover, it has a compact, spreading habit and is slow-growing, reaching perhaps 1m (3ft) in height after ten years' growth. I can think of no other white-variegated conifer so well suited to massing. This one is even tolerant of a little abuse. It will respond well to a little clipping, if needed to keep it down to size.

The reason, incidentally, for having the white conifer near the house is that white is a colour that always looks nearer to you than it actually is. If you put it at the top of the garden, it will bring the garden in, making it seem smaller. By putting it close to the house this closing effect is minimized.

Since we have split the colour band in front of 'Blue Heaven', using both *Microbiota decussata* and *Chamaecyparis lawsoniana* 'Albovariegata', we need to link that split by a further small curve of colour. In this case *Thujopsis dolabrata* 'Nana' would make an ideal linking plant. It is quite different in foliage from either of the other two plants, and changes from a good mid-green in summer to a rich bronze in winter. The colour is lighter and brighter than that of *Microbiota decussata* and the foliage is held in more or less erect sprays, as compared with the rather flattened sprays of the *Microbiota*.

Going back to the left-hand side of the garden, where we already have *Picea pungens* 'Thomsen' and *Pinus sylvestris* 'Aurea', we need a further two colour bands to complete the picture. In front of the *Pinus sylvestris* 'Aurea' I would plant a band of *Juniperus communis* 'Depressa Aurea' which is to my mind the best of the junipers which turn yellow in winter, though *Juniperus media* 'Old Gold' runs a close second. There are several other good ones, but this is lower-growing than most of them, and the winter colour is particularly fine. It is a somewhat bronzy yellow which goes well with the clear bright yellow of the pine behind it. The summer colour is a slightly greyish green. In front of that we need a plant that is very low-growing indeed to take the levels down to the lawn. Again I would choose a juniper, partly because the different foliages to be found among the junipers is fascinating in itself, but also because there are few better coniferous carpeters than the prostrate junipers. I think the one to go for here is *Juniperus horizantalis* 'Bar Harbour', an older introduction but still one of the most distinct. It is, in any case, a winning plant, with rather finer needles than most of the junipers and very flexible stems that trail flat along the ground or follow the contours of rocks, while the side branches are held somewhat upswept, so that the overall effect is of a deep-pile carpet. The foliage in summer is a similar grey-green to that of the juniper in the colour band behind it, but its winter colour is quite different: it is a deep rich mauve.

Once again we have broken the continuity of a colour band and so need a linking filler. I think that here I would use *Thuja orientalis* 'Juniperoides', a thuja with foliage remarkably like that of a juniper. What is more interesting from the colour point of view is that the winter colour is quite remarkably like that of the prostrate juniper next to which it will be planted. It is quite definitely mauve in winter – though probably a bluer mauve than the juniper. In summer the leaves are a soft blue-green. It is altogether an excellent complement to the juniper, the more so in that most people on first meeting it would think that it was one anyway, so like a juniper's are the needles. The only problem with this plant is that it grows a little taller than is ideal in this position – ultimately about 2m (6½ft), but it can be kept in check by trimming.

Behind this patch of 'Juniperoides', we need a patch of contrasting blue, a little taller than the two junipers just discussed. A highly desirable plant for this position would be *Pseudotsuga menziesii* 'Fletcheri', a curious form of the Douglas fir which never makes a leader and which consequently grows into a semi-dwarf flat-topped bush, invariably wider than high. It is not the bluest of blue conifers, but somehow has a quality of blue that makes up for that. The blue is certainly a complete contrast to any of the other blues being used in this garden. To finish off the bottom left-hand corner of the garden, we are going to have a single specimen conifer, quite a large-grower at that: *Chamaecyparis lawsoniana* 'Silver Queen'. This is ultimately a tall and relatively narrow conical tree of typical lawson growth and habit, but in this case of a curious whitish colour: I can think of no other conifer that is quite this shade. Again, because it is white or at least whitish it is being grown near the house. It would look completely wrong at the other end of the garden. Besides, we have other plans for that.

The far end of the garden is dominated by a single colour band stretching right across the fence or boundary. That single colour band is made up of the indescrib-ably horrible *Thuja occidentalis* 'Rheingold'. 'Rheingold' is at all seasons the most horrifically shocking colour imaginable in a conifer. It is a sort of vibrant orange-gold that can be relied on to 'sock it to you' every time you see it. Even when you have lived with it for years, it still has this effect. The colour is so strong that it will dominate even among the brilliant blues and yellows in other parts of the garden. Even when you look away from massed 'Rheingold', you are still inescapably aware that it is there. To soften the blow a little, it is perhaps wise to put a plant of a sophisticated colour next to it, and for this reason the top left-hand corner is of a pure clean silver – almost platinum – to go with the vulgarity of gold. Oddly enough, the two complement each other really rather well.

Now we need to go back to where the colour band of *Juniperus communis* 'Depressa Aurea' bulges out to its furthest extent. At the thickest point of this bulge we need a specimen conifer that will not only complement the juniper out of which it rises, but also the backdrop against which the eye will see it – the 'Rheingold'. It needs to be a tall, narrow conifer to break up the low, flat, horizontal nature of the colour bands, and preferably a yellow to contrast with the blue dominants on this side of the garden. There are two choices: there is the very tall and narrow *Cupressus sempervirens* 'Swane's Gold', a slow-growing plant of a good, rich yellow; or there is *Juniperus chinensis* 'Aurea', which is probably preferable here. It is a naturally narrow-growing conifer, of a pale creamy yellow turning to a richer yellow in summer. The colour is quite unlike that of any other yellow conifer, and it is this that makes it so ideal as a specimen. It is a quality plant of the first water, somewhat rare, and that too is exactly what one wants in a specimen.

Finally, there is a group of three tall and narrow specimen conifers to go in the top right-hand corner between the 'Winston Churchill' and 'Donard Gold'. The first tall narrow conifer that springs to mind is, I suppose, *Juniperus virginiana* var. *scopulorum* 'Skyrocket'. The fact that it is probably the most widely planted tall, narrow specimen conifer is a sufficient deterrent to planting it here (not that there is anything against using plants merely because they are very popular and everyone else has them: the point is that if everyone else has them, you can enjoy them in other people's gardens, and plant something a little more unusual in your own). In this case I would break up the two big clumps of yellow by using a green conifer, but one of a singularly dark, almost sinister green, *Cupressus sempervirens* 'Cost of Living' – so called, its raisers claim, because, like the cost of living, it just keeps on going up and up and up: and it really does. It is a quite remarkably narrow clone of the Italian cypress and, even more in its favour, it is extremely hardy – unlike most *Cupressus sempervirens*.

That of course only leaves you with a smooth green lawn in the middle to mow, unless you would like to add in a couple of colour bands of your own. You could use *Erica carnea* 'Anne Sparkes', which goes a bright orange in winter, and the bright yellow *Erica vagans* 'Valerie Proudley', the best of the yellows, just for starters. Try them at the front of one of the low-growing coniferous colour bands, and mow them with a hover mower: once established they will stand such treatment well.

A garden like this is, of course, very easy to maintain once made. There is little to do to it except enjoy it. This is all right if all you want from a garden is a picture to look at out of a window, but for most gardeners it is not enough.

So let's have a water garden. By a water garden I mean an area that contains both an open surface of water (complete with gold fish, if they take your fancy) and areas of relative degrees of bogginess. If you're going to have a wet area, keep it all in one place. After all, every good gardener learns from what happens in the wild, and one of the realities of the natural world is that ponds do not just suddenly happen in the middle of, for example, your lawn or herbaceous border. They occur in such a way that they are invariably surrounded by a wet or boggy area, and there is a gradation from normal soil to wet soil to soil that is submerged in winter to soil that is permanently under water. So let's try to arrange for all those things to happen in roughly that sequence in a multi-coloured style.

Start with the pond itself – the area of clear surface water. Like everything else in the multi-coloured garden, it should be made up of interlocking curves and curls. The shape is too difficult to describe in plain English without resorting to complex mathematics and algebraic calculations, so we'll take the short cut and use a diagram (Fig. 6A) – that is the shape of your pond. On to that complicated series of curves, the bog areas interlock (Fig. 6B), and the whole area is then tied together with a further, outer band of coloured curves, these being more simple than the curves and curls of the pond or bog area (Fig. 6C, overleaf).

If you're going to have a bog garden, you've got to grow gunnera: a bog garden without gunnera would be like a sitting-room with nothing to sit on. Besides, there is no other plant you can grow out of doors in the cool to temperate regions of the world that can match its sheer breathtaking magnificence, those vast leaves – far, far larger than the leaves of any other hardy plant – riding on their tall, red-prickled stems, and those curious, almost revolting flower spikes. The gunnera, of course, is *Gunnera manicata*. In an ideal situation, such as we have for it here, it will send up leaves that will tower above your head, borne on petioles perhaps 3m (10ft) or more tall, and it will spread at least as much. If you haven't the room for something on this

FIGURE 6A
The pond only

FIGURE 6B
The pond with bog areas added

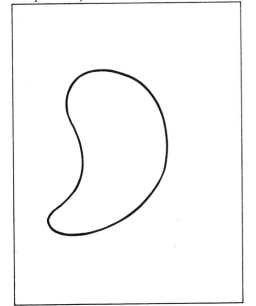

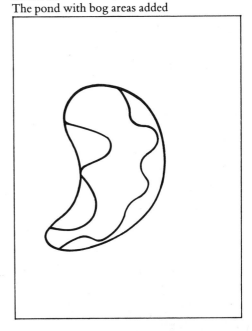

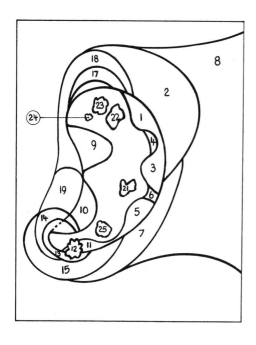

FIGURE 6C
1 *Gunnera manicata*
2 *Miscanthus sinensis* or *M. s.* 'Variegata'
3 *Scirpus* 'Albescens'
4 *Filipendula ulmaria* 'Aurea'
5 *Lobelia cardinalis*
6 *Phormium* 'Maori Maiden'
7 *Phragmites australis* 'Variegata'
8 *Cotinus coggygria* 'Royal Purple'
9 *Glycera maxima* 'Variegata'
10 *Azolla foliculoides*
11 *Helxine soleiroli* 'Aureus'
12 *Acer palmatum* 'Dissectum Atropurpureum'
13 *Ophiopogon planiscarpus* 'Nigrescens'
14 *Carex stricta* 'Aurea'
15 *Cupressus macrocarpa* 'Gold Spreader'
16 *Acorus calamus* 'Variegatus'
17 *Hosta fortunei* 'Aurea'
18 *Hosta sieboldiana* 'Elegans'
19 *Acaena saccaticupula*
20 *Zantedeschia aethiopica* 'Crowborough'
21 *Polypodium vulgare* 'Cristata'
22 *Arundinaria variegata* 'Dwarf Form'
23 *Pinus mugo* 'Ophir'
24 *Uncinia egmontiana*
25 Rock

scale, there is *Gunnera chilense*, which is a somewhat smaller version, but in the same idiom. It grows to perhaps 2m (6½ft) in the fullness of time. If, however, you are forced by circumstances to think on the smallest scale, and you still want to grow gunnera, try *Gunnera magellanica*, probably the most easily obtained of a number of dwarf species. This one has leaves about 5cm (2ins.) across, borne on stems perhaps barely 5cm tall, and it runs rapidly over the surface of the ground. It is really delightful.

Now, if you're going to grow gunnera you have got to have some shelter. So, to the north-west of it, plant the large, clump-forming grass, *Miscanthus sinensis* 'Variegata'. This is a grass that will grow, given good conditions, to nearly 3m (10ft), and it has long, narrow leaves springing alternately from the culms, each leaf dramatically striped with white. Even more exciting, though you need a mild climate to grow it successfully, is *Arundo donax* 'Variegata', which will grow well over 3m and has leaves over 5cm (2ins.) broad, each with a broad white stripe along the margin and some lesser striping within the leaf blade. It would be my first choice in such a position, but experience has proved it too tender to be relied upon.

Next to the gunnera, in front of it as you look from the house, you again need something rather light, but different from the miscanthus. An almost ideal plant here would be *Scirpus* 'Albescens', a curious reed with typical tall, straight, leafless stems, often wholly bleached white but showing an occasional vertical green stripe. It will in time form a large clump, but for effect it may be better to plant several in the first place. The very strong vertical accent is just perfect in front of the rounded shape of the gunnera. My only hesitation in commending it for this position is that it is not yellow: if there were a yellow version of *Scirpus* 'Albescens' that would be even better.

The lack of yellow may be compensated for, however, by the simple device of interposing a yellow plant between the gunnera and the reed. An ideal plant for this position would be the little bright golden-yellow *Filipendula ulmaria* 'Aurea', ideal because it not only enjoys an abundance of moisture at the roots, but also because it benefits from the shade cast in high summer by both the reed in the morning and the gunnera in the afternoon. This is one of those plants that people are inclined to condemn when it flowers, saying that the flowers let it down. They certainly do, for they are a drab, greyish-at-best off-white; but worse, they spoil the colour of the plant. To keep it at its best, bright golden-yellow it really is necessary to remove the flowers as they begin to appear.

In complete contrast to all these, the bottom bulge on the plan is going to be filled with a plant with really purple leaves, of a magnificent rich colouring – *Lobelia cardinalis*. There are two forms of this, one with red flowers and one with pink. I would go for the pink: they are the perfect flowers to go with that foliage. This again is a rather upright grower, so that we need something with a more spreading emphasis to put between it and the white reed. In a way the perfect linking plant would be something with arching leaves, and a phormium springs to mind. The ideal one here would be the rather newly introduced *Phormium* 'Maori Maiden', the only one so far to have a basically pink variegation to the leaf. The pink will complement the lobelia in much the same way as the pink flowers do. It also looks well against the white reed, the curve of the leaves cutting across the military erectness of the stems of the reed.

Behind the scirpus, lobelia and phormium we need another tall plant that will readily fill a large area. *Phragmites australis* 'Variegata' has almost every quality to commend it in such a position. It is naturally a plant that runs by means of stolons and in the wild forms vast, monotypic stands: where it occurs naturally you tend to find it covering large areas. The plant has the typical growth of the rushes with straight, tall stems, the leaves held out sideways making a curious mixture of vertical and semi-horizontal accents. The variegation in this case is a bright yellow striping, and the overall effect of a large planting is yellow.

All the plants mentioned so far in this group need a backdrop. Because most of them are rather light in colour, a dark backdrop would show them off best. The simplest and quickest dark backdrop one could go for would be *Corylus maxima* 'Purpurea', with its rich, purplish-brown leaves. It is, however, a rank grower, and altogether rather coarse, good enough when seen massed from 0.4km (¼ mile) away, but not impressive at close quarters. Of far more quality would be one of the smoke bushes, *Cotinus coggygria* 'Royal Purple', or any of the other purple forms. And if you have space and can add down at the eastern end of this area a further planting of *Pyrus salicifolia* 'Pendula', the weeping silver pear, then the contrasts you will have created within this group alone would be enough to make your garden remarkable. But we still have the rest of the pond to plant yet.

.There are two further bog areas to the left of the pond which can each be treated quite differently. In the more westerly of the two we'll grow *Glycera maxima* 'Variegata', an elegant variegated grass which loses none of its beauty through being widely planted and rightly popular. Its appeal lies largely in the way it changes its colours through the season: the leaves when they first emerge are dominantly pink; then a yellowish variegation appears through early summer; and later in the year the colouring fades to whitish. It is a strongly-spreading plant that needs to be controlled. In the other bay we are going to plant something else that, in its own way, is so rampant that it could be counted as pestilential menace in any ordinary pond: but contained as it is here, it is a joy. This is *Azolla filiculoides*. If you have only ever grown this in an indoor aquarium, you will probably dismiss it as merely green. Grown out of doors in full sunlight, it assumes the most extraordinary orange colouring, quite unlike anything else growing in or around the pond. This quaint little plant is, incidentally, a fern, and is popularly known as fairy moss.

There is one last, very small bay, down at the eastern end of the pond, which could be kept a little drier than the other bog bays. Right in the centre of this a large boulder should be placed. This is partly because big boulders and water look good together (and there are other big boulders to follow), but mainly because we need it there for cultural reasons. The plant we want to grow in this area was at one time considered tender and only ever grown in greenhouses (usually to cover the bare earth under the staging). This is *Helxine soleiroli*, a familiar enough plant, but the form we are going to grow has bright golden-yellow leaves. It is a plant that enjoys a damp situation and a high degree of atmospheric humidity, so would be ideal here – the rock helps to overcome the tenderness problem. While the plant, or most of it, will come through most winters without too much harm, in severe weather it does tend to be killed back; but the bits that have taken shelter under the rock will grow again as soon as mild weather comes in spring, and it will quickly spread out to fill its allotted span. It is a plant that is also helped by shade, and it is mainly for this reason that we are going to put a single specimen small tree, *Acer palmatum* 'Dissectum Atropurpureum', in the colour band behind the helxine. Not only will this cast some shade, it will also, with its purple colouring and brilliant autumn hues, add a different dimension to the general planting. The colour band under the purple cut-leaf maple will be *Ophiopogon planiscarpus* 'Nigrescens', whose glossy, jet-black leaves are a joy in any colour group but will be particularly effective here, contrasting with the yellow helxine and with the next yellow we come to. This is *Carex stricta* 'Aurea', Bowles' golden sedge. This is a most exciting plant (at least it was exciting enough to make the revered Mr Bowles give up hunting butterflies and take up hunting plants), for the gold is really gold, not just yellow: it has that touch of reddishness in the colouring that lifts it way above the ordinary. And just to emphasize that point, we will have as the outer linking band in this section another yellow, a much more typical garden yellow, a carpet of *Cupressus macrocarpa* 'Gold Spreader'. There is one rock sticking up out of this colour band, relating to the rock we used to give a little winter protection to the helxine.

Going now to the northern end of the pond, we have more big and bold plants – furthest away from the house – with the tiny gems closest to the house. The block nearest the water will be *Acorus calamus* 'Variegatus', which, in common with me and most other people, you will probably dismiss as an iris when you first see it, so great is the similarity of leaf. It is usually only when it flowers that people realize its true identity, and it seldom flowers. The particular appeal of this plant, beyond its bold white-variegated leaves, is the fact that the leaves come through a bright reddish colour in earliest spring. Behind this we have a bold planting of *Hosta fortunei* 'Aurea', of a good, clear, if somewhat transparent, yellow (always at its best, incidentally, when seen with the sun shining through the leaves). Beyond that the biggest, boldest hosta of them all, *Hosta sieboldiana elegans*, forming huge clumps of metallic grey-blue leaves. This sweeps round in a bold curve to end just behind the glycera. As a final linking patch of colour, but very low so that it does not seem out of proportion with the fairy moss, there is a block of *Acaena saccaticupula*. This is a New Zealand burr of a most extraordinary colour, quite unlike anything else I have ever seen in the plant kingdom, and probably best described as *café au lait*, but with only a touch of *lait*. It is the perfect plant to contrast with the orange of the azolla, complement the blue of the hosta, and make seem even more brilliant the yellow of Bowles' golden sedge.

Finally, we come to those little touches, those delicate refinements, that make all the difference between a garden and a gardener's garden. In the curve of water between the gunnera and the *Scirpus* 'Albescens', we'll plant a group of the hardy arum, *Zantedeschia aethiopica* 'Crowborough'. This plant seems to be perfectly hardy so long as it is covered by about 10cm (4ins.) of water through winter to protect it from the frosts. The arrow-shaped leaves, on their long stems, have a unique appeal when striding out across the flat, reflecting surface of water. The white flowers have a sumptuous quality, and are of the purest white. Then there is a further rock, standing in the water, in the bay between the helxine and the lobelia. This is of a soft stone: it should be relatively porous. And on it let's grow a fern: I would go for the common polypody, *Polypodium vulgare*, or one of its forms, preferably a crested one. The idea here is to cover the rock completely with the fern, so that it looks like a large ball of fern rising from the water. Quite emphatically it should not look like a rock with a few pieces of fern sticking out of it. It is true that the polypody is not variegated, but it is ideal for its purpose. The only variegated fern that might succeed here, if your garden is not too exposed, is the Japanese painted fern, *Athyrium nipponicum* 'Metallicum' (= *A. goeringianum* 'Pictum'), beautiful with its greys and crimson markings. It does spread by stolons, but is slow to do so, so that if you were to want to cover a whole rock with it you would need to start with quite a number of smallish plants.

Right at the other end of the pond there are three further rock clumps. The largest of these should be hollowed out, but the others simply left solid. In the hollow rock you can grow *Arundinaria variegata* 'Dwarf Form' – a delightful little bamboo with white-variegated leaves. On the island next to that you can grow a dwarf conifer: a miniature pine would make the ideal contrast with the bamboo, especially if the two rocks are very close together. The pine I would go for here is *Pinus mugo* 'Ophir', which is a dwarf bun-shaped pine whose needles turn yellow through winter. And on the last of the rock islands I would have one of the bronze sedges, probably *Uncinia egmontiana*, which is the brightest in this colour group, and whose arching narrow leaves make a further contrast to foliage type within this grouping. It is just such touches as these island rocks with their plantings that make a gardener's garden so much more interesting than anyone else's.

If you are sufficiently interested in your garden to have a water feature, chances are you will probably want rocks in it as well. You may even want a rock garden, and a conventional one at that. There should be room enough for that in the multi-coloured garden. What I am suggesting is something a little different, not at all the conventional rock garden, nor even a suburban plum pudding. It is something as carefully contrived as a good rock garden, but in quite a different idiom. Instead of the sort of rocks that people at garden centres sell you for rock gardens, take yourself

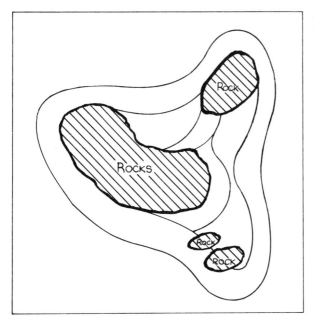

FIGURE 7
Rock feature

down to the coast and find some large, oval, sea-washed rocks, nothing less than 60cm (2ft) long and the majority at least 1m (3ft) long. Seek out some round rocks as well, even larger. To arrange these in your garden, place the large, round rocks first, and then within the framework you have created with them, lay the oval rocks, but lay them all obliquely so that they all lie at the same angle, and are all pointing in the same direction. Ram the spaces with soil and then, instead of planting the sort of gems that people like to cultivate in rock gardens (or, come to that, the sort of carpeting plants with which less knowledgeable gardeners smother their rocks) plant a carefully selected arrangement of grasses and sedges. Use the soft lines of such sedges as *Carex comans* and *Carex albula*, and grasses like *Stipa pennata* to contrast with the spikier lines of such grasses as the blue porcupine *Helictotrichon sempervirens*, or that curled hedgehog, *Festuca punctoria*. You will find that the contrast between the hardness of the rock and the softness of the grasses and sedges will be deeply satisfying at all seasons. Whatever other complexities you add to the scheme, it's all there for you in Fig. 7. Do be sure to contain the whole concept within a single band of colour, preferably a species that is almost as low-growing as your lawn.

The last of the features which could be fun to create is a doline – a key-hole-shaped hollow in the ground (see Fig. 8). The rounded part is where you grow your rock plants, and the adjoining straight part is the passageway by which you enter it. The whole thing is walled up with rock, not only to keep it secure, but also to provide suitable places in which to grow a quite remarkable collection of plants. In our case

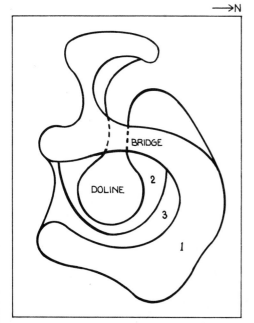

FIGURE 8
Key
1 *Acaena* 'Blue Haze'
2 *Raoulia australis*
3 *Carex petriei*

we are going to curve the entrance passageway just slightly, to add an air of mystery, and we are going to add yet another feature, a bridge across the passageway at the place where the passage meets the 'bowl'. The bridge will have to be quite substantially constructed since it has to carry the weight of soil and another colour band. It also creates a further illusion: as you come down the passageway, you see under the bridge into the bowl, as though you were looking into a brightly-lit cave. It is a most effective device. The doline and its entrance are both for growing the widest diversity of plants you can find and accommodate. It is for this reason that the planting around it should be singularly simple. I would embrace the whole of the doline in one vast curve of colour – nothing too violent, though. An acaena, one of the New Zealand burrs, would be ideal, vigorous enough to make a weed-proof ground cover without being so rampant as to become troublesome. There are many to choose from. *Acaena* 'Blue Haze' seems to be the best-known and most popular, with its grey-blue foliage and bronzy burrs. It is, perhaps, a little too rampant, and I would go for the smaller mat-forming *Acaena microphylla*, which again has grey-blue leaves (perhaps more grey than blue), and an abundance of brilliant red burrs. And if you want a second colour band, one of the bronze New Zealand sedges would be ideal. As a final touch to try your skill as a cultivator, make the innermost band, that nearest the edge of the doline itself, a band of a plant which is itself a rock-garden gem, needing a really gritty soil with absolutely perfect drainage (which is what it would get at the edge of the doline): *Raoulia australis*. When well grown this will make a tight

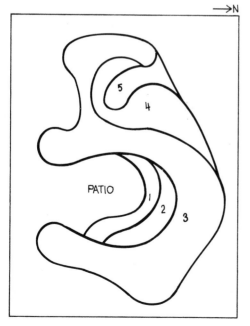

→N

FIGURE 9
Key
1 *Festuca caesia*
2 *Uncinia egmontiana*
3 *Thuja occidentalis* 'Rheingold'
4 *Senecio laxifolius*
5 *Bergenia* 'Sunningdale'

PATIO

silver carpet quite unlike anything else you could grow in such a position. If you've only ever seen this raoulia grown in a pot or a crevice on a rock garden, try growing it this way and you will be amazed by the way it performs.

The same scheme can, by a quick re-adjustment of one's mental horizons, be readily turned into the setting for a patio (Fig. 9). The whole scheme is then executed on level ground, and the sitting area of the patio replaces the doline itself. Plainly, there is no longer the need for a bridge. A rethink of the plant material enables the provision of a colourful backdrop to the patio, while at the same time providing screening. The combination of *Festuca caesia*, *Uncinia egmontiana* and *Thuja occidentalis* 'Rheingold' is singularly striking and pleasing at all seasons. It has the further advantage in a patio surround that it will not suffer too much if people accidentally tread on it – provided that they do not make a habit of it. The rounded grey leaves of *Senecio laxifolius* are a natural complement to the 'Rheingold', while the bergenia not only fills in where the pathway to the doline might have been, but also adds an effective contrast in its own right. Seen either from the patio side or from the side away from the patio, the scheme builds up from ground level to the centre, and that is a mode of planting that is always effective.

Our final working plan (see Fig. 10) is a perfect example of the multi-coloured garden in practice. Its simplicity is its main strength; and it is capable of being planted in a great variety of different ways. It was originally drawn in response to a particular problem. The garden belongs to a house on a corner site and only the back garden, to

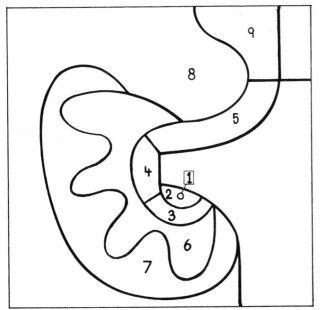

FIGURE 10
Key
1 *Ilex* x *altaclarensis* 'Golden King'
2 *Bergenia* 'Sunningdale'
3 *Juniperus sabina* 'Blue Danube'
4 *Juniperus* x *media* 'Pfitzeriana Glauca'
5 *Juniperus* x *media* 'Hetzii'
6 *Microbiota decussata*
7 *Erica carnea* 'Aurea'
8 Normal lawn grasses
9 Shrub border

the west, is fenced. The front garden is separated from a metalled footpath by a thin strip of concrete edging blocks. In the design it was necessary to accommodate a turning wedge, and to make a planting surround it that would look good from all sides. It was also a fundamental of the concept that it should appear to screen the house, without creating a solid blocking effect. The essence of the design is therefore the screen, which is composed of elements 3, 4 and 5. Element 3 is *Juniperus sabina* 'Blue Danube', which grows little more than 30cm (1ft) high; 4 is *Juniperus* x *media* 'Pfiteriana Glauca', which grows to about 1m (3ft) in height; while 5 is *Juniperus* x *media* 'Hetzii', which grows to about 2m (6ft). All are of very similar colour, form and foliage and they therefore create the illusion that the same plant has been used all along, but that those at one end are larger than those at the other. In contrast with the blue-grey of the junipers there is a bold shape of *Microbiota decussata*, which is a spreading, low-growing conifer of a lovely feathery texture, bright green in summer and brilliant bronze in winter. The pattern made with the microbiota is contained within a planting of a yellow heather, in this case, since the soil is chalky, *Erica carnea* 'Aurea', that in itself being contained within the area of ordinary lawn. On the turning wedge side of the junipers there is a planting of bergenia, chosen partly for its early flowers, partly for its plum-purple winter colouring and partly for the fine effect the big bold leaves make against the foliage of the junipers. The centre point is *Ilex* x *altaclarensis* 'Golden King', a marvellously golden holly of a good, compact habit and relatively tall but narrow. An alternative for the centre point, which I personally prefer is *Corylus avellana* 'Contorta'. This would still have given height (it grows to about 4.5m/15ft) and is a joy in winter with its contorted twigs and branches. You really need to plant it in a position such as this so that you can enjoy at close quarters the contrast between the vertically-drooping catkins and the curly twigs; and you need to be this close to it even to see the tiny red flowers.

There are various very simple changes you could ring on this theme. You could run blocks 3, 4 and 5 together and plant a simple curve of *Senecio laxifolius*. You could plant, instead of the microbiota, *Erica erigena* (*mediterranea*) 'Golden Lady', and at ground level, instead of *Erica carnea* 'Aurea', the prostrate blue *Hebe albicans*, which only ever seems to look effective used in quantity. But it's your garden: the choice is yours.

All of this, you may say, is fine, but how does one actually do it? How does one, for example, get enough plants, clear the ground sufficiently and, most of all, stop one band of colour running into the next? Plainly, we have to consider the practicalities of the matter.

CHAPTER ELEVEN

Some Practicalities

If you are going to create a multi-coloured garden you are going to run into one or two problems which will probably seem new to you. In fact, most of them are already with you; it is merely that you will be meeting them on a new scale. So let's start with some fundamentals and work our way through them to the rest.

Perhaps the first thing you need to appreciate about multi-coloured gardening is that you are, in effect, making a garden with ground-cover plants, but ground-cover plants that have coloured foliage. From a cultural point of view that is very important. In the temperate regions of the world, wherever the soil is fertile it is covered with an abundance of plants: there is not a bare patch of soil to be seen. And this cover of plants is self-supporting and self-maintaining. It is fed by decaying leaves, dying roots, the detritus of dead birds, animals and micro-organisms in the soil: the cover is so complete that it traps any passing leaves or vegetation on which it can feed, and it binds the soil, preventing erosion. The moment a patch of bare earth is exposed, it is instantly invaded by plants striving to cover the ground again as quickly as possible.

The weed problem of a conventional garden arises wholly because there is bare earth visible – bare earth which every local wild plant will be trying to invade. It is the natural driving force of plants to attempt to occupy every available corner of fertile soil. But wild ground cover is infinitely varied, different soils supporting different communities of plants. The whole concept of the multi-coloured garden runs in quite the opposite direction: its essence is to have great monospecific curves and curls of colour-leaved ground cover, each monospecific colour band being clearly differentiated from its neighbours. So the invasion of natural ground cover (better known as weeds) needs controlling. There are really only a very small number of cultivated ground-cover plants that, once planted and established in conditions in which they can thrive, will spread and suppress the weeds that were there before them – *Trachystemon orientale*, *Petasites giganteus*, and possibly *Peltatum peltiphyllum* and one or two rhododendrons, but very few others. Therefore, if you are to get your multi-coloured garden off to a good start, you will first have to clear the ground.

In the so-called good old days clearing the ground was a back-breaking task, weekend after weekend of laboriously digging over ground to remove weeds which seemed to grow again as fast as you dug them out. Modern science and technology have made that approach a bit of an anachronism. These days you can use machines or weedkillers to do the work for you: you probably need to use both for the best results.

First, kill the weeds. Modern weedkillers are invaluable, provided you use them properly. Start with a modern contact weedkiller, such as paraquat, simply to clear the ground so that you can see what further weed problems lie before you. You may find that you need more than one application, since contact weedkillers literally only kill off what they come into contact with, and if your ground is very fertile and your weeds are thriving, they may be growing so densely that one leaf covers another and another and another and those others underneath will not come into contact with the first dose of contact weedkiller. It is only when that first application has killed off the upper leaves that the second layer is exposed ready for a further treatment of the same weedkiller.

Having cleared the worst of the weeds by this method, you will be left with the more persistent weeds – everyone seems to have some – couch grass, bindweed, ground elder, ground ivy, mare's tail: the usual catalogue of enemies. These can be dealt a death-blow with one of the translocating weedkillers based on glyphosates. The way these work is that they are absorbed by the leaf (and sometimes the stem) and translocated to the roots, where they do the killing. If you are not familiar with these weedkillers they can be a bit disconcerting. When you use a contact weedkiller you know it is working within twenty-four hours: you can see the leaves of the weeds burning up in the sunlight. With the translocating weedkillers nothing seems to happen for days or weeks, and that's just as it should be, for while nothing is apparently going on, the chemical is being translocated to the roots. After anything from three to six weeks, the plants will just keel over and die. These translocating weedkillers should work in one application: in practice it may take as many as three to get rid of vigorous invasions of the more pernicious weeds.

One great advantage of both types of weedkiller described is that they are neutralized on contact with the soil. This means effectively that you can plant the ground as soon as the weeds seem to be dead, and the plants will thrive.

Of course, many people are firmly convinced that these new weedkillers are a seven-day wonder, and stick stubbornly with sodium chlorate. The problem with sodium chlorate is that it can remain active in the soil for a year (longer on heavy ground) after its initial application; it can also move laterally through the soil to kill plants that you never intended to kill. If you use sodium chlorate, you will have to wait a year or even two before you can plant the ground, and very few people want to wait that long these days.

Having cleared your ground, you need to till it. I know it brings new weed seeds to the surface (there are simple ways of killing those) but it really is necessary. On clay soils, for example, all you are left with once you have killed the weeds is a slippery, slimy surface that pans as soon as it rains; light sandy soils simply wash away. So some cultivation really is necessary. All you need to do is hire yourself an efficient mechanical cultivator, and turn the ground with that. Learn how to use it in the middle of a patch you have weedkilled, and then systematically rotovate the whole area you want to plant.

A particular technique that has evolved with the multi-coloured garden is to weedkill the perimeter of a colour band with a contact weedkiller, just to mark it out, then weedkill the whole of that colour band and rotovate it. Do this to each band as you come to it, at intervals through a single growing season, over the years. And if you want to obliterate a colour band you no longer like, don't be squeamish: resort to the same weedkill-and-rotovate technique. Life's not long enough for being sentimental about what was once a good idea.

Your preliminary work doesn't end with rotovating the ground. That will improve aeration and drainage. You also need to increase the fertility of the soil. To do that you need to add humus, preferably plenty of it, as well as some fertilizer such as bone meal or hoof-and-horn. The form in which you add your humus is not particularly important – it all helps. Leaf-mould, farmyard manure or horse manure and good garden compost are the best sources of humus. Apply them thickly, 8–10cm (3–4ins.) at a time, and then rotovate them into the ground.

Finally, apply a pre-emergent weedkiller, such as simazine, to stop weeds coming up. The way these weed-killers work is by forming a layer of gas in the top few centimetres or so of the soil, and any tender young seedling trying to get up through that layer of gas is killed by it.

Now you have killed your weeds, tilled your land, dug in the leaf-mould and/or manure, your garden is ready for planting. After treatment like that, you can reasonably expect most of what you plant to thrive; and therein lies a problem. Because if everything thrives, everything is going to run into everything else and you are going to finish up, in time, with exactly the sort of promiscuous muddle that the multi-coloured garden seeks to avoid. The very essence of the multi-coloured garden is simplicity, the simplicity of bold blocks or curves of colour, each clearly differentiated from the next.

Before we try to stop the plants running into each other, let's try to get them into the ground in the right place to start with. If you draw your plan on squared paper and use a scale that you can relatively easily convert – 1cm = 1m, for example – you can use lengths of string, attached to pegs, stretched across the ground so that you form squares 1m each way, these squares corresponding to the ones on your drawing. Having done that, you would expect it to be terribly easy just to go out into the garden, look at your plan, and reproduce the curls and swirls of your drawing on the ground. In practice it hardly ever works quite like that. The proper procedure is to make a little red mark on your drawing where each curve crosses one of the sides of the squares, measure these as precisely as possible from a corner, scale them up, and then drive red pegs into the ground to correspond to the red marks on the drawing. You then take a length of clothes'-line cord and curve it so that it links up the red pegs in exactly the same curve that you have on your drawing. It should all work, and most of the time it does. Where the deception occurs is that you draw your plan looking down on it from above, but you look at the curves in your garden standing on the ground. The perspective changes, and with it the emphasis of the curve. You may find you need to fiddle with your dividing lines, to increase a bulge here, and make a hollow recede a little there. If after trying to readjust the curve you are still not quite sure, leave it for a few days, then look at it again. It may immediately strike you what is wrong; it may not, in which case you simply have to have the courage to go ahead and plant it, and make the adjustments later.

The other advantage of working to scale is that it helps you calculate the number of plants you need for a particular area. This is actually quite important. It is no good buzzing down to your local garden centre and picking up half a dozen heathers and three *Hebe pinguifolia* 'Pagei' and repeating the journey again and again until you have sufficient plants. It is much better to start by knowing that you need thirty-seven heathers and forty-two of the hebe, and getting them on your first visit. It is even more important to be aware of how many plants you need if you are going to propagate them yourself.

The way to work out the number of plants you require for a given area is to find out what their spread is. If a plant has a spread of 1m (3ft), and you want to mass it, the individual plants should be set 60cm (2ft) apart so that they run into each other. If they have a spread of 23cm (9ins.), plant them 15cm (6ins.) apart. The golden rule is to place the plants two-thirds of their spread apart.

The most difficult plants for which to assess the initial spacing are those whose spread is indefinite, for example the trailing rubuses, or the periwinkles. In such cases the spacing really depends upon how fast you want to fill the ground between the plants, and how vigorously the plants spread, which is largely a matter of knowing your plants. I would always err, with such plants, on the side of getting them too close together rather than too far apart. To simplify your task, however, there is a table at the back of the book giving approximate planting distances. Remember that it is for guidance only: you can always fill a given space quicker by using twice as many plants.

Having spaced your plants correctly and allowed them to settle down and get established, you may then come up against the problem of different rates of growth and start wondering how to stop the vinca smothering the heather, or the other way about. The simplest way of controlling lateral spread is to take edging shears and simply clip your way along the division between one plant group and the next, clipping both plants and leaving a clean gap of about 5cm (a couple of inches) all along the line as you go. With plants that spread by underground runners, redefine the curve or line by making a vertical cut into the ground with a well-sharpened spade to sever the runners. You also need to trace any runners that have made top-growth and detach them.

With many plants, however, it is helpful to make a permanent dividing line between one group and the next. In a small garden you can sink either zinc or plastic lawn-edging strips into the ground: that will effectively prevent plants running into each other. If you are working on a vast scale, such as a municipal planting, you can define the curves with 5cm (2in.) widths of concrete set in the ground. You need a minimum of 10cm (4ins.) sunk in the ground, and if you are using concrete a 30cm (1ft) depth is more practicable. In both cases the plants will throw their foliage over the dividing line, so you need have no worries about the dividing line itself being unsightly.

Another point to bear in mind is that if you are propagating your own plants, you should always take more cuttings or sow more seed than the number of plants you need to fulfil your plan – one-third more, to be precise. Even if you have green fingers and a hundred-per-cent success in rooting your cuttings, there is always the chance that there may be a drought while you are on holiday, or the neighbour's cat will dig a few up or for one reason or another you will lose some between taking the cuttings and planting the established propagules. One-third over the top is the rule which the professionals follow. You can always swap or sell the surplus.

However, before you get as far as actually planting anything, there are a number of limiting factors to consider, and the most important of these is the pH of your soil, that is, whether your soil is acid or alkaline. This is measured on a logarithmic scale (like the f numbers on a camera) running from 0 to 14. 0 and 14 are hypothetical extremes: at pH 0 the soil would be as acid as sulphuric acid; at pH 14 it would be as caustic as caustic soda. At either extreme it would burn your skin. In practice the soil of most gardens falls between pH 4.5 and pH 8. pH 7, half-way along the scale, is considered to be neutral. Any pH number lower than 7 indicates an acid soil, which means you can grow rhododendrons, camellias, azaleas and so on; and pH numbers above 7 indicate a soil in which you cannot grow these plants. You can grow the widest possible range of plants well between pH 5.5 and 6.5. The nearer to the extremes you get, the more limiting your soil becomes. At a pH of over 8 the sheer chalkiness of your soil is really starting to limit what you can grow, and a lot of the foliage in your garden will look yellow even when it should not. But acidity can be just as limiting: I once gardened on a soil of pH 3.5 or less and had to add lime to get even rhododendrons to grow. The problem of pH extremes is one of mineral deficiencies.

The quickest way of working out whether your soil is acid or alkaline is to check on the plants in your neighbour's gardens. If they have an abundance of rhododendrons, azaleas, camellias, and related ericaceous plants, such as kalmias and the more showy magnolias, your soil is acid. If none of these plants is growing anywhere near you, but instead there is an abundance of viburnums, hydrangeas, and roses, the chances are your soil is alkaline. If you are well up in your native flora, you can also tell from the weeds what your soil will or won't grow.

Of course, the only accurate way of determining whether your soil is acid or alkaline is by the use of a soil-testing kit. The simplest of these merely tells you whether the soil is one or the other and is relatively inexpensive. There are more sophisticated soil-testing kits that will also enable you to determine whether you have any trace-element deficiencies. Such kits, if used correctly, are usually accurate enough for most practical purposes, but if you run into problems it is well worth sending off soil samples and having them tested at a testing station. The Royal Horticultural Society in Britain will do this, for a fee, and in the USA the state agricultural research station will do it.

In general when discussing multi-coloured plants I have mentioned only an intolerance of lime or a particular preference for chalk. There are other limiting factors, however. Some plants will only grow well in shade, while others only grow well in sun. In general the colouring of coloured leaves is to some extent influenced by the amount of sunlight reaching the plant. Many purple-leaved plants, for example, only reach their fullest colouring in full sunlight; almost all silver-leaved plants need full sun (and good drainage) to thrive. The great majority of yellow-leaved plants prefer full sunlight, otherwise they tend to turn to a drab sickly green. Nearly all white-variegated plants do their best when grown in partial shade: ironically, their brilliance is often best seen only at those times when the sun is low in the sky and can be seen shining through from the far side of the leaves. So again, I have mentioned such preferences.

It is important, when considering the general layout of your garden to note those places which are in sun and which are in shade. All too often people planting in the winter think that a particular spot is shaded, only to find half-way into the summer that it is in full blazing sunlight, and getting scorched around the edges. If you possibly can, make some sort of note – even if it is only a matter of driving in a stake – as to where maximum shade is cast in winter and minimum shade in summer. You need to do this at true noon on mid-summer's day and on the shortest day of the year: it may be inconvenient to be in your garden at noon on those days but that is the ideal. You will be amazed at just how much the amount of shade cast by, for example, a fence, varies.

Many gardeners, accustomed to growing borders of colourful bedding plants, are inclined to be given over to a gnashing of teeth and wringing of hands when they find that they have to move to a garden which is heavily shaded. They should rejoice: there is a wealth of plants that will thrive only in shade. Indeed, if your garden is bereft of trees, from a gardening point of view you are the loser, and the sooner you plant some the sooner you will be able to grow a greater diversity of good plants. But choose your trees with care: small gardens demand small trees. While *Cedrus atlantica* 'Glauca' may look marvellous in the spacious rolling landscape of a great garden, it is quite out of scale in a small one. I have mentioned a number of colour-leaved trees, but for further guidance I would commend to you *Trees for Smaller Gardens* (J. M. Dent & Sons Ltd), a little book I wrote a few years ago which still has some merits.

It is worth giving careful thought to the siting of your trees, even small ones. Obviously you need to avoid putting them too close to windows, doors and drains, but beyond that there are certain arrangements of trees which will enable you to take greater advantage of the shade they cast than other arrangements. A particularly useful grouping in a small garden is a clump of three trees (see Fig. 11) since this gives you not only the density of shade that a single tree would give you, but also an area of

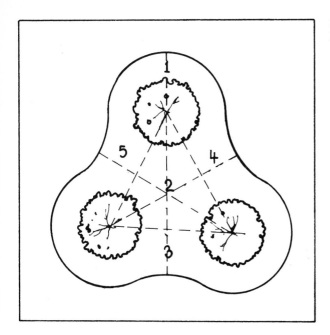

FIGURE 11
Key
  1 Deep shade
  2 Shade all day
  3 Sun all day
  4 Sun early, shade later
  5 Shade early, sun later

permanent shade – whereas the shade from a single tree moves as the sun moves across the sky, so that relatively few of the plants grown in the shade of a single small tree are in shade the whole day through. This particular grouping also gives you areas of dense shade as opposed to merely shade. There is also, of course, an area under a tree which, while sheltered by overhead branches, is not actually in the shade.

Other limitations on what you can grow are climatic. Frost is the one factor that immediately springs to mind, but severity of frost is not in fact the only climatic limitation. You also need to consider how exposed your garden is, since exposure to wind, particularly in winter, can be every bit as killing as frost. And the combination of the two is quite lethal to a vast number of plants that might otherwise be considered hardy. If you have a 0°C (32°F) frost on a still night, that is a 0°C frost and that is that. But if you have a 0°C frost and the wind is 35km (22 miles) per hour, as far as the plant is concerned that is equivalent to perhaps −7°C (20°F). In the USA this combination of wind and cold is called a chill factor; the British, with more flair and less precision, tend to overlook the problem.

So long as you take into account from the very outset the sort of practicalities discussed in this chapter, you will find that the multi-coloured garden presents you, on the whole, with rather fewer problems than a conventional, promiscuous garden in the suburban traditional style; and with a very great deal more satisfaction. Once it is established you will find it so rewarding and sustaining that you will wonder why you never set about making a garden of this sort long, long ago.

Summary of Recommended Plants

Key

D   = Deciduous
E   = Evergreen
†   = Continues increasing in spread
††   = Spreads vigorously
Note: The height given for conifers is for ten years' growth, not their ultimate size.

Plant name and page ref.	Height	Spread	Plant type	Habit	Colour	Spacing	Increase
Abies concolor 'Candicans' 94	60m	10m	Tree E	Pyramidal	Blue	10m	Graft
A.c. 'Glauca Compacta' 94	1m	1m	Bush E	Bun	Blue	1m	Graft
A. lasiocarpa var. *arizonica* 'Compacta' 94	1.5m	30cm	Shrub E	Pyramid	Blue	30cm	Graft
Acaena 'Blue Haze' 78	15cm	30cm†	Carpeter E	Prostrate	Grey	25cm	Proles
A. buchananii 78	10cm	25cm†	Carpeter E	Prostrate	Grey	20cm	Proles
A. microphylla 78	10cm	25cm†	Carpeter E	Prostrate	Grey	20cm	Proles
A. saccaticupula 78	5cm	15cm†	Carpeter E	Prostrate	Grey	15cm	Proles
Acer circinatum 'Little Gem' 24	1.5m	1.5m	Shrub D	Ball	Vari	1m	Graft
A. ginnala 'Durand Dwarf' 24	2m	1.5m	Shrub D	Dome	Vari	1.5m	Graft
A. japonicum 'Aureum' 59	10m	6m	Tree D	Rounded	Yellow	5m	Graft
A. palmatum 'Dissectum' forms 23	3m	4m	Shrub D	Mushroom	Various	2m	Graft
Acorus calamus 'Variegatus' 30	45cm	50cm	Herb D	Vase	White	30cm	Divide
A. gramineus 'Variegatus' 30	10cm	15cm	Herb E	Vase	White	10cm	Divide
Aegopodium podagaria 'Aurea Variegatum' 59	15cm	1m†	Herb D	Spreading	Yellow	50cm	Divide
A.p. 'Variegatum' 30	15cm	1m†	Herb D	Spreading	White	50cm	Divide
Agave gracillima 78	45cm	45cm	Succulent E	Rosette	Grey	50cm	Proles
A. parryi 79	30cm	45cm	Succulent E	Rosette	Grey	50cm	Proles
A. schottii 79	30cm	30cm	Succulent E	Rosette	Grey	50cm	Proles
A. shawii 79	30cm	30cm	Succulent E	Rosette	Grey	50cm	Proles
A. utahensis var. *eborispina* 79	15cm	15cm	Succulent E	Rosette	Grey	10cm	Proles
A.u. var. *kaibabensis* 79	45cm	1m	Succulent E	Rosette	Grey	1m	Proles
A.u. var. *nevadensis* 79	10cm	15cm	Succulent E	Rosette	Grey	10cm	Proles
A.u. var. *utahensis* 79	10cm	15cm	Succulent E	Rosette	Grey	10cm	Proles
Agropyron glaucum 94	45cm	50cm	Grass D	Tussock	Blue	30cm	Division
Ajuga reptans 'Atropurpurea' 101	10cm	25cm†	Herb E	Carpet	Purple	20cm	Proles
A.r. 'Burgundy Glow' 19	12cm	25cm†	Herb E	Carpet	Multi	20cm	Proles
A.r. 'Multicolour' 19	10cm	25cm†	Herb E	Carpet	Multi	20cm	Proles
Alchemilla erythropoda 79	3cm	5cm	Herb D	Clump	Grey	5cm	Division
A. mollis 79	45cm	50cm	Herb D	Clump	Grey	30cm	Seed
Alopecurus pratensis 'Aureus' 59	30cm	50cm	Grass D	Tuft	Yellow	30cm	Division
Aptenia cordifolia 'Variegata' 60	5cm	30cm†	Succulent E	Carpet	Yellow	10cm	Cuttings
Arrhenatherum elatius forma *bulbosum* 'Variegatum' 31	30cm	25cm	Grass D	Clump	White	20cm	Bulbils
Artemesia absinthium 'Lambrook Silver' 80	45cm	40cm	Herb D	Rounded	Silver	30cm	Cuttings

Plant name and page ref.	Height	Spread	Plant type	Habit	Colour	Spacing	Increase
A. arborescens 80	1.3m	1.3m	Shrub D	Clump	Silver	1m	Cuttings
A. canescens 80	45cm	30cm	Herb D	Rounded	Silver	25cm	Cuttings
A. ludoviciana & forms 80	60cm	45cm	Herb D	Flopping	Silver	30cm	Proles
A. purshiana 80	60cm	1m	Shrub D	Clump	Silver	75cm	Cuttings
A. schmidtiana 80	10cm	10cm	Herb D	Clump	Silver	10cm	Cuttings
A. stelleriana 80	20cm	25cm	Herb D	Clump	Silver	15cm	Cuttings
Arundinaria variegata 31	1m	3m	Bamboo E	Clump	White	1m	Division
A. viridistriata 60	1.5m	3m	Bamboo E	Clump	Yellow	1.5m	Division
Arundo donax 81	3m	1m†	Grass D	Clump	Grey	1m	Division
A.d. 'Variegata' 32	2m	1m†	Grass D	Clump	White	1.5m	Division
Astelia chatamica 81	1.5m	3m	Herb E	Clump	Silver	1m	Division
A. nervosa 81	60cm	1.5m	Herb E	Clump	Silver	1m	Division
A. petriei 81	1m	1.5m	Herb E	Clump	Silver	1m	Division
Athyrium nipponicum 'Metallicum' 80	15cm	30cm†	Fern D	Tufted	Silver	15cm	Division
Atriplex hortensis 101	1m†	30cm	Biennial	Spire	Purple	30cm	Seed
Aucuba japonica 'Crotonifolia' 61	3m	3m	Shrub E	Rounded	Yellow	1.5m	Cuttings
A.j. 'Gold Dust' 61	3m	3m	Shrub E	Rounded	Yellow	1.5m	Cuttings
A.j. 'Gold Splash' 61	2.5m	2.5m	Shrub E	Rounded	Yellow	1m	Cuttings
Berberis thunbergii 'Atropurpurea' 103	2.5m	2m	Shrub D	Rounded	Purple	1m	Cuttings
B.t. 'Atropurpurea Nana' 103	45cm	45cm	Shrub D	Rounded	Purple	30cm	Cuttings
B.t. 'Rose Glow' 103	1m	1m	Shrub D	Rounded	Purple	75cm	Cuttings
Bergenia beesianum 25	15cm	25cm†	Herb E	Spreading	Vari	25cm	Proles
B. cordifolia 'Purpurea' 24	45cm	60cm†	Herb E	Spreading	Vari	50cm	Proles
B. crassifolia 24	30cm	45cm†	Herb E	Spreading	Vari	30cm	Proles
B. purpurascens 25	25cm	50cm†	Herb E	Spreading	Vari	25cm	Proles
B. x 'Ballawley' 25	45cm	60cm†	Herb E	Spreading	Vari	45cm	Proles
B. x 'Sunningdale' 25	30cm	45cm†	Herb E	Spreading	Vari	30cm	Proles
Brunnera macrophylla 'Variegata' 32	45cm	30cm†	Herb D	Clump	White	25cm	Division
Buddleia davidii 'Harlequin' 32	3m	2m	Shrub D	Vase	Cream	2m	Cuttings
B.d. 'Variegata' 32	3m	2m	Shrub D	Vase	White	2m	Cuttings
Calluna vulgaris 'Beoley Gold' 61	30cm	45cm†	Shrub E	Hump	Gold	20cm	Cuttings
C.v. 'Golden Carpet' 61	15cm	25cm†	Shrub E	Hump	Gold	15cm	Cuttings

Plant name and page ref.	Height	Spread	Plant type	Habit	Colour	Spacing	Increase
C.v. 'Golden Haze' 61	45cm	60cm†	Shrub E	Hump	Gold	45cm	Cuttings
C.v. 'Multicolour' 19	15cm	30cm†	Shrub E	Hump	Multi	35cm	Cuttings
C.v. 'Robert Chapman' 61	25cm	45cm†	Shrub E	Hump	Gold	30cm	Cuttings
C.v. 'Silver Knight' 81	30cm	45cm†	Shrub E	Hump	Grey	30cm	Cuttings
C.v. 'Silver Queen' 81	25cm	30cm†	Shrub E	Hump	Grey	20cm	Cuttings
C.v. 'Silver Rose' 82	40cm	60cm†	Shrub E	Hump	Silver	45cm	Cuttings
C.v. 'Sir John Charrington' 61	45cm	60cm†	Shrub E	Hump	Gold	45cm	Cuttings
C.v. 'Sister Anne' 82	10cm	30cm	Shrub E	Hump	Silver	20cm	Cuttings
C.v. 'Sunset' 61	30cm	45cm†	Shrub E	Hump	Gold	30cm	Cuttings
Calocephalus brownii 82	30cm	30cm	Succulent E	Twiggy	Silver	10cm	Cuttings
Camellia japonica 'Benten' 33	4m†	3m†	Shrub E	Bushy	White	1.5m	Cuttings
C.j. 'Variegata' 33	4m†	3m†	Shrub E	Bushy	Cream	1.5m	Cuttings
C. sasanqua 'Variegata' 33	3m	3m	Shrub E	Leggy	Whitish	1.5m	Cuttings
Canna indica 'Egandale' 103	2m	45cm	Bedder	Upright	Purple	30cm	Division
C.i. 'Purpurea' 103	2.5m	45cm	Bedder	Upright	Purple	30cm	Division
Carex albula 33	45cm	45cm	Sedge	Tufted	White	30cm	Division
C. buchananii 102	60cm	20cm	Sedge	Tufted	Bronze	15cm	Division
C. comans 33	20cm	45cm	Sedge	Tufted	White	30cm	Division
C. c. 'Bronze Form' 102	45cm	45cm	Sedge	Tufted	Bronze	30cm	Division
C. flagellifera 102	60cm	50cm	Sedge	Tufted	Bronze	30cm	Division
C. ornithopoda 'Variegata' 33	15cm	15cm	Sedge	Tufted	White	10cm	Division
C. petriei 102	30cm	30cm	Sedge	Tufted	Bronze	15cm	Division
C. reticulosa 'Aurea' 61	45cm	30cm†	Sedge	Tufted	Yellow	30cm	Division
C. riparia 'Variegata' 34	1m	1m††	Sedge	Running	White	50cm	Division
C. siderostica 'Variegata' 34	10cm	20cm	Sedge	Tufted	White	10cm	Division
C. stricta 'Aurea' 61	60cm	45cm	Sedge	Tufted	Yellow	30cm	Division
C. uncinifolia 102	5cm	10cm	Sedge	Tufted	Bronze	5cm	Division
Catalpa bignonioides 'Aurea' 62	12m	15m	Tree D	Shrubby	Yellow	10m	Cuttings
C.b. 'Variegata' 34	10m	12m	Tree D	Shrubby	White	10m	Cuttings
C. duclouxii 'Variegata' 35	7m	10m	Tree D	Shrubby	White	10m	Cuttings
Centaurea candidissima 83	25cm	60cm	Bedder	Rounded	Grey	45cm	Cuttings
C. gymnocarpa 82	30cm	9cm	Bedder	Rounded	Grey	15cm	Cuttings
Chamaecyparis lawsoniana 'Albovariegata' 36	70cm	50cm	Conifer E	Bun	White	45cm	Cuttings
C.l. 'Albospica' 36	3m	1m	Conifer E	Vase	White	75cm	Cuttings
C.l. 'Blom' 95	2m	40cm	Conifer E	Spire	Blue	1m	Cuttings

Plant name and page ref.	Height	Spread	Plant type	Habit	Colour	Spacing	Increase
C.l. 'Columnaris' 95	2.5m	80cm	Conifer E	Flame	Blue	1m	Cuttings
C.l. 'Erecta Aurea' 62	1m	50cm	Conifer E	Oval	Gold	40cm	Cuttings
C.l. 'Flecher's White' 36	1.5m	75cm	Conifer E	Upright	White	50cm	Cuttings
C.l. 'Gold Splash' 36	1.5m	80cm	Conifer E	Mushroom	Yellow	60cm	Cuttings
C.l. 'Hillieri' 62	15m	3m	Conifer E	Pyramid	Yellow	2m	Cuttings
C.l. 'Lanei' 62	20m	2.5m	Conifer E	Pyramid	Yellow	2m	Cuttings
C.l. 'Luteo-compacta' 62	1.5m	1m	Conifer E	Bun	Yellow	75cm	Cuttings
C.l. 'Minima Aurea' 62	50cm	40cm	Conifer E	Globe	Yellow	30cm	Cuttings
C.l. 'Pembury Blue' 95	3m	1.5m	Conifer E	Spire	Blue	1m	Cuttings
C.l. 'Pygmaea Argentea' 36	40cm	40cm	Conifer E	Bun	White	30cm	Cuttings
C.l. 'Silver Queen' 36	3m	1.2m	Conifer E	Pyramid	White	1m	Cuttings
C.l. 'Smithii' 62	3m	1.2m	Conifer E	Pyramid	Yellow	1m	Cuttings
C.l. 'Snow Flurry' 36	3m	1m	Conifer E	Bush	White	75cm	Cuttings
C.l. 'Stewartii' 62	3m	1.2m	Conifer E	Pyramid	Yellow	1m	Cuttings
C. obtusa 'Blue Surprise' 95	2m	50cm	Conifer E	Narrow	Blue	35cm	Cuttings
C.o. 'Boulevard' 95	3m	2m	Conifer E	Bushy	Blue	1m	Cuttings
C.o. 'Nana Aurea' 63	50cm	30cm	Conifer E	Bun	Yellow	25cm	Cuttings
C.o. 'Tetragona Aurea' 63	2m	1m	Conifer E	Scarecrow	Yellow	75cm	Cuttings
C. pisifera 'Filifera Aurea' 63	1m	1.3m	Conifer E	Mushroom	Yellow	1m	Cuttings
C.p. 'Gold Spangle' 63	50cm	1m	Conifer E	Bun	Yellow	75cm	Cuttings
C.p. 'Snow' 37	1.5m	1.5m	Conifer E	Upright	White	1m	Cuttings
C.p. 'Squarrosa Intermedia' 95	1.5m	1.5m	Conifer E	Mushroom	Blue	1m	Cuttings
C.p. 'Squarrosa Sulphurea' 37	2m	1m	Conifer E	Tiered	White	75cm	Cuttings
C.p. 'Strathmore' 63	1.5m	1m	Conifer E	Bun	Yellow	75cm	Cuttings
Chrysanthemum foeniculaceum 83	60cm	15cm	Bedder	Spray	Silver	15cm	Cuttings
C. ptarmaciflorum 83	60cm	60cm	Bedder	Bushy	Silver	30cm	Cuttings
Coleus 'Roi des Noires' 111	50cm	30cm	Bedder	Bushy	Black	20cm	Cuttings
Cornus alba 29	2m	4m†	Shrub D	Twiggy	Red	3m	Cuttings
C.a. 'Elegantissima' 37	3m	3m	Shrub D	Twiggy	White	2.5m	Cuttings
C.a. 'Kesselringii' 29	2m	3m	Shrub D	Twiggy	Black	2.5m	Cuttings
C.a. 'Sibirica' 29	2m	3m	Shrub D	Twiggy	Red	2.5m	Cuttings
C.a. 'Spaethii' 63	2m	3m	Shrub D	Twiggy	Gold	2.5m	Cuttings
C.a. 'Variegata' 37	3m	3m	Shrub D	Twiggy	White	2.5m	Cuttings
C. alternifolia 'Variegata' 38	3m	2m	Tree D	Tiered	White	2m	Layers
C. controversa 'Variegata' 38	4m	2.5m	Tree D	Rounded	White	2m	Cuttings
C. florida 'Rainbow' 19	3m	3m	Shrub D	Bushy	Multi	2m	Cuttings

Plant name and page ref.	Height	Spread	Plant type	Habit	Colour	Spacing	Increase
C.f. 'Tricolor' 20	3m	3m	Shrub D	Bushy	Multi	2m	Cuttings
C. mas 'Aurea' 64	3m	3m	Shrub D	Twiggy	Yellow	2m	Cuttings
C.m. 'Elegantissima' 20	2.5m	2m	Shrub D	Twiggy	Multi	1.5m	Cuttings
C.m. 'Variegata' 38	3m	3m	Shrub D	Twiggy	White	2m	Cuttings
C. paliophylla 29	1.5m	1m	Shrub D	Bushy	Green	1m	Cuttings
C. stolonifera 29	3m	4m†	Shrub D	Bushy	Red	2m	Cuttings
C.s. 'Flaviramea' 29	2.5m	3m†	Shrub D	Bushy	Gold	2m	Cuttings
C.s. var. nitida 29	2.5m	2.5m	Shrub D	Bushy	Green	2m	Cuttings
Cortaderia sellowana 'Albo-marginata' 39	2m	2m	Grass E	Tussock	White	1.5m	Division
C.s. 'Gold Banded' 64	2m	2m	Grass E	Tussock	Yellow	1.5m	Division
Corylus maxima 'Purpurea' 102	3m	2m	Shrub E	Upright	Purple	1.5m	Cuttings
Cotinus coggyria 'Atropurpurea' 103	3m	3m	Shrub D	Rounded	Purple	2m	Cuttings
C.c. 'Notcutts Variety' 103	3m	3m	Shrub D	Rounded	Purple	2m	Cuttings
C.c. 'Royal Purple' 103	3m	3m	Shrub D	Rounded	Purple	2m	Cuttings
Cryptomeria japonica 'Compressa' 25	1m	1m	Conifer E	Bun	Vari	75cm	Cuttings
C.j. 'Elegans' 25	4m	4m	Conifer E	Splayed	Vari	3m	Cuttings
C.j. 'Elegans Compacta' 25	3m	2m	Conifer E	Splayed	Vari	2m	Cuttings
C.j. 'Knaptonensis' 39	30cm	1m	Conifer E	Congested	White	50cm	Cuttings
C.j. 'Vilmoriniana' 25	1m	1m	Conifer E	Bun	Vari	75cm	Cuttings
Cupressus arizonica 'Blue Pyramid' 96	4m	2m	Conifer E	Pyramid	Blue	1.5m	Cuttings
C.a. 'Compacta' 96	45cm	40cm	Conifer E	Bun	Blue	30cm	Cuttings
C.a. 'Hodginsii' 96	4m	2m	Conifer E	Pyramid	Blue	1.5m	Cuttings
C. macrocarpa 'Donard Gold' 64	4m	1.5m	Conifer E	Flame	Gold	1m	Cuttings
C.m. 'Goldcrest' 64	4m	1.5m	Conifer E	Flame	Gold	1m	Cuttings
C.m. 'Gold Spreader' 64	1m	3m	Conifer E	Wide	Yellow	2.5m	Cuttings
C. sempervirens 'Swane's Gold' 64	2m	50cm	Conifer E	Flame	Yellow	1m	Cuttings
Cynara cardunculus 84	1.75m	2m	Vegetable E	Bold	Grey	60cm	Division
C. scolymus 84	1.5m	1.5m	Vegetable E	Bold	Grey	60cm	Division
Dacrydium laxifolium 25	12cm	50cm	Conifer E	Prostrate	Vari	25cm	Cuttings
Dicentra oregana 84	45cm	60cm	Herb D	Floppy	Grey	30 cm	Division

Plant name and page ref.	Height	Spread	Plant type	Habit	Colour	Spacing	Increase
Eleagnus x ebbingei 'Gilt Edge' 65	2m	2m	Shrub E	Bushy	Yellow	1.5m	Cuttings
E. pungens 'Maculata' 65	3m	3m	Shrub E	Bushy	Yellow	1.5m	Cuttings
Elymus arenarius 96	1m	2m††	Grass E	Spiky	Blue	1m	Division
Erica carnea 'Anne Sparkes' 65	25cm	30cm	Shrub E	Low	Yellow	25cm	Cuttings
E.c. 'Aurea' 65	25cm	30cm	Shrub E	Low	Yellow	25cm	Cuttings
E. cineraria 'Rock Pool' 65	15cm	30cm	Shrub E	Low	Yellow	25cm	Cuttings
E.c. 'Windlebroke' 65	25cm	30cm	Shrub E	Low	Yellow	25cm	Cuttings
E. x darleyensis 'Jack H. Brummage' 65	45cm	45cm	Shrub E	Low	Yellow	30cm	Cuttings
E. erigena 'Golden Lady' 65	1m	60cm	Shrub E	Bushy	Yellow	45cm	Cuttings
E. vagans 'Valerie Proudley' 65	20cm	30cm	Shrub E	Low	Yellow	25cm	Cuttings
Euphorbia characias 84	1.3m	1.5m	Sub-shrub D	Bushy	Grey	1m	Division
E. myrsinites 85	30cm	20cm	Sub-shrub D	Spreading	Grey	15cm	Division
E. wulfenii 84	2m†	2m†	Sub-shrub D	Upright	Grey	1.5m	Division
Euonymus fortunei 'Emerald 'n Gold' 66	30cm	45cm	Shrub E	Bushy	Yellow	30cm	Cuttings
E.f. 'Emerald Gaiety' 39	30cm	45cm	Shrub E	Bushy	White	30cm	Cuttings
E.f. radicans 'Silver Pillar' 39	45cm	30cm	Shrub E	Bushy	White	20cm	Cuttings
E.f.r. 'Silver Queen' 39	30cm	45cm	Shrub E	Bushy	White	30cm	Cuttings
E.f. 'Variegatus' 39	30cm	45cm	Shrub E	Bushy	White	30cm	Cuttings
E. japonicus 'Macrophyllus Albus' 40	2m	1.5m	Shrub E	Bushy	White	1m	Cuttings
E.j. 'Ovatus Aureus' 66	1.5m	1m	Shrub E	Upright	Yellow	75cm	Cuttings
Fascicularia bicolor 85	45cm	60cm	Bromeliad E	Spiky	Grey	60cm	Division
F. pitcairniifolia 85	45cm	1m	Bromeliad E	Spiky	Grey	75cm	Division
Festuca caesia 96	20cm	20cm	Grass E	Tufted	Blue	15cm	Division
F. punctoria 97	25cm	30cm†	Grass E	Whorled	Blue	25cm	Division
Filipendula ulmaria 'Aurea' 66	45cm	30cm	Herb D	Low	Yellow	20cm	Division
Fuchsia 'Golden Treasure' 66	30cm	40cm	Shrub D	Rounded	Yellow	25cm	Cuttings
Fragraria vesca 'Variegata' 40	5cm	1m†	Herb D	Spreading	White	25cm	Proles
Gazania 'Silver Beauty' 85	15cm	30cm	Bedder	Spreading	Grey	20cm	Cuttings
Glechoma hederacea 'Variegata' 40	5cm	1m†	Herb D	Spreading	White	25cm	Proles
Glycera maxima 'Variegata' 40	1.3m	1m††	Grass D	Running	Creamy	75cm	Proles

Plant name and page ref.	Height	Spread	Plant type	Habit	Colour	Spacing	Increase
Griselina littoralis 'Dixon's Cream' 41	3m	2m	Shrub E	Rounded	Yellow	2m	Cuttings
G.l. 'Variegata' 41	3m	2m	Shrub E	Rounded	White	2m	Cuttings
Hakonechloa macra 'Albo-aurea' 66	25cm	15cm	Grass D	Spraying	Yellow	10cm	Division
Hebe albicans var. *prostrata* 86	15cm	30cm	Shrub E	Spreading	Grey	25cm	Cuttings
H. andersonii 'Variegata' 41	2m	2m	Shrub E	Rounded	White	25cm	Cuttings
H. franciscana 'Variegata' 41	15cm	25cm	Shrub E	Rounded	White	15cm	Cuttings
H. pinguifolia 'Pagei' 86	5cm	25cm	Shrub E	Flat	Grey	15cm	Cuttings
Hedera canariensis 'Gloire de Marengo' 42	30cm	30m	Vine E	Climber	White	3m	Cuttings
H.c. 'Margino-maculata' 42	30cm	30m	Vine E	Climber	White	3m	Cuttings
H. colchica 'Dentato-variegata' 42	30cm	45m	Vine E	Climber	White	3m	Cuttings
H.c. 'Sulphur Heart' 67	30cm	45m	Vine E	Climber	Yellow	3m	Cuttings
H. helix 'Adam' 42	5cm	1m†	Vine E	Climber	White	75cm	Cuttings
H.h. 'Ardingly' 42	5cm	1m†	Vine E	Climber	White	75cm	Cuttings
H.h. 'Buttercup' 67	5cm	1m†	Vine E	Climber	Yellow	75cm	Cuttings
H.h. 'Cavendishii' 42	5cm	1m†	Vine E	Climber	White	75cm	Cuttings
H.h. 'Chicago Variegated' 43	5cm	1m†	Vine E	Climber	White	75cm	Cuttings
H.h. 'Glacier' 43	5cm	1m†	Vine E	Climber	White	75cm	Cuttings
H.h. 'Gold Heart' 67	5cm	1m†	Vine E	Climber	Yellow	75cm	Cuttings
H.h. 'Harald' 43	5cm	1m†	Vine E	Climber	White	75cm	Cuttings
H.h. 'Heise' 43	5cm	1m†	Vine E	Climber	White	75cm	Cuttings
H.h. 'Little Diamond' 43	5cm	1m†	Vine E	Climber	White	75cm	Cuttings
H.h. 'Lutzii' 43	5cm	1m†	Vine-E	Climber	White	75cm	Cuttings
H.h. 'Pedata Variegata' 43	5cm	1m†	Vine E	Climber	White	75cm	Cuttings
H.h. 'Saggitifolia Variegata' 43	5cm	1m†	Vine E	Climber	White	75cm	Cuttings
H.h. 'Trinity' 43	5cm	1m†	Vine E	Climber	White	75cm	Cuttings
Helichrysum angustifolium 86	60cm	60cm	Shrub E	Rounded	Silver	45cm	Cuttings
H. fontanesisi 86	1.3m	1m	Shrub E	Rounded	Silver	75cm	Cuttings
H. microphyllum 86	10cm	1m†	Bedder	Trailing	Grey	30cm	Cuttings
H. petiolatum 86	15cm	1m†	Bedder	Trailing	Grey	45cm	Cuttings
Helictotrichon sempervirens 97	45cm	60cm	Grass E	Dome	Blue	1m	Division
Helxine soleirolii 'Albo-Variegata' 44	1cm	45cm†	Herb E	Flat	White	30cm	Division
H.s. 'Aureus' 67	1cm	45cm†	Herb E	Flat	Yellow	30cm	Division

Plant name and page ref.	Height	Spread	Plant type	Habit	Colour	Spacing	Increase
Heuchera americana 'Purple Form' 104	30cm	30cm	Herb D	Rounded	Purple	15cm	Division
H. sanguinea 'Taff's Joy' 44	30cm	45cm	Herb E	Tufted	White	20cm	Division
Holcus mollis 'Variegatus' 44	15cm	30cm†	Grass D	Spreading	White	15cm	Division
Hosta albomarginata 45	50cm	45cm	Herb D	Rounded	White	30cm	Division
H. decorata 46	60cm	45cm	Herb D	Rounded	White	30cm	Division
H. fortunei 67	75cm	60cm	Herb D	Rounded	Grey	50cm	Division
H.f. 'Albopicta' 67	75cm	60cm	Herb D	Rounded	Yellow	50cm	Division
H.f. 'Aurea' 67	75cm	60cm	Herb D	Rounded	Yellow	50cm	Division
H.f. 'Gold Edge' 68	75cm	60cm	Herb D	Rounded	Yellow	50cm	Division
H.f. 'Marginato-Alba' 46	75cm	60cm	Herb D	Rounded	White	50cm	Division
H. sieboldiana 97	75cm	60cm	Herb D	Rounded	Grey	45cm	Division
H.s. elegans 97	75cm	60cm	Herb D	Rounded	Grey	45cm	Division
H.s. 'Frances Williams' 68	75cm	60cm	Herb D	Rounded	Yellow	45cm	Division
H. x 'Thomas Hogg' 46	60cm	45cm	Herb D	Rounded	White	30cm	Division
H. tokudama 97	45cm	45cm	Herb D	Rounded	Grey	30cm	Division
H.t 'Aurea-nebulosa' 68	45cm	45cm	Herb D	Rounded	Yellow	30cm	Division
H. undulata 46	45cm	30cm	Herb D	Rounded	White	25cm	Division
H.u. univittata 46	45cm	30cm	Herb D	Rounded	White	25cm	Division
H. ventricosa 'Variegata' 46	60cm	60cm	Herb D	Rounded	White	45cm	Division
H. 'Wogan Giboshi' 68	30cm	30cm	Herb D	Rounded	Yellow	15cm	Division
Hypericum x moserianum 'Tricolor' 20	45cm	1m	Shrub D	Leggy	White	30cm	Cuttings
Ilex x altaclarensis 'Silver Sentinel' 46	4m	2m	Tree E	Pyramid	White	1.5m	Cuttings
I. aquifolium 'Argentea Pendula' 47	4m	3m	Tree E	Weeping	White	1.5m	Cuttings
I.a. 'Ferox Argentea' 47	2m	1.5m	Tree E	Bushy	White	1m	Cuttings
I.a. 'Handsworth New Silver' 47	5m	3m	Tree E	Spire	White	1.5m	Cuttings
I.a. 'Silver Milkboy' 47	4m	3m	Tree E	Rounded	White	1.5m	Cuttings
I.a. 'Somerset Cream' 47	5m	3m	Tree E	Rounded	White	1.5m	Cuttings
I. crenata 'Golden Gem' 68	1m	1.5m	Shrub E	Mushroom	Yellow	75cm	Cuttings
Iresine herbstii 104	30cm	15cm	Bedder	Upright	Purple	15cm	Cuttings
I. lindenii 104	30cm	15cm	Bedder	Upright	Purple	15cm	Cuttings

Plant name and page ref.	Height	Spread	Plant type	Habit	Colour	Spacing	Increase
Iris foetidissima 'Variegata' 48	30cm	30cm	Herb E	Fan	White	15cm	Division
I. japonica 'Variegata' 48	45cm	45cm	Herb E	Fan	White	25cm	Division
I. pallida 'Aurea-Variegata' 48	45cm	45cm	Herb D	Fan	Yellow	25cm	Division
I.p. 'Variegata' 48	45cm	45cm	Herb D	Fan	White	25cm	Division
Jasminum officinale 'Aureo-variegatum' 68	4m	4m	Climber D	Scandent	Yellow	2m	Cuttings
Juniperus chinensis 'Aurea' 69	2m	75cm	Conifer E	Pillar	Yellow	3m	Cuttings
J. communis 'Depressa Aurea' 69	30cm	1.5m	Conifer E	Spreading	Yellow	1m	Cuttings
J. horizantalis 'Bar Harbour' 98	15cm	3m	Conifer E	Flat	Grey	2m	Cuttings
J.h. 'Douglasii' 98	30cm	2.5m	Conifer E	Flat	Grey	2m	Cuttings
J.h. 'Wiltonii' 98	15cm	3.5m	Conifer E	Flat	Grey	2.5m	Cuttings
J. x media 'Gold Coast' 69	60cm	2m	Conifer E	Flat	Gold	1.5m	Cuttings
J. x m. 'Hetzii' 98	2m	2m	Conifer E	V-shape	Grey	1.5m	Cuttings
J. x m. 'Old Gold' 118	60cm	2m	Conifer E	V-shape	Yellow	1.5m	Cuttings
J. x m. 'Pfitzeriana Glauca' 98	1m	2m	Conifer E	Arching	Grey	1.5m	Cuttings
J. x m. 'Plumosa Aurea' 69	75cm	2m	Conifer E	V-shape	Yellow	1.5m	Cuttings
J. scopulorum 'Blue Heaven' 98	1m	25cm	Conifer E	Flame	Grey	3m	Cuttings
J.s. 'Skyrocket' 18	2m	30cm	Conifer E	Spire	Grey	2.5m	Cuttings
J. squamata 'Chinese Silver' 86/7	2m	1.5m	Conifer E	Arching	Silver	1m	Cuttings
Kerria japonica 'Variegata' 48	1m	1m	Shrub D	Twiggy	White	75cm	Cuttings
Kniphofia caulescens 87	30cm	60cm	Herb E	Rounded	Grey	45cm	Division
Lamium maculatum 'Aureum' 69	12cm	30cm†	Herb D	Creeping	Yellow	15cm	Proles
L.m. 'Silver Beacon' 89	10cm	25cm†	Herb D	Creeping	Grey	20cm	Proles
L. galeobdolon 'Variegatum' 49	25cm	45cm†	Herb D	Creeping	Grey	30cm	Proles
Larix decidua 'Corley' 26	1m	1.5m	Conifer D	Rounded	Vari	1m	Grafting
Leptospermum cunninghamii 87	2m	1.5m	Shrub E	Upright	Vari	1m	Seed
L. lanigerum 87	2m	1m	Shrub E	Bushy	Grey	75cm	Seed
Ligularia dentata 'Desdemona' 105	45cm	60cm	Herb D	Robust	Purple	30cm	Division
Liquidambar styracifula 'Golden Treasure' 70	10m†	3m	Tree D	Spire	Yellow	5m	Grafting
L.s. 'Red Dwarf' 26	1m	1m	Shrub D	Round	Vari	75cm	Cuttings
Liriope platyphylla 'Gold Banded' 70	30cm	30cm	Herb E	Grassy	Yellow	15cm	Division
L.p. 'John Burch' 49	30cm	30cm	Herb E	Grassy	Yellow	15cm	Division

Plant name and page ref.	Height	Spread	Plant type	Habit	Colour	Spacing	Increase
L.p. 'Silvery Midget' 49	15cm	15cm	Herb E	Grassy	White	8cm	Division
L.p. 'Silvery Sunproof' 50	30cm	30cm	Herb E	Grassy	White	15cm	Division
Lonicera nitida 'Baggesen's Gold' 70	2m	3m	Shrub E	Twiggy	Yellow	1m	Cuttings
Lotus berthelotii 87	30cm	1m†	Bedder	Pendulous	Grey	45cm	Cuttings
Lysimachia nummularia 'Aurea' 71	5cm	1m†	Herb D	Creeping	Yellow	45cm	Proles
Melissa officinalis 'Aurea' 71	15cm	20cm	Herb E	Bushy	Yellow	10cm	Seed
Microbiota decussata 26	30cm	1m†	Conifer E	Spreading	Vari	45cm	Cuttings
Millium effusum 'Aureum' 71	45cm	30cm	Grass D	Arching	Yellow	15cm	Seed
Miscanthus sinensis 'Variegata' 50	2m	45cm	Grass D	Upright	White	45cm	Division
Molinia caerulea 'Variegata' 50	30cm	15cm	Grass D	Arching	Yellow	15cm	Division
Ochagavia lindleyana 85	60cm	1m	Bromeliad E	Spiky	Grey	45cm	Division
Ophiopogon jaburan 'Variegatus' 50	30cm	30cm	Herb E	Grassy	White	15cm	Division
O. intermedius 'Variegatus' 50	10cm	10cm	Herb E	Grassy	White	5cm	Division
O. planiscarpus 'Nigrescens' 111	30cm	30cm	Herb E	Grassy	Black	15cm	Division
Opuntia cantabrigiensis 88	1m	2m†	Cactus E	Shrubby	Grey	1m	Cuttings
O. haematocarpa 88	1m	1.5m	Cactus E	Shrubby	Grey	1m	Cuttings
O. phaeacantha 88	1m	2m	Cactus E	Shrubby	Grey	1m	Cuttings
Origanum vulgare 'Aureum' 71	30cm	15cm	Herb D	Upright	Yellow	10cm	Division
Pachysandra terminalis 'Variegata' 51	15cm	1m†	Herb E	Spreading	White	45cm	Cuttings
Parrotia persica 'Pendula' 27	1m	3m	Tree D	Weeping	Vari	1.5m	Cuttings
Pelargonium x hortorum 'Mrs Henry Cox' 20	30cm	25cm	Bedder E	Gaunt	Multi	10cm	Cuttings
P. x h. 'The Czar' 21	30cm	30cm	Bedder	Rounded	Multi	15cm	Cuttings
Perilla atropurpurea 105	45cm	30cm	Bedder	Bushy	Purple	15cm	Seed
Phalaris arundinacea 'Picta' 51	1.5m	2m†	Grass D	Grassy	White	1m	Division
Philadelphus coronarius 'Aureus' 72	3m	2m	Shrub D	Bushy	Yellow	1.5m	Cuttings
P.c. 'Variegatus' 51	2.5m	2m	Shrub D	Bushy	White	1.5m	Cuttings
Phlox paniculata 'Harlequin' 52	75cm	30cm	Herb D	Upright	White	15cm	Division
P.p. 'Nora Leigh' 52	75cm	30cm	Herb D	Upright	White	15cm	Division

Plant name and page ref.	Height	Spread	Plant type	Habit	Colour	Spacing	Increase
Phormium tenax 'Bronze Baby' 105	30cm	30cm	Shrub E	Arching	Bronze	15cm	Division
P.t. 'Dazzler' 106	60cm	60cm	Shrub E	Arching	Purple	30cm	Division
P.t. 'Maori Chief' 106	1m	1m	Shrub E	Arching	Yellow	45cm	Division
P.t. 'Maori Sunrise' 106	50cm	60cm	Shrub E	Arching	Purple	30cm	Division
P.t. 'Purpureum' 105	2m	2m	Shrub E	Arching	Purple	1m	Division
P.t. 'Variegatum' 52	3m	2m	Shrub E	Upright	White	1.5m	Division
Picea abies 'Aurea' 28	10m	3m	Conifer E	Pyramid	Vari	2m	Grafting
P. orientalis 'Aurea' 28	8m	3m	Conifer E	Pyramid	Vari	2m	Grafting
P. pungens 'Glauca' 98	8m	3m	Conifer E	Pyramid	Blue	2m	Grafting
P.p. 'Glauca Pendula' 99	5m	8m	Conifer E	Weeping	Blue	2m	Grafting
P.p. 'Glauca Prostrata' 99	1m	1.5m	Conifer E	Spreading	Blue	1m	Grafting
P.p. 'Koster' 99	8m	3m	Conifer E	Pyramid	Blue	3m	Grafting
P.p. 'Hoopsii' 99	9m	3m	Conifer E	Pyramid	Blue	3m	Grafting
P.p. 'Moerheimii' 99	8m	3m	Conifer E	Pyramid	Blue	3m	Grafting
P.p. 'Thomsen' 99	8m	3m	Conifer E	Pyramid	Blue	3m	Grafting
Pieris formosa forrestii and forms 27	4m	3m	Shrub E	Bushy	Vari	1.5m	Cuttings
P. japonica 27	2m	2m	Shrub E	Bushy	Vari	1m	Cuttings
Pinus sylvestris 'Aurea' 28	10m	5m	Conifer E	Gnarled	Vari	1m	Grafting
Pittosporum tenuifolium 'Garnetii' 53	5m	3m	Shrub E	Twiggy	White	1.5m	Cuttings
P.t. 'Irene Paterson' 53	4m	2.5m	Shrub E	Twiggy	White	1m	Cuttings
P.t. 'Purpureum' 106	5m	3m	Shrub E	Twiggy	Purple	1.5m	Cuttings
P.t. 'Silver Queen' 53	5m	3m	Shrub E	Twiggy	White	1.5m	Cuttings
P.t. 'Variegatum' 53	5m	3m	Shrub E	Twiggy	White	1.5m	Cuttings
Plantago lanceolata 'Streaker' 53	15cm	15cm	Herb D	Clump	White	10cm	Division
P. major var. rubrifolia 106	20cm	20cm	Herb D	Clump	Purple	15cm	Division
Pleioblastus chino f. angustifolia 32	30cm	1m	Bamboo	Clump	White	50cm	Proles
Poa colensoi 99	25cm	25cm	Grass E	Tuft	Blue	15cm	Division
P. tasmanica 99	5cm	10cm	Grass E	Carpet	Grey	5cm	Division
Prunus cerasifera 'Diversifolia' 106	5m	4m	Tree D	Rounded	Purple	4m	Cuttings
P.c. 'Nigra' 106	5m	4m	Tree D	Rounded	Purple	4m	Cuttings
P.c. 'Pissardii' 106	5m	4m	Tree D	Rounded	Purple	4m	Cuttings
P.c. 'Rosea' 107	5m	4m	Tree D	Rounded	Purple	4m	Cuttings
P.c. 'Trailblazer' 107	5m	4m	Tree D	Rounded	Purplish	4m	Cuttings

Plant name and page ref.	Height	Spread	Plant type	Habit	Colour	Spacing	Increase
P. x cistena 107	2m	3m	Shrub D	Twiggy	Purple	2m	Proles
P. laurocerasus 'Green Marble' 53	3m	3m	Shrub E	Rounded	White	1.5m	Cuttings
P. lusitanica 'Variegata' 54	2.5m	3m	Shrub E	Rounded	White	1.5m	Cuttings
Pseudotsuga menziesii 'Caesia' 100	4m	2.5m	Conifer E	Pyramid	Blue	1.5m	Grafting
P.m. 'Fletcheri' 100	1m	1.5m	Conifer E	Bush	Blue	1m	Grafting
Pseudowintera colorata 21	1m	2m	Shrub E	Obese	Multi	1m	Cuttings
Pulmonaria saccharata 'Silver Heart' 88	30cm	30cm	Herb D	Flat	Grey	15cm	Division
Pyracantha coccinea 'Harlequin' 21	2.5m	2m	Shrub E	Spiky	White	1m	Cuttings
Pyrus salicifolius 'Pendula' 89	3m	2m	Tree D	Weeping	Grey	1.5m	Grafting
Rhamnus alternata 'Variegata' 54	5m	2.5m	Tree E	Pyramid	White	1.5m	Cuttings
Rhododendron x 'Blue Diamond' 89	1.5m	1.5m	Shrub E	Rounded	Grey	1m	Cuttings
Rh. campanulatum var. aeriginosum 89	2m	1.5m	Shrub E	Rounded	Grey	1.5m	Layers
Rh. concatenans 89	2m	2m	Shrub E	Rounded	Grey	1.5m	Cuttings
Rh. x 'Elizabeth Lockhart' 107	1m	75cm	Shrub E	Rounded	Purple	50cm	Cuttings
Rh. impeditum 89	75cm	75cm	Shrub E	Rounded	Grey	50cm	Cuttings
Rh. lepidostylum 89	45cm	75cm	Shrub E	Spreading	Grey	45cm	Cuttings
Rh. ponticum 'Purple' 107	4m	4m†	Shrub E	Rounded	Purple	2m	Cuttings
Rh. scintillans 90	60cm	1m	Shrub E	Rounded	Grey	75cm	Cuttings
Ribes sanguineum 'Brocklebankii' 72	1m	1.5m	Shrub D	Spreading	Yellow	75cm	Cuttings
Ricinus communis 'Gibsonii' 107	1.5m	2m	Bedder	Rounded	Purple	1m	Seed
Robinia pseudoacacia 'Aurea' 72	10m†	5m	Tree D	Tree	Yellow	2.5m	Grafting
R.p. 'Frisia' 72	10m†	5m	Tree D	Tree	Yellow	2.5m	Grafting
Rosa rubrifolia 108	2.5m	2m	Shrub D	Arching	Grey	1m	Seed
R. wichuriana 'Variegata' 54	1m	3m	Shrub D	Spreading	White	1.5m	Cuttings
Rubus idaeus 'Aureus' 72	1.5m	2m††	Shrub D	Thicket	Yellow	1m	Proles
R. microphyllus 'Variegatus' 22	60cm	75cm†	Shrub D	Thicket	Multi	50cm	Proles
Ruta graveolens 100	60cm	1m	Shrub D	Rounded	Grey	50cm	Cuttings
R.g. 'Jackman's Blue' 100	75cm	1m	Shrub D	Rounded	Blue	50cm	Cuttings
R.g. 'Variegata' 54	75cm	1m	Shrub D	Rounded	White	50cm	Cuttings

Plant name and page ref.	Height	Spread	Plant type	Habit	Colour	Spacing	Increase
Salix alba 'Sericea' 90	10m	7m	Tree D	Rounded	Grey	5m	Cuttings
S. x boydii 90	15cm	10cm	Shrub D	Gnarled	Grey	5cm	Cuttings
S. exigua 90	3m	2.5m	Shrub D	Lax	Grey	2m	Cuttings
S. hastata 90	1.5m	1.5m	Shrub D	Bushy	Grey	75cm	Cuttings
S. lanata 90	2m	1.5m	Shrub D	Bushy	Grey	75cm	Cuttings
S. lapponum 90	3m	4m	Shrub D	Willowy	Grey	2m	Cuttings
Salvia officinalis 'Purpurasceus' 108	1.5m	2m	Sub-shrub E	Rounded	Purple	1m	Cuttings
Sambucus nigra 'Aurea' 73	3m	2m	Shrub D	Leggy	Yellow	1.5m	Cuttings
S.n. 'Pulverulenta' 55	1.5m	1m	Shrub D	Bushy	White	75cm	Cuttings
S.n. 'Purpurea' 108	3m	2m	Shrub D	Leggy	Purple	1.5m	Cuttings
S.n. 'Variegata' 55	3m	2m	Shrub D	Leggy	White	1.5m	Cuttings
S. racemosa 'Plumosa Aurea' 73	3m	3m	Shrub D	Bushy	Yellow	1m	Cuttings
Santolina chamaecyparissus 90	60cm	45cm	Shrub E	Bushy	Silver	30cm	Cuttings
S. corsica 91	15cm	75cm	Sub-shrub E	Feathery	Grey	50cm	Cuttings
S. neapolitana 91	75cm	75cm	Sub-shrub E	Feathery	Grey	50cm	Cuttings
Saxifraga 'Cloth of Gold' 73	5cm	25cm	Herb D	Mossy	Yellow	15cm	Division
S. cuscutiformis 108	10cm	1m†	Herb E	Running	Purple	15cm	Proles
S. fortunei 'Rubra' 108	30cm	30cm	Herb D	Tufted	Purple	15cm	Division
S.f. 'Wada's Form' 108	40cm	40cm	Herb D	Tufted	Purple	20cm	Division
S. stolonifera 22	15cm	1m	Herb E	Running	Grey	20cm	Proles
Scrophularia aquatica 'Variegata' 55	60cm	30cm	Herb D	Tufted	White	30cm	Division
Senecio cineraria & cvs 91	60cm	60cm	Bedder	Bushy	Silver	30cm	Cuttings
S. x 'Leonard Cockayne' 91	2m	3m	Shrub E	Leggy	Grey	1.5m	Cuttings
S. monroi 92	60cm	60cm	Shrub E	Rounded	Grey	45cm	Cuttings
S. reynoldii 92	60cm	1m	Shrub E	Leggy	Grey	75cm	Cuttings
S. x 'Sunshine'	1.5m	2m	Shrub E	Round	Grey	1m	Cuttings
Setcreasea purpurea 109	30cm	75cm	Bedder	Sprawling	Purple	30cm	Cuttings
Sisyrinchium striatum 'Variegatum' 56	45cm	60cm	Herb E	Tufted	Cream	30cm	Division
Spartina pectinata 'Aureo-marginata' 73	1m	1m	Grass E	Clump	Yellow	75cm	Division
Spirea bumalda 'Goldflame' 73	45cm	1m	Shrub D	Mound	Gold	75cm	Cuttings
Stachys lanata 92	30cm	60cm	Herb E	Spreading	Grey	30cm	Proles
S.l. 'Silver Carpet' 92	20cm	60cm	Herb E	Spreading	Grey	30cm	Proles

Plant name and page ref.	Height	Spread	Plant type	Habit	Colour	Spacing	Increase
Symphytum x uplandicum 'Variegatum' 56	1m	1m	Herb D	Clump	White	75cm	Division
Tanacetum densum 92	15cm	30cm	Herb E	Carpet	Grey	15cm	Proles
Taxus baccata 'Aurea' 74	3m	4m	Conifer E	Bushy	Yellow	1.5m	Cuttings
T.b. 'Adpressa Aurea' 74	1.3m	1.6m	Conifer E	Bushy	Yellow	1m	Cuttings
T.b. 'Dovestoniana Aurea' 74	3m	6m	Conifer E	Arching	Yellow	2m	Cuttings
T.b. 'Elegantissima' 74	3m	4m	Conifer E	Bushy	Yellow	1.5m	Cuttings
T.b. 'Fastigiata Aurea' 74	4m	1.5m	Conifer E	Erect	Yellow	4m	Cuttings
T.b. 'Golden Gem' 74	1m	1.5m	Conifer E	Bushy	Yellow	1m	Cuttings
T.b. 'Repens Aurea' 74	75cm	2m	Conifer E	Creeping	Yellow	1m	Cuttings
T.b. 'Semperaurea' 75	3m	4m	Conifer E	Bushy	Yellow	1m	Cuttings
T.b. 'Standishii' 75	4m	1.5m	Conifer E	Erect	Yellow	1m	Cuttings
Tellima grandiflora 'Purpurea' 109	30cm	60cm	Herb D	Tufted	Purple	45cm	Division
Thuja occidentalis 'Columbia' 75	2.5m	1.2m	Conifer E	Pyramid	Yellow	75cm	Cuttings
T.o. 'Ellwangeriana Aurea' 75	3m	4m	Conifer E	Bush	Yellow	1m	Cuttings
T.o. 'Lutea' 75	2.5m	1m	Conifer E	Pyramid	Yellow	1m	Cuttings
T.o. 'Rheingold' 75	75cm	1.5m	Conifer E	Bun	Yellow	1m	Cuttings
T.o. 'Wareana Lutescens' 75	2.5m	1.5m	Conifer E	Pyramid	Yellow	1m	Cuttings
T. orientalis 'Beverlyensis' 75	2m	75cm	Conifer E	Flame	Vari	50cm	Cuttings
T.o. 'Juniperoides' 28	2m	1m	Conifer E	Pyramid	Vari	50cm	Cuttings
T.o. 'Rosedalis' 28	1m	50cm	Conifer E	Bun	Yellow	45cm	Cuttings
T.o. 'Semperaurea' 76	1.6m	1m	Conifer E	Globe	Yellow	75cm	Cuttings
T.o. 'Westmont' 76	1.5m	1m	Conifer E	Flame	Yellow	75cm	Cuttings
T. plicata 'Cuprea' 76	1m	60cm	Conifer E	Pyramid	Yellow	45cm	Cuttings
T.p. 'Irish Gold' 76	4m	2m	Conifer E	Pyramid	Yellow	1m	Cuttings
T.p. 'Old Gold' 76	3m	2m	Conifer E	Pyramid	Yellow	1m	Cuttings
T.p. 'Stoneham Gold' 76	2m	1m	Conifer E	Spire	Yellow	1m	Cuttings
T.p. 'Zebrina' 76	3m	1.5m	Conifer E	Pyramid	Yellow	1m	Cuttings
T.p. 'Wansdyke Silver' 56	1m	1.5m	Conifer E	Bun	White	1m	Cuttings
Thujopsis dolabrata 'Nana' 28	50cm	1.5m	Conifer E	Bun	Vari	1m	Cuttings
Tolmeia menzesii 'Taff's Gold' 76	30cm	45cm	Herb E	Tufted	Yellow	30cm	Cuttings
Tovara virginiana 'Painter's Palette' 22	45cm	60cm	Herb D	Bushy	Multi	45cm	Division
Tsuga canadensis 'Aurea' 76	4m	3m	Conifer E	Pyramid	Yellow	2m	Grafting
T.c. 'Dwarf Whitetip' 57	4m	3m	Conifer E	Pyramid	White	2m	Grafting

Plant name and page ref.	Height	Spread	Plant type	Habit	Colour	Spacing	Increase
Uncinia egmontiana 109	15cm	15cm	Sedge E	Tufted	Purple	10cm	Seed
U. unciniata 109	15cm	20cm	Sedge E	Tufted	Purple	10cm	Division
Vinca major 'Albo-reticulata' 57	30cm	1m††	Herb E	Running	White	50cm	Proles
V.m. 'Aureo-maculata' 76	30cm	1m††	Herb E	Running	Yellow	50cm	Proles
V.m. 'Elegantissima' 57	30cm	1m††	Herb E	Running	White	50cm	Proles
V. minor 'Aureovariegata' 76	15cm	1m††	Herb E	Running	Yellow	50cm	Proles
V.m. 'Variegata' 57	15cm	1m††	Herb E	Running	White	50cm	Proles
Viola labradorica 110	10cm	25cm	Herb D	Running	Purple	15cm	Seed
Vitis vinifera 'Purpurea' 110	6m	5m	Vine D	Scandent	Purple	3m	Cuttings
Weigela florida 'Purpurea' 109	2m	2.5m	Shrub D	Bushy	Purple	1.5m	Cuttings
W.f. 'Variegata' 77	2m	2.5m	Shrub D	Bushy	Cream	1.5m	Cuttings
W. japonica 'Looysmansii Aurea' 77	2m	3m	Shrub D	Arching	Yellow	1.5m	Cuttings
Yucca filamentosa 'Variegata' 58	75cm	1m	Shrub E	Rosette	White	75cm	Division
Y. flaccida 'Bright Edge' 77	60cm	60cm	Shrub E	Rosette	Yellow	45cm	Division
Y.f. 'Variegata' 77	60cm	60cm	Shrub E	Rosette	Yellow	45cm	Division
Y. gloriosa 'Variegata' 58	2m	1m	Shrub E	Rosette	Multi	1m	Division
Y. whipplei 92	2m	2m	Shrub E	Rosette	Grey	2m	Seed

Index